Living in Sheffield

1000 YEARS OF CHANGE

The Star
Living in Sheffield
1000 YEARS OF CHANGE

Author
Bob Horton

Illustrations and Editing
Ian Nettleton

The Breedon Books
Publishing Company
Derby

First published in Great Britain by
The Breedon Books Publishing Company Limited
Breedon House, 44 Friar Gate, Derby, DE1 1DA.
1999

Modern photographs by Bob Horton

Other photographs reproduced by kind permission of
The Star newspaper, Sheffield.

ISBN 1 85983 175 3

Printed and bound by Butler & Tanner Ltd., Selwood Printing
Works, Caxton Road, Frome, Somerset.

Colour separations and jacket printing by GreenShires Group
Ltd, Leicester.

Contents

Acknowledgements 6

Introduction 7

Sheffield – "A Right Mixture" 8

In the Beginning: The Field by the Sheaf 12

The First Hundred Years 14
1000 Anno Domini 18

The Second Hundred Years 25
1100 to 1200 27

The Third Hundred Years 33
1200 to 1300 36

The Fourth Hundred Years 41
1300 to 1400 44

The Fifth Hundred Years: 50
1400 to 1500 52

The Sixth Hundred Years 56
1500 to 1600 62

The Seventh Hundred Years 69
1600 to 1700 74

The Eighth Hundred Years 80
1700 to 1800 91

The Ninth Hundred Years 97
1800 to 1900 116

The Last Hundred Years 125
1900 to 2000 168

Appendices 179

Susbscribers 182

Acknowledgements

Research for this book has necessitated reference to about 100 publications of one sort of another. These include history books, technical books, reference books, fact books, magazines and newspapers.

In addition, I have spoken in length to residents of this great city, many of whom are elderly, as well as those who work here.

It would be impossible to mention all the sources of my information, for which I am extremely grateful, but I would like to thank a few people who have been of particular assistance. These are: John Spencer for his help in getting the book off the ground; Pat Bohane for his contribution on cutlery and silverware trades; Joe Castle for his help in many areas; Arthur Faulkner for his valuable reminiscences on cutlery manufacture; Judy Broughton for her general and detailed help in many areas; Susan Woods for her help in photograph selection; Marie Sparling for sharing her father's wartime and sporting experiences with me; Sheffield City Library staff for their help and patience.

I would also like to thank Sheffield City Libraries Local Studies Department for permission to print old maps copied from them; Sheffield Galleries & Museums Trust for permission to print an old 1650 map prepared by them, and two photographs of exhibits taken by myself; Sheffield Industrial Museums Trust for permission to print several photographs of exhibits taken by myself.

Readers will be acutely aware, however, of the value of the excellent and sometimes amusing illustrations which appear on most of the pages of this book. They bring the history of Sheffield to life and give an exciting, visual impact to the story as it unfolds. I would, therefore, like to thank Ian Nettleton, the talented illustrator, for his major contribution towards this publication and for his imaginative interpretation of this text.

In addition, I was also fortunate enough to be able to obtain Ian's services to edit the book, as he is also a writer as well as an artist. He unselfishly dedicated much of his very limited spare time to this important task, for which again I am very grateful.

Last but not least, I would like to thank Janet Proctor for her untiring efforts in typing the manuscript on time. Being "last in the line" is often a thankless task, and her helpful, friendly manner was much appreciated.

Introduction

BEFORE we take our interesting stroll through a thousand years of changing Sheffield and find out first hand how people lived, I thought it would be useful to explain the basis upon which this book has been written.

First, I feel that there was a need to write something about our city that not only explains its dramatic and ever changing history, but also gives you, the reader, the opportunity to understand how our ancestors really lived. To achieve this, each century begins with an outline of the historical changes which have taken place over its hundred year span. Immediately following this, I have selected several interesting events, typical of that century, which I have related in story form through the lives of Mr and Mrs S, and their children. This family represents the average Sheffielder, and you are able to share their experiences over the whole of the one thousand years.

Second, whilst the history section of each century deals with the whole spectrum of society, the story line concentrates on the working classes, who make up the vast majority of Sheffielders throughout the millennium. This has the effect of often portraying the life of the average Sheffielder as being harsh, difficult, and sometimes quite tragic. But that is how life was; and that is how it must be told.

Third, I must explain the authenticity of the story line. In the earlier centuries, during which time detailed records of actual events do not exist, I have created a story around the factual history. Thus, for example, Mr and Mrs S are involved in adventures typical of that time which show how a typical family would have lived. As the centuries progress, many fictional characters appear in factual situations. I have also been able to identify more detail of actual events which took place. These once again have been re-created in story form, and in many instances are true to life. Some of the more recent adventures of Mr & Mrs S have been based on old newspaper reports, records from archives, or discussions with elderly people, the oldest being a man in his nineties. In such instances, names have been changed, where appropriate, in order to respect the privacy of individuals.

I must also point out, that in researching this interesting history of Sheffield, I have found that on occasions, some historians give differing news regarding the same historical "facts". In addition, some of the history in the earlier times is based on personal interpretation by historians, as facts are simply not available. My presentation therefore, has, of necessity, had to be based on my interpretation of the best information available to me. Should this differ with any other that is written, please understand the reason why.

Finally, the many facts which are contained in this book have been obtained from over 100 different sources. I have tried to present them fairly and creatively, with no intention of simply reproducing the work of others. I trust that I have been successful in achieving this.

Sheffield – "A Right Mixture"

The Stone Age (40,000 BC-2000 BC)

Many thousands of years ago, Britain had been physically joined to and was obviously part of Europe.

As we now enter this new millennium with anticipation and hope, it is strange to think that shortly we may have gone "full circle" and once again be part of a united Europe. We shall have to wait and see.

However, looking back into the distant past it appears that Britain, as it now exists, was probably occupied by a mixture of European tribes who lived in those times, some of whom may have travelled to and possibly infiltrated the densely forested area we know as Sheffield.

Evidence of modern man living in caves has been found at Creswell Crags in Derbyshire (about 10,000 BC), and even nearer to home the earliest house known in Britain (a ring of stones in the shape of a hut or tent base) was found in Deepcar dating back to about 8000 BC.

By about 6000 BC, Britain was cut off from the rest of Europe by rising sea levels (which formed the English Channel) and became an island. Whilst there is little evidence of who lived in this area and what their life-style might have been like, we do know that game was plentiful, fish were in the rivers and berries and nuts were on the trees. We could hazard a guess, therefore, that the pace of life was probably relaxing with the odd bit of hunting, fishing or fruit and berry picking taking the place of today's supermarket shopping spree!

As time moved on some animals became domesticated and by about 3000 BC farming was taking place as sheep, cows, pigs and goats were brought over from Europe together with crops such as barley and wheat. By the end of the Stone Age, the Sheffielder's ancestors were possibly a mixture of hunters and farmers of mixed origin, although there is little evidence to support any definite conclusions.

The Bronze Age (2000 BC – 700 BC)

The next 1,300 years was known as the Bronze Age, when farming became more sophisticated and tools and weapons were made both from copper and bronze (a mixture of copper and tin).

It was during this time that (from about 800 BC) the Britonic Tribes of the Celts came over from continental Europe and began to settle in our country. Most of these were farmers, skilled in the working of bronze.

The Iron Age (700 BC-70 BC) and The Celts (800 BC-43 BC)

Over the next few hundred years (which takes us into the Iron Age), the Celtic tribes continued to arrive and by about 400 BC they decided on a full scale invasion.

These warriors, unlike their more peaceful forefathers, were a quarrelling, fighting group of people who overran the whole country. They settled in several different territories and had a hierarchy in each, comprising a Chieftain and warriors ruling over farmers, craftsmen and slaves.

The local tribes in the "Sheffield" area who arrived with iron weapons, were known as the Brigantes.

Of particular significance is that the Celts brought over a new language called BRITONIC and it was from these Britonic tribes that BRITAIN as we know it today obtained its name.

The Celts occupied the area for the remainder of the first millennium BC, although Julius Caesar did make two brief attempts to conquer Britain in 55 and 54 BC, only to leave again.

So, by the year ZERO (the birth of Christ) the area which would one day become Sheffield was occupied by Celtic invaders from Germany and it is from here that our true ancestry starts.

Reminders of their existence remain in the known location of the fortress built on Wincobank Hill by the Brigantes, the existence of Britonic river names (e.g. the Don) and the name Eccle (meaning church) as in **Ecclesall** (Church Hill) and **Ecclesfield** (Church field).

The Romans (43 AD-410 AD)

As we enter the FIRST MILLENNIUM AD, it is the turn of the Romans (from Italy) to influence the history of the people of our area. The Roman Invasion from across the waters began about 43 AD and had advanced to meet the Celtic Brigantes in our area by about 71 AD. Over the next ten years or so, the Roman Conquest was complete and Britain became part of the Roman Empire for nearly 400 years.

Anglo-Saxons (450-865 AD)

To the dismay of its people, there was to be no respite for the British and by the middle of the 5th century our country was invaded yet again. This time it was the Anglo-Saxons from Germany and Denmark.

These all-conquering invaders found a Romano-British population somewhat weakened by plague and famine and by 600 AD the British had been killed or pushed out of the country, to remain only in Wales and Scotland.

The country became known as Angle-land or ENGLAND as the new occupants took control.

These new "English" people loved the land and were here to stay. They were, however, more basic than their predecessors and, disliking towns and the whole structure set up by the Romans, they destroyed everything in sight and built little villages over the country instead.

They also created seven Kingdoms with the Angles settling mainly in the northern half of the country and the Saxons settling mainly in the South. Most were farmers and they built settlements mainly in the valleys.

A map of England showing the heptarchy — the seven kingdoms into which the country was divided by the 7th century. Wessex had become the most important kingdom by Alfred's reign. 1 Celtic Territories (not part of the heptarchy) 2 Mercia 3 Northumbria 4 East Anglia 5 Essex 6 Kent 7 Sussex 8 Wessex

The Anglian names identified in the area of what is now Sheffield paint the early picture of our city. Names ending in "ley" (meaning forest clearing) and "ton" (meaning enclosed farmstead) are of Anglian origin from which can be identified many familiar settlements which were probably established between 600 and 800 AD. These include **Heeley, Longley, Southey, Tinsley, Totley, Wadsley, Walkley, Norton** and **Owlerton.**

Other known Anglian settlements which probably emerged during this period had also been established, these being **Attercliffe, Shirecliffe, Brincliffe, Brightside, Darnall, Fulwood, Gleadless, Handsworth** and **Woodseats.**

The most significant historical reference is that of **Dore,** which was situated near the border between the two Kingdoms of Mercia and Northumbria and which for part of its length was formed by the River "Sheaf" (an Anglian word meaning a dividing line). It was at **Dore** in 829 that Ecgbert

Whilst life under the Romans changed dramatically in many parts of the country with new towns, houses, villas, roads and efficient government creating an environment of greater wealth, peace and stability, there is little evidence of much Roman influence in the area of the future Sheffield. Most Celtic Britons living in villages and farms remained there, although a few rich ones probably moved to the luxury of the new towns.

Roman forts were, however, built at Templeborough (near Rotherham), Doncaster, Chesterfield and the Hope Valley village of Brough (near Castleton) and a road linking the Templeborough and Brough forts (and onwards to Buxton) was built via what is now Sheffield City. This road is thought to have followed a route from Templeborough along the south bank of the Don, which it forded somewhere around Bridge-houses, climbing up the approximate line of the present Corporation Street to Broad Lane – Brookhill – Western Bank – Witham Road – Crookes – Lydgate Lane – Crosspool – Lodgemoor and skirting Stannage Pole out to Brough and Buxton.

Let us not lose sight, however, of the fact that we are trying to establish who we Sheffield people are.

The significance of the 400-year Roman occupation of the country, ruling and living alongside the Celtic Britons, is that during that extremely long period, integration between the two races (Celtic Britons and Italian Romans) would have been considerable, resulting in many Romano-Britons across the country.

Included in these would be some living in, around or near to the area later to be called Sheffield.

By the end of the 4th century, however, the Roman Empire elsewhere in the world was being challenged by other countries, and by 410 AD the Roman Army had left Britain which subsequently reverted to Celtic-British and Romano British control for the next half century.

became the first King of all England by "defeating" the Northumbrian army (who actually submitted to him without a fight).

Last, but not least, however, is a later reference to a small settlement at the junction of the rivers Don and Sheaf called ESCAFELD or SCEATHFELD which are Anglo-Saxon names meaning "field or clearing by the Sheaf". This evidence, which is contained in a historical reference of 1086 called the DOMESDAY book, identifies the origins of our city as being probably a family of Angles who settled on the banks of the River Sheaf about 700 to 800 AD.

The Vikings (Norsemen) (865 AD-1000-1066 AD)

The story of the identity of Sheffielders is, however, far from complete.

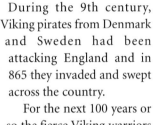

During the 9th century, Viking pirates from Denmark and Sweden had been attacking England and in 865 they invaded and swept across the country.

For the next 100 years or so the fierce Viking warriors and the Anglo-Saxons fought, resulting in the Vikings controlling most of the north of the country and the Saxons the south.

By the beginning of the second millennium, 1000 AD, the Danish Vikings controlled most of the country, and for 60 years there was a time of relatively peaceful co-existence between them and the Anglo-Saxons.

The impact of this Viking (Danish) invasion was of varying significance in this area. The Danes preferred hilltops for their settlements and records indicate that they established hamlets such as **Jordanthorpe** ("thorpe" meaning small farmstead), **Osgathorpe, Grimesthorpe, Hackenthorpe, Upperthorpe, Crookes, High Storrs** and **Ranmoor.**

The small settlement of Sheffield, however, is unlikely to have been affected to any significant degree by the Danish occupation. It is probable, therefore, that neighbouring settlements of hilltop Danes and river valley Angles lived together in this area along with a few groups of Celtic British or Romano British descendants which may have survived the continual invasion of our lands. As time progressed, Anglo-Danish descendants would evolve to further enrich the Sheffielder's ancestral mix.

The Normans and William The Conqueror (1066)

The final stage of our identity build-up took place in the well-known year of 1066 when yet another mighty force invaded our shores.

This time it was William the Conqueror who chose to

bring his Norman army to our beleaguered country and defeat the English King Harold at the Battle of Hastings.

It is interesting to note that William, who now became the new King of England, was the Duke of Normandy in northern France. Normandy had in fact been established in that area about 200 years previously (when the Vikings were invading Britain) when a group of Danes, led by Rollo the Norseman, went to live there.

Thus the Normans, who were now to rule England for the next 100 years or so, were of Danish origin with French connections developed over 200 years. Their influence on Sheffield in terms of its growth and development was considerable through successive Lords of the Manor.

However, the number of Normans who actually came to this area to rule and settle was relatively small and their impact on the Sheffielder's ancestry was probably quite modest, particularly amongst the working classes.

Summary of Sheffielder's Ancestral Mix

This was the last of the successful foreign invasions and we can now draw together the strands which make up the identity of the Sheffielder.

First, let us summarise the chronological process:

40,000 BC-2,000 BC (The Stone Age)	Possibly the odd family or two from mixed European tribes. Not much evidence.
2,000 BC-700 BC (The Bronze Age)	A few CELTS from Germany may have appeared as their peaceful invasion of Britain began about 800 BC.
700 BC-70 BC (The Iron Age)	CELTIC warriors (BRITONS) invaded and the Brigante Tribe settled in this area.
70 BC-43AD	The CELTS remained and our country became known as Britain.
43AD-410 AD	ROMANS (from Italy) arrive and rule. CELTIC BRITONS remain.

410 AD-450 AD	The Romans have left. BRITONS and ROMANO BRITONS remain.
450 AD-865 AD	ANGLO-SAXONS arrive from Germany and Denmark. Most of the Britons/Romano-Britons are killed or pushed out of area. ANGLES settle in Sheffield.
865 AD-1066 AD	VIKINGS arrive from Denmark and Sweden and live alongside the Angles (English) and any remaining Britons.
1066 AD-1154 AD	The NORMANS arrive from Normandy (Danish-French origin) and become Lords of the Manor in the Sheffield area.

Second, let us consider who to include in our Sheffielder identity kit:

(1) Those who settled in the area as a whole (Celts).

(2) Those who settled in the area or nearby (Romans).

(3) Those who settled in the Sheffield Valleys (Angles).

(4) Those who settled on the Sheffield Hill Tops (Danes-Vikings).

(5) Those who latterly ruled the Sheffield Area (Normans).

(6) Those who migrated to Sheffield from neighbouring villages, towns and cities, as well as from Ireland, Scotland and Wales, particularly from 1800 onwards, when Sheffield's growth escalated and its population increased from about 30,000 to over half a million today.

(7) Last but not least, we include all our friends from across the seas who migrated to Sheffield in the 20th century from places such as India, Pakistan, the Afro-Caribbean countries, China and Poland to create the multi-cultural society of today.

Finally, from all we have examined, let us try and define the end result by putting all the ingredients together which make the SHEFFIELD PIE:

The Sheffielder of today is mainly Anglo-Saxon with a good helping of Viking, a dash or two of Celtic Briton and a sprinkling of Roman all topped off with a touch of Norman influence, into which, for added flavour and satisfaction, have been added spices from across the world.

So, now we know who we all are. The whole Sheffield "Pie" is undoubtedly what we now call English, but there is little doubt that today's Sheffielder is a RIGHT MIXTURE!

In the Beginning – The Field by the Sheaf

AS I STOOD at the bottom of Commercial Street adjacent to the busy Park Square roundabout and gazed upwards to view the huge steel bow bridge carrying Sheffield's new Supertram, I found it difficult to imagine that this is more or less where our great city began about 1,200 years ago.

Compare the scene in your mind. A small attractive clearing on the banks of the gently flowing River Sheaf which burbled its way with some excitement towards its meeting with deeper, faster flowing waters of the Don which beckoned in the distance.

The view from the river bank over the thatched rooftops of the two wooden huts which gave shelter to a family of simply-clad peasant farmers was breathtaking. The subtle greenery of the open field gave way to deeper shades as an ocean of heavily-leafed trees with swaying branches whispered to each other as they reached for the clouds before disappearing over the horizon.

Closer examination of the quaint thatched homes showed that their walls consisted of woven branches covered in mud. There were no windows as the thatch almost reached the ground, but an opening was left for a doorway which was covered by further strong branches to keep out the two goats and the clucking hens which all foraged happily close-by.

Surrounding this haven of peace and contentment was a stout wooden fence, again interwoven by supple branches from the abundance of nearby trees. This was provided to safely enclose the primitive homestead and keep out unwanted intruders which might stray from the forest after dark. Wolves were not unusual visitors in these times.

As I gazed into the distance, the forests of the past melted

Bow bridge, over Park Square roundabout.

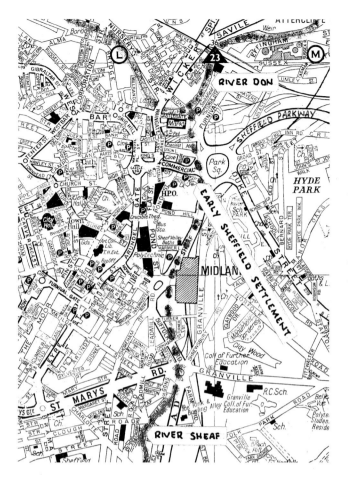

Early Sheffield Settlement.

away and I was conscious of the fact that two piercing red eyes had been staring at me for some time. Their sudden change through amber to a fiercely glowing green was greeted by the deafening roar of a lumbering juggernaut which belched out clouds of angry fumes as it lunged forward.

My dreams of yesteryear were further shattered by the intermittent screech of a frustrated fire engine which teased its way through the platoons of anxious commuters who religiously shuffled and spluttered their way around this steel and concrete jungle every day. This is today's reality. This is the year 2000, the beginning of the new millennium.

But how had this change of such enormity come about? Have we really progressed from serenity to chaos?

Let us find out by taking a stroll through the last one thousand years, century by century, and briefly examine such change.

The First Hundred Years (1000-1100 AD)

(a) Size and General Growth

BY THE year 1000, the family of peasant farmers which had formed the settlement of Escafeld (or Sceathfeld) on the banks of the River Sheaf 200 years or so ago, had grown into a small village with its cluster of thatched wooden huts built around a wooden hall.

The mud-covered woven branch walls had been replaced by more solid timber in the newer buildings, the largest of which was now used for meetings and occasional feasts. Many more trees had been felled and the small forest clearing had slowly grown to include large, open cultivated fields.

Downstream of the village, further tree clearance was taking place at the junction of the River Sheaf and the River Don. Rumour had it that a Manor House was to be built there for the local Danish landowner whose Viking forefathers had invaded the land nearly a century and a half earlier. (History is rather vague on this point and we can only conjecture that the Danish Lord of the Manor did in fact choose this location for his home.)

Sheffield's population at this time is difficult to estimate but was probably between 100 and 200 rising to about 500 by the end of the century. Its area did not of course include any of the districts of which it is now comprised, many of these existing at this time as separate valley or hilltop hamlets of Angle or Danish farmers. Some of these have already been identified earlier.

Following the invasion of England by William the Conqueror in 1066, Sheffield and its surrounding areas were

> **Did You Know** that domestic cats were introduced to Britain in about 1066, the year that William the Conqueror invaded our shores? There are now about eight million of them in the country and they kill about 75 million birds every year. There are also about six million dogs doing their "bits and bobs" in the streets, parks and gardens.

attacked by his Norman troops a few years later in retaliation for an uprising of Danish Lords wishing to overthrow the new King. Many villages and hamlets suffered in this onslaught and much of the population was probably killed or driven off.

The size of Sheffield at this time is referred to in the Domesday Book of 1086 which William the Conqueror had prepared in order to find out how much land and property he owned. Our fair city at that time appeared to be a small sub-manor of a larger manor referred to as Hallam (as was also Attercliffe) under the ownership of an Anglo-Danish Lord called Sweyn. The entry in the Doomsday Book reads:

"In Ateclive and Escafeld (two manors) Sweyn had five carucates of land to be taxed. There may be have been about three ploughs. This land is said to have been inland, demesne land of the manor of Hallam". (Demesne land means it is part of the estate of Hallam.)

It has been suggested that "five carucates of land" is about 500 acres, and if this is the total area owned by Lord Sweyn, then Sheffield and Attercliffe probably occupied about 250 acres each, about twice the size of the Meadowhall Shopping Centre complex.

(b) Local Rule and Government

Even though the Danish Vikings had invaded the country in the year 865 and penetrated South Yorkshire over the next 100 years or so, the Anglo-Saxon Kings still ruled the country until early into the year 1000.

In the Sheffield area, the last major battle between the Anglo-Saxons and the Danish Viking invaders took place in the year 942 when the Anglo-Saxon King Edmund conquered the Danes of Mercia "as far as where Dore divides the Kingdoms of Mercia and Northumbria".

After this time, the Angles and the Danes lived relatively peacefully together, with Anglo-Saxon and later Danish Earls owning the lands and controlling the people on it.

Sheffield had a succession of noble rulers for many centuries to come, the first of whom we know something about being the Danish Earl Waltheof who was Lord of the Manor around the year 1050. He was a powerful warrior who submitted to William the Conqueror in 1066 but was allowed to keep his lands and property as a gesture of goodwill.

> **Did You Know that the Danes were scoffed at by the British as being too soft because they combed their hair once a day, bathed every Saturday and often changed their clothes?**

However, within ten years, Earl Waltheof had betrayed this trust and friendship and, following two incidents of conspiracy against the King, was beheaded by him for treason.

The next Lord of the Manor was a wealthy knight called Roger de Busli, the first Norman Lord of this area, who retained the position to the end of the century.

Along with the Norman Conquest and rule came a new way of life, in particular relating to the way people held their land. It was called the FEUDAL SYSTEM and was to continue for several hundred years. This social system, introduced by William, produced a pyramid-like structure of society and gave free men the right to land in return for services and allegiance to superiors. ("Free" means those who are not slaves, the latter being entitled to nothing.) It can best be represented with the following diagram:

The King Holds all the land.
He grants most of it to his Barons in return for service (soldiers for fighting) or money. Some lands are also granted to Bishops and Leading Churchmen.
Barons grant some lands to knights (and lesser nobles) in return for service. The knight has to follow his Lord to war for 40 days a year, armed and on horseback together with the required number of soldiers.
The Knights in turn grant land to Yeomen and other Freemen (mostly farmers) in return for working on their Lord's farms for prescribed times or for being available fight if so required.
SERFS or <u>SLAVES</u> work for the freemen for their keep. This class of people (i.e. the labourers) probably made up about two-thirds of the population.

As has always appeared to be the case throughout history, the deprived working classes make up the vast majority of the population. In this and succeeding centuries, such labouring classes remained as slaves. Their persons, families and goods were the property of their Lord who could dispose of them as he pleased either by gift or sale.

This way of life was introduced rigidly by the Normans and its severe laws were rigorously enforced. The King held courts as did the Lord of the Manor (who exercised powers for all crimes), and punishment by death, torture, whippings or fines were common.

One benefit of this system, however, was that the lower ranks of the "pyramid" were given a certain amount of protection in return for their services to their overlord. This could be important when armed strength usually determined power in these medieval times.

(c) Working Life

There were two main areas of work in these early days of Sheffield. You were either fighting or farming!

All the men helped to run the little manor and either ploughed and cultivated their fields (and those of the Lord of the Manor), or bred farm animals which needed rough pasture for grazing and woodlands or common lands for pig feeding.

Within the manor, a group of men was also identified as being available to be called upon by the overlord to fight for the king as and when necessary.

As the whole country appeared to be in a nearly permanent state of war for nine and a half centuries of this millennium, soldiers and armies were always on the move and played a major factor in the everyday lives of most people.

(d) Domestic and Social Life

It was in 1016 that the wise Danish King Canute came to the throne. This was the king who reputedly tried to control the tides and waves on the shores of England, although it is probable that it was more likely to be his advisers who tried to persuade him to try against his better judgement. He now introduced Laws which had an important impact on domestic life.

These laws complimented those introduced nearly 100 years earlier by the Anglo-Saxon King Athelston, which required that every peasant who hadn't got a home of his own must reside with a householder without whose surety he would not be regarded as a member of the community nor be entitled to its protection.

Canute's law reinforced this by imposing a duty on every householder to be responsible for all individuals in his household (whether a freeman or a slave), and for any stranger whom he had admitted under his roof.

The idea of these laws was to try and prevent homeless people wandering about, begging for food and probably turning to crime and violence. It may have succeeded in this aim to some degree, but it also established the divide between those with property and those without, those who had money and those who were poor; in other words a reinforcement of class discrimination.

The fact that the law imposed a duty on one party of supervising the behaviour of the other as well as providing for his or her necessities of life (work, food and shelter), meant that some of the poor tried to work as little as possible for the maximum amount of assistance, whilst some householders tried to get as much work out of the poor as possible for the minimum amount of support and assistance. This situation, combined with the feeling of inferiority by the "underdog" must have created friction in the household.

The general picture which sums up the life of those living and working on the land was one of hardship. This

was in stark contrast to that of the nobility and gentry which was generally considered to be one of riotous living and excesses.

The homes of the average people, you will recall, were only simple thatched wooden huts and these were run by the women of the village or manor who also brought up the children and made clothes by weaving and the sewing of animal skins.

Food supplies were not a big problem for the lucky riverside dwellers of Sheffield who were able to obtain a plentiful supply of fresh fish, although game was not allowed to be caught in the forests which were in the strict ownership of the Lord of the Manor. Grain crops were the staple diet of the poor from which course brown bread made from barley or rye together with primitive stews of peas, oatmeal and a few herbs would form the basis of most meals.

The rich were able to afford game meat from the Lord's

forests, together with fruit such as apples, pears and a few grapes and even the luxury of a little white bread made from wheat. Whilst sheep and cows' milk was drunk by all, ale was the ordinary man's beverage with mead (made from honeycombs) and latterly wine being preferred by the rich.

Buying and selling of goods in these early days was usually the privilege of the better off. One pound (£1) in the year 1000 would be the equivalent of about £500 in today's money, and although silver pennies and gold coins were in use, the main method of "sale" amongst the average Sheffielder was bartering or exchange of goods of similar value.

Life in the open was of course more healthy, but as there were no doctors, illness was only cured by natural handed-down herbal and plant remedies if you were lucky. Serious illness would almost certainly have been fatal. Polluted water

> **Did You Know that the first known bath was made in 1700 BC in Crete? It was almost identical to that of today's modern bath, and water was supplied to it through terracotta (earthenware) pipes interlocked and "cemented" at their joints.**

wasn't a problem in these early days and the clean flowing rivers and natural springs provided adequately for drinking, pleasure and even occasional personal washing for those so inclined.

(e) Travel and Communications

Sheffield from its infancy was a remote, rather isolated little community without any means of proper communication for hundreds of years.

Messages requiring to be taken anywhere were sent with personal servants of the wealthy who used horseback as the only mode of transport other than walking.

Travelling by water was also popular, again mainly for local journeys and the Angles were skilled at making boats which could be used for either fishing or leisure.

Chapter 1
1000 Anno Domini

WE KNOW that Sheffield started about 200 years earlier when a family or two of Angles settled in a small clearing on the banks of the River Sheaf. As we begin our stroll through time at the turn of the first millennium, we can join Mr and Mrs Average Sheffielder and their baby daughter as the little village of Sheffield awakens to a new era.

It was a chilly start to the morning as Mrs S (as her friends liked to call her) shook her long dark hair to rid herself of the clinging straw upon which she had been lying on the cold floor of her sleeping quarters. It wasn't so much the hardness of her bed that irritated her or even the ever-present company of hundreds of insects. She just didn't like the infuriating problem of shedding wisps of straw for the next few hours, particularly when Mr S objected to them floating about in his morning cuppa!

She shivered a little and pulled the sheepskin shawl tightly over her weathered shoulders before braving the morning frost to find brittle sticks and "sugar-coated" brown leaves with which to rekindle the fire outside the entrance to her thatched humble little home.

The crackling of the hot embers and the brightness of the yellow-red flames which licked hungrily around the black iron pot of water now suspended bravely over the inferno awoke baby S from her sleep. Without waiting to be asked, and in a language as yet alien to everyone, she demanded breakfast with increasingly loud cries and shrieks, these being interrupted by choking spasms as the morning breeze wafted in mischievous clouds of smoke which snaked across the room in search of a vulnerable victim to torment.

As an accomplished mother and wife, Mrs S was easily able to cope with this latest demand on her time without having to suspend breakfast-making for herself and her husband. From the old brown sack lounging contentedly in the corner of the room she scooped three large handfuls of oats and dropped them into the water which was now bubbling merrily in the pot over the fire. With wooden spoon in one hand and baby S clutched to her breast with the other, she carried on with the family breakfast.

By this time, unable to sleep through the unwelcome dawn chorus, Mr S was grumbling nicely and wondering why his head felt as heavy as iron. After all, he'd only drunk six pints of ale last night, a mere nothing for a hard working farmer of his calibre.

Now the only thing which irritated Mrs S in a morning more than clinging wisps of straw was her spouse's usual comment when his eyes eventually opened wide enough to focus.

"Well wife, where's my breakfast? I'm hungry."

"The bowl's on the table, husband," she responded trying to control her feelings as she pointed to the centre of the room where flat sections of oak were proudly supported by two gnarled pillars cut from the wide-girthed trunk of the same fallen tree. "And you can help yourself to the oats whilst I go and feed the animals."

With baby S now slung firmly over her back, Mrs S made her way over to the compound where a pig, three hens and a goat paced up and down impatiently whilst awaiting their breakfast. En route, and out of sight of the thatched wooden shack which was their home, she squatted behind a tree to water the brown tufts of grass which struggled in vain to resist the daily urine attack which nature deemed a necessary part of Mrs S's routine. Later, of course, she would visit the nearby woods for a bit of privacy but, first thing in the morning she preferred this easier course of action.

Arriving at the compound, mother and baby were greeted by the grunting and squawking residents who only relented from their noisy outburst when the remains of yesterday's breakfast, lunch and evening meal had been tossed in. As usual the goat had been too impatient to wait and Mrs S had to carefully extricate the end of her shawl from it's mouth as it obviously preferred the flavour of well-worn sheepskin to beef bones, turnip ends and left-over sticky porridge.

The sudden bellowing roar of her beloved husband's voice signalled the fact that he was off to work in the open fields with colleagues from the village and would not return until dusk. Scurrying quickly back home, she dodged the cooking fires which were now burning brightly outside the entrance to every shack and, being careful not to fall into the storage trenches dug out between the dwellings, she exchanged greetings with her neighbours as she hurried past.

"About time too" complained Mr S "I can't go without me snap can I?"

Mrs S glanced at her husband's strong hands and arms which only a few years ago had successfully wielded a mighty sword against fierce Viking warriors who had invaded the area. Although now living peacefully with the Danes, she wondered how such a once accomplished soldier could not even get himself a bit of lunch before going to work.

"I've given you a piece of bread, a chunk of cheese and a baked egg, and you can get a drink from the river," she said, pushing the still grumbling worker out of the shack. "And mind you bring back a hare with you after work or there'll only be cabbage stew for supper."

Did You Know that the working man in Sheffield in the year 1000 was predominantly a farmer?

Clothes were similar for both men and women, being simple tunics and cloaks.

Women wore their hair under a head veil, although single girls could wear theirs loose.

Materials used were mainly coarsely woven wool, although the upper class used linen.

For outdoor working, clothes made from animal skins and leather (usually cowhide) were worn.

The staple diet of these early Sheffielders was an oatmeal, barley or rye stew complete with cabbage or peas. This was supplemented by fish from the river, and game from the forest, together with hen's eggs and cow's milk.

Joining the other villagers who were also leaving their shacks, Mr S made his way over to the clearing to collect his oxen for ploughing. He had two such beasts which formed part of a team of eight used to pull the heavy iron plough over the open fields which the local nobleman had granted to the village farmers.

Each was responsible for his own strip of land and at this time of year nearly everyone from the village came to help as successful ploughing and the sowing of seed for wheat, barley, oats and rye crops were important times in the farmers' diary.

Ploughing was later than usual as January was the normal month for such a task. However, the long cold winter spell had kept the ground in a grip of ice and it was only now that the early spring sunshine had given out sufficient warmth to make the land workable. In order not to miss the sowing season, the little army of villagers would concentrate on breaking up the soil with an assortment of spades, long handled axes and rakes not unlike those used by today's gardeners.

Mrs S, with a very young baby to care for, was happy to be able to stay behind along with two or three other mothers and the village elderly to do domestic chores and child-minding at home.

The sun was now bursting through the fast disappearing clouds and had already dispersed the morning frost. It's golden rays were playfully dancing on the clear blue water of the River Sheaf on the banks of which the village settlement was built. This calm and beautiful setting was just too tempting for Mrs S and she quickly decided to leave the housework until later and take baby and her other young charges to the river to see if she could tempt them to remove some of the dirt and grime from their faces.

Not wishing to miss an opportunity, the resourceful young mum arrived at the river bank with fishing line and a few clothes to wash. A bit of grilled or boiled trout for lunch was always appetising and there were plenty of these in the river just waiting to be caught.

It was later than intended when the happy band arrived back home looking clean and refreshed. One little helper carried the bag of clean wet washing whilst another marched proudly in with a large rainbow-bellied fish slung over his tiny shoulder. They all crowded round while mum slit open it's belly and cut off it's head before popping it into the ever ready boiling pot over the fire.

Baby S had already had her second breakfast at the riverside and was now sleeping. Making sure that the children were playing happily within earshot, Mrs S set about sweeping the shack floor with the birch broom which lived at the entrance to the shack. This was never as easy as one might expect as it was always a battle with several mice and often a wandering water rat for the discarded crumbs and scraps of unwanted food scattered amongst the ever-present strands of straw.

She noticed that a bowl of fresh milk had been placed on the table since her adventure down to the river with the children, this having been provided by a kindly neighbour who had a share in one of several cows which grazed contentedly on the stubble outside the stout timber fence encircling the little village. It reminded her that she was thirsty, but the five little insects who were having a race in the "cross-bowl milk-swimming championships" put her off for the time being!

A sudden scream of pain penetrated Mrs S's thoughts and she rushed outside to find her neighbour's son writhing on the ground clutching his leg. Several other children were wildly swinging sticks and branches at the long, dark object which swiftly and silently snaked its way to the safety of the stockade boundary.

An adder bite was dangerous and prompt action was required. Grasping the young victim's leg, Mrs S put her mouth on the two small puncture marks showing slightly pink on the skin's surface and sucked as hard as she could, hoping to rid the wound of some of its poisonous venom. Having spit out the contents of her mouth she produced a small knife and paused for a moment whilst she looked reassuringly into the frightened eyes staring up at her!

"Bleeding" was the main cure for most ailments at this time, as it was believed that it would rid the body of all poisons, which in turn were the cause of most illnesses. In this instance it was probably true, although the poor boy, already in pain, was not at all grateful for the additional agony caused by two sharp thrusts of the knife which set his "poisonous" blood running freely down his quivering leg.

The boy's mother had been busy weaving cloth on an ingenious wooden loom (which was the pride of the village) when the incident occurred. Upon hearing of her son's distress, Mrs Weaver quickly but calmly proceeded to her thatched home to collect a cold poultice of crushed herbs and plants which was probably the equivalent of today's tube of "cure-all" antiseptic cream. As she emerged from the entrance with her tried and tested natural remedy, Mrs S arrived carrying the whimpering child in her slender but powerful arms, followed, as one might have guessed, by nearly all the children in the village who never expected such excitement on a Monday afternoon.

"Put him down here love and get me one of yonder leaves so that I can bandage the poor little beggar".

Mrs S obliged, and between them, they doctored the child's leg with mum's special poultice carefully contained by a broad green leaf and two strips of hessian.

With all the excitement over and mum's medical view being that "he'll soon be alright, don't you worry," life got back to normal in "little Sheffield" as the tiny patient rested from his ordeal.

Mrs Weaver's husband had built the loom upon which she was now an expert from a few stout branches taken from the nearby woods. The wool and hessian thread from which the cloth was being made had been obtained by bartering with the merchant from his Lordship's nearby Manor House who had insisted on taking only the fattest pig in exchange for his wares.

"Come on love, I'll show you how it works," she said to Mrs S "It's simple when you know how."

Now whilst Mrs S was as good as anyone at making clothes and could turn a "mean hand" to sewing with her specially sharp bone needle and thread, she found weaving rather boring. Back and forth went the little shuttle as the wooden arms of the loom were repeatedly adjusted to form the coarsely woven cloth to the obvious delight of its operator. Mrs S looked on in feigned admiration, whilst at the same time wishing she could be elsewhere.

"I'll have to go now Mrs Weaver," she suddenly blurted out. "The children will be missing me and the men will be home from the fields before long".

In what seemed no time at all, the evening light began to fade and the faint glimmer of the moon cast a silvery shadow over the distant treetops. The villagers began to return, the older children being rewarded for their help by being allowed to lead the oxen back ahead of the straggling crowd. Some of the menfolk had a hare or two slung over their broad backs, whilst others had reduced the pigeon population in their endeavours to provide a good supper for them and their families.

The women who had remained in the village stoked up the fires which now burned merrily outside the huts, giving off welcoming warmth and light to the returning workers. The pale grey clouds of steam from the near-bubbling stew pots began to intermingle with the darker smoke of the fires to create a hovering grey blanket which spread slowly over the thatched rooftops. This was bonfire night on a grand scale, and the crackle of the chattering fires, together with the startling effects of the firelight absorbed and reflected by the blanket of steamy smoke was better than any fireworks display.

Ale flowed freely as the tired workers enjoyed their vegetable broths and fish or meat stew. Even the youngsters tried a "tipple" or two as mum and dad tried anything to ensure a good night's sleep.

All the animals had by now been herded back to the safety of the village enclosure, with those most fortunate making their way to a large wooden hall situated in the centre of the village.

Although used as a meeting hall, it was also the home of the head man and his family together with their servants and slaves. In addition, it provided a warm sanctuary for his personal animals such as dogs, pigs and cattle.

If we take a careful look at this unusual home we can see that its walls are built of logs standing vertically next to each other and its thatched roof has a hole in the centre through which smoke was curling from the open-fired hearth beneath it.

Small openings in the walls formed windows and, whilst not wishing to be nosy, a long look through one of these makes most interesting viewing. The "Thane", as the head-man was called, was entertaining friends in the large eating area within which several wooden tables supported on V-shaped trestles are located around the central hearth. A skewered pig was slowly roasting over the open fire whilst two lean mongrel dogs chased around the room after several rats who had arrived uninvited to the party. Oblivious of this pandemonium, which was seriously spoiling the shape of the rushes and straw "carpet" which had previously been laid on the bare earth with some care by the household servants, the group of ale-swilling men bellowed and guffawed as they recounted previous conquests they had made in battle in years gone past.

There was no shortage of food or drink as the Thane was relatively well off when compared to the rest of the villagers and could afford to supplement his home produced meats, cheese and bread with a few barrels of ale and a basketful or two of apples and plums bought from the Lord's orchards.

An unusual noise to the right of the hall was also ignored by the merrymakers as an irritated cow thrust its head over a low wooden partition to protest that her mother's fine horns were now being used as cups to hold alcoholic drink, a sad sign of disrespect to such a fine old lady.

The women were not, of course, allowed to join in the "men's talk", and indeed would not wish to do so. They had plenty to talk about themselves, particularly relating to the disgraceful way that the Lord of the Manor's wife "parades outside their new mansion showing off her new clothes." Jealousy was just as rife in those days as it is now!

It wasn't just the fine clothes that separated the nobility from the rest. A glance inside the Manor House bedroom shows us that her ladyship would sleep at night in a bed of modest comfort whilst the Thane's wife and family would manage quite well on hard wooden slats softened by a layer of straw and animal skins.

As we already know, the small simple huts of the villager (the average "Sheffielders" of these times) provided the most basic facilities of all, and cuddling up together for warmth on the straw covered floor at least saved the hard-pressed housewife from having to make the bed every morning.

* * * * * * * * *

The relatively peaceful life of our new-millennium ancestors was soon to be shattered by the arrival in England in 1066 of this chap called William the Conqueror with a huge army of Norman soldiers.

Rumours were rife that King Harold had been killed in battle, and the comings and goings at Earl Waltheof's Manor House just along the river certainly indicated that something was seriously amiss.

A group of the strongest men in the village had already been summoned by the Earl to join his growing army of fighting men, and Mrs S watched in tears as her husband

strode out amongst them into the evening darkness of uncertainty. She took her daughter by the hand and gazed up into the star spangled sky wondering whether to pray to the mythical gods of old or to the single, all powerful God associated with the "newer" religion of Christianity. She didn't mind which of them listened as long as someone would ensure that her husband would be kept safe and well.

As if in answer to her desperate prayer, Mrs S was suddenly aware of a most unusual and very bright light travelling slowly across the sky. Unlike the twinkling stars, it dragged a long bright tail behind it which gradually faded out into the darkness. With mixed emotions of joy, fear and disbelief, she picked up little S and, hugging her with all her might, shouted "Thank you!"

Halley's Comet, photographed in the 20th century.

She would never know, of course, that what she had seen was a rare sighting of what would later be known as Halley's Comet which, whether by chance or design, chose this night in the year 1066 to grace our sky with its presence!

It was several days later when Mrs S awoke from a troubled sleep to the sounds of screaming and laughter, and at first she thought she was dreaming. Brushing aside a large, evil-looking spider which was hovering ominously above her, she ran her fingers carelessly through her hair to rid herself of any other little creatures which preferred her thatch to that of their own in the roof above.

A gentle movement in the doorway suddenly caught her attention and, catching her breath, she realised someone was watching her.

"It's only me lass. I'm home."

With a cry of disbelief Mrs S sprang to her feet and threw her arms around her husband, not knowing or even caring why he was home so early.

A rustling in the corner of the dark little hut was accompanied by a tired, gentle voice which sounded like magic to Mr S's ears.

"You've not been long daddy", followed after a hesitant pause by "Mummy promised that I could have one of Mrs Weaver's puppies because you'd gone away. Can I still have it?"

"Of course you can child" came the roar of consent as all three hugged each other at this unexpected but very welcome, early reunion.

Later, as they sat down to breakfast, eating their bowls of

porridge, Mr S explained that Earl Waltheof had met the Norman conqueror, now established as King William, who had agreed to let him keep his lands and property in return for his promise of allegiance and loyalty in the future. The Earl had given such a pledge, upon which the King had promised peace between them. Little did our family know in their hour of relief that power and greed would soon break the Earl's fragile pledge to the cost not only of himself but also of those he was supposed to protect.

In the absence of such foresight, however, our little family of Sheffielders, together with all their friends and neighbours, continued with their regular yearly chores. April and May were lambing times and the constant threat from wolves demanded much of their attention. The midsummer month of June was usually taken up with cutting and gathering wood for many uses. The nearby woods provided a

plentiful supply for the villagers, who, armed with long handled axes and two-wheeled, oxen drawn wagons, felled trees and chopped branches for building new homes and repairing old ones. Trestle tables and stools were also needed, and whilst not being the medieval equivalent of today's "G-Plan" or "Ercol" furniture, they served their purpose for the great majority of the people. Last, but not least, wood was required as fuel for heating and cooking, and good stocks for all these uses were essential.

July and August saw much activity with haymaking (using scythes with long wooden handles and heavy iron blades) and the harvesting of corn (using much smaller hand sickles) which was gathered and put in two-wheeled wagons for transporting back to the village store.

As autumn approached many of the farm animals were put out to pasture to fatten up for the "winter kill", the cattle and sheep going on grazing land and the pigs to the forest where acorns were in abundance. Housing and feeding these animals during the winter months was a difficult and costly task, so the best breeding stock and those supplying constant food such as dairy cattle were kept, whilst many of the remainder were slaughtered and salted for winter storage and use.

A task which had been left to the winter month of December was the threshing of the corn with hinged wooden sticks (called flails) which separated the seeds from the head (or ear) of the plant harvested three or more months previously. The chaff (small husks in which the seed grows and is protected) was then sifted out and the resulting seed corn (which may be wheat, barley or oats) then bagged and either taken back for grinding into flour from which to make bread, or simply added to stews for bulk and goodness.

The little village had no corn mill at this time but Mrs S was quite skilled at making flour from the stone hand-quorn which her DIY husband had made for her birthday some years previously. The two round pieces of stone, one raised in the centre and the other hollowed out, were fairly easy to rotate once the smooth seeds were spread between their surfaces, although lifting off or replacing the heavy top stone had resulted in many a trapped finger, not to mention the uttering of the medieval version of "chuffin 'eck" on such occasions. Could it be that the expression "chaffin 'eck" was its originator?

In these times of self sufficiency, seldom was anything left to waste. Not only was Mrs S able to adequately use the corn seed, she was also able to put the chaff from which it had been separated to good use. Many a good pillow or mattress for the young one was able to be produced by stuffing these little husks into hessian or woollen bags and sacks.

Three years had passed since the uncertain time of King William's conquest and rumours of discontent amongst the Danish Lords in the north of the country had been circulating for some time. Mr S had been put on "Red Alert" once more but this time it was more serious. His loyalty and allegiance to Earl Waltheof was not in doubt but fighting for him was supposed to be in the name of the King. Unfortunately the Earl and his fellow nobles were rising up against William and news was filtering through that skirmishes had already started in more northern parts.

The news then broke that Norman soldiers were advancing on the area, this being evidenced by the sinister plumes of grey smoke which twisted their way up from the hilltops as if to warn those watching to be aware. A hurried meeting was called in the Thane's hall at which a decision was soon taken to abandon the village and make for the woods. Panic abounded as sobbing mothers and frightened children were ushered out first, whilst the menfolk gathered a few bare essentials and followed them.

Mrs S was breathless by the time she reached the relative safety of the dense trees, having half dragged little S most of the way. She glanced back and noticed that a group of the strongest men, armed with swords and axes, had remained until the last to ensure the safety of the elderly and infirm who were not able to travel with any degree of speed. As she expected, Mr S was one of them.

"Mummy, what's that strange noise?" asked little S nervously as a distant pulsating rumble steadily increased to match the pounding of her heart.

Before Mrs S was able to reply, a flurry of movement to her left was suddenly transformed into a crescendo of thundering hooves and shrieking cries as Norman warriors on horseback charged wildly towards the village.

Flailing feet and flashing blades tore indiscriminately through the fleeing village stragglers and the accompanying brave menfolk who tried in vain to stop them, leaving a trail of destruction and despair which would etch itself on Mrs S's mind for ever.

Billowing smoke and raging flames confirmed that the King's uncompromising servants had reached their destination, and for what seemed like an age, they metered out "rough justice" for the indiscretion of their foolish Lord.

With their task fulfilled, the marauding aggressors left as suddenly as they had arrived and for a minute or two a deathly silence hung over the shocked and disbelieving Sheffielders as they cowered in the sanctuary of the forest.

The smoke from the village was now drifting towards them on a gentle breeze which kindly picked up and carried the plaintiff cries of the surviving wounded to their waiting loved ones.

Mrs S was the first to move as, with a cry of desperation, she staggered and stumbled over the rough stubble towards the fallen victims, hoping against hope to see the face and hear the voice she so desperately loved.

"I'm still here lass. You can't get rid of me that easily."

The faltering, deep voice which drifted slowly up from the huddled figure on the ground was too much for this usually strong Sheffield lady, and she sobbed uncontrollably, as she knelt down and cradled her husband's head in her arms.

The next few hours were a mixture of joy and sadness for the village population as some were re-united with their loved ones and others suffered loss. Make-shift stretchers were hurriedly constructed from those stocks of timber which had not been torched and the dead and wounded were either carried by hand or pulled by oxen back to the confines of their once proud home.

Many of the little thatched huts had been reduced to smouldering ash and charred timbers although many more were left intact. Things could have been worse, but for those who lost both home and family life did not seem worth living.

Tending for the wounded was also a major task as herbs, plants, rough bandages and prayer were the only medical aids available, although, as today, a good dose of loving tender care always seemed to work wonders.

Arising from the ashes of this tragedy, however, came an even greater strength of community spirit as families took in friends, neighbours helped to rebuild homes and no one was left to go hungry.

The extent of the devastation wrought by the ruthless Normans also became evident as the next few days unfolded. Lone hilltop farmers, themselves once cruel Viking pirates, staggered into the village with tales of slaughter and destruction even more devastating than that which had happened here.

No one had been spared in this calculated act of reprisal by the new conqueror, but that gritty, stubborn nature which personifies the Sheffielder deepened their determination to carry on and succeed.

There is little doubt that strength of character would remain an essential part of survival as the first century of this new millennium came to a close.

The King had spared Earl Waltheof's personal home and property and even consented to him marrying his niece, such an event bringing with it even more power and wealth. Such unusual circumstances can only be put down to the Earl's ability to skilfully convince William that he hadn't really been part of the plot by his peers to overthrow him. Either the King was gullible (which I doubt) or the Earl could "talk the hind leg off a donkey" in the fashion of a true Sheffielder.

However, skilful talking was no compensation for outright foolishness, and after once again plotting to get rid of the King, he was beheaded for treason.

"That's torn it" exclaimed Mr S as he dunked his bread in the bowl of chicken broth which had been placed before him for supper on the evening that the dreadful news had been announced.

"You can bet your boots that we'll get a Norman as Lord of the Manor now. I hear that they're tipping this bloke Roger de Busi for the job; fat lot he knows about running a Manor!"

Her husband's words of wisdom would be recalled with trepidation by Mrs S in the years to come as a new and more tyrannical regime controlled the villagers lives and made them wish for better things to come. We shall see!

The Second Hundred Years (1100-1200 AD)

(a) Size and General Growth

THIS century saw significant progress in the growth of Sheffield with its population increasing from about 400 to 700.

A wooden castle was built by the Lord of the Manor at the point where the River Sheaf met the River Don on the site now occupied by Castle Market, and a Parish Church was built on the site of the present Cathedral to serve the religious needs of the slowly growing population.

In between these two landmarks, the little town of Sheffield gradually began to take shape with a cluster of thatched wooden houses being built initially in the area around the castle walls.

A cornmill, called the Town Mill for many centuries to come, was built at Millsands (which runs off Bridge Street), and close by the town's first wooden bridge was built over the River Don at what is now called Lady's Bridge.

To accommodate the sick poor of the town, a hospital (called St Leonard's) was also built outside the town on fields in an area which became known as Hospital Hill (later shortened to Spital Hill). Although called a hospital, St Leonard's was really an almshouse for the elderly and infirm, as hospitals and medical treatment as we know it did not arrive for several hundred years.

Sheffield of today, of course, encompassed many districts which, as already explained, were simply separate homesteads, hamlets or villages at this time.

Beauchief, or "beautiful headland" was the name given to one such area which was established during this century by the Norman monks who occupied the new Abbey founded about the 1180s.

The nearby hamlet of Ecclesall already had its own little chapel, built in 1046, to which the Beauchief Abbey Monks walked over beautiful countryside to take the service. The derivation of this little hamlet's name appears, however, to

Beauchief Abbey.

have given historians some problems as it varies from "Hecksel Hall" (the witches hill or slope), to "Ecklishal or Eccleshale" meaning land or slope on which an ancient British church stood. I favour the latter interpretation.

(b) Local Rule and Government

Local rule during this century was probably one of the most important in Sheffield's history. It encompassed three generations of the de Lovetot family as Lords of the Manor and began in about the year 1116 with William de Lovetot, acknowledged as the real founder of Sheffield.

This Norman baron from Huntingdonshire succeeded from Roger de Busli and was responsible for all the building and growth which took place over the first half of the century. By all accounts he was, unlike most Norman nobility of the time, a relatively caring Lord who showed some concern regarding the welfare of the people of his town. This was evident by his building of the hospital and the church, the latter being his most long lasting memorial, as by founding the church he established its parish boundaries.

These boundaries drawn round the little church in the mid-1100s encompassed a large area which included many homesteads, hamlets and villages, the whole of which was the same as the area of the City of Sheffield in the year 1900. Thus, the area for which the Church and its clergy were responsible (which may be the whole or part of a town, city or village, or may encompass many villages over a wide area) did not change with regard to Sheffield for about 750 years.

For clarity, it should be pointed out that the physical and welfare needs of a society are provided by its local government organisation (Lords of the Manor to Local Councils), whilst the spiritual needs of such society are provided by the Church and clergy whose area of responsibility (its parish) is often different to that covered by local government.

The new social system or way of life (feudal system) had begun to have significant effect by the end of this century. Although the de Lovetot dynasty ruled with reputed consideration for the people of their town for 70 years or so, the emphasis of the Norman Kings (Henry I and Henry II during this time) was that of even stricter enforcement of law and order. Even breaches of the peace were severely punished and hanging for robbery was common.

The last few years of this century saw the marriage of Maude, the daughter of the last surviving member of the de Lovetot family, to a Norman Knight Gerard de Furnival who became the new Lord of the Manor in about 1190.

Gerard was one of many who went on the Crusades to Jerusalem to rid the area of the Saracens (Arabs and Moslems) during the very lengthy "Holy War". Richard the "Lionheart" was King of England at this time and Gerard de Furnival followed his popular King to war and unfortunately to his death in 1219.

(c) Working Life

Farming was still the predominant occupation of Sheffielders and took up most of their time although towards the end of the century early iron smelting was being carried out in one or two locations in the outer areas. This very early beginning of industry took place in the open air and required local iron ore, a supply of charcoal provided by charcoal burners in the forest and a good wind for several days to keep up a well heated primitive furnace. Arrowhead Smiths also began working in the area at this time, one such hearth being recorded at Brightside.

Evidence of farming in the outlying areas and of the existence of what eventually were to become Districts of Sheffield is gained from records made in 1184 which identified Fulwood Booth and Old Booth, Bradfield (booth being an old Danish word meaning shelter) as being restocked with 40 cows, four bulls and eight oxen. The cows and bulls clearly identify the existence of thriving dairy farms which breed from their own stock, whilst the oxen (usually eight to a plough) show that the farms also undertake agriculture.

(d) Domestic and Social Life

Homelife was still very basic and difficult during this age of strict rule by the Norman Lords and little time was left other than for working and sleeping.

The old Anglo-Saxon and Danish laws had been abolished which required the poor to work for and be the responsibility of house-holders and did, in fact, result in the lessening of tensions and unrest which had built up with this arrangement. In its place, however, were left many poor people with nowhere to call home who were left to starve if unable to obtain food by begging or stealing.

The village community was growing, nevertheless, and the children helped their parents at work from a very early age doing farmyard chores, fetching water and helping to make clothes and baskets. These tasks, coupled with evening storytelling by their tired mother or father, also formed the basis of their limited education as schooling would not be available for at least another 400 years!

If time did become available for entertainment, competitive games such as running and wrestling were probably the most popular whilst an evening firelight sing-along over a pot of ale would always end the day well.

For those who were better off, a little more variety of food was becoming available with fruits now including gooseberries and damsons. Unfortunately, their popularity, caused by a glut during many good harvests, resulted in an alarming increase in diarrhoea amongst many of the population, possibly a fitting punishment for their greed!

The poorer working class, however, still had to be content with simple broth's of meal, vegetables and herbs, together with home-baked, hard bread and cheese, although the occasional rabbit or pigeon for roasting was a delicacy to look forward to. Fish was still very popular and was made more so by the introduction of compulsory fish days during lent and on Wednesdays, Fridays and Saturdays in an attempt to keep the nation's fishing fleet busy. It is hardly likely that remote little Sheffield complied with this directive to any great degree.

Shopping, of course, was still an activity of the future and although money in the form of silver pennies were in circulation, "fair exchange" was still the common form of obtaining food and goods, at least as far as the working classes were concerned.

There was little, if any, improvement in the prevention or cure of illness and infirmity and only the clean, wholesome air and unpolluted water aided a relatively healthy survival. Sanitation was still unheard of amongst the average townspeople, although the Lord of the Manor probably had servants willing and able to dispose of his natural waste and prepare a weekly bath for him.

(e) Travel and Communications

Walking and riding on horseback were still the only methods of travel, the latter not being available to those other than the better off. Except for the very slow development of streets in the little townships, roads into or out of the area were not in existence and rough tracks over rocky terrain had to be used by the nobility to communicate with their peers and King when such was necessary.

Local transport within the Manor usually entailed the pulling of wooden carts, either by the villagers themselves or by harnessing to an oxen.

Chapter Two
1100 to 1200

THE dawn of the new century was one of mixed feelings for the villagers of Sheffield. Their determination to succeed had resulted in the creation of new and better homes for many of the hard-working population who could now enjoy the luxury of an "inside fire" to brighten up their lives. However, opportunities to earn enough to live on had reduced and times were certainly hard.

Moving house, as we all know, is an exciting time for anyone, and for Mr & Mrs S it was no exception. Standing in the doorway of their new home with his arm placed lovingly around his wife's shoulders, Mr S admired the new 12th-century layout, with its high-class central stone hearth and two little shuttered windows. The high timber walls were particularly impressive and certainly appealed to Mrs S.

"Its big enough to hold a dance in here, isn't it love?" she said to Mr S.

"Well, I wouldn't go so far as to say that, but at least we can move around without knocking our heads against the thatch now. It always irritated me that did."

Mrs S smiled quietly to herself as she recalled that most things irritated her husband, and she always kept out of his way when he was building or making anything.

"I think I'll light a fire to warm the place up. It feels a bit nippy in here, don't you think so love?"

A grunt was the best response that could be expected as Mr S critically examined his handiwork, particularly the smoke-hole in the centre of the thatched roof, above which he'd constructed a cover to prevent water coming in during heavy rainfall.

Now lighting a fire was not the easiest job in the world for our ancestors and, indeed, matches were not destined to be invented for another 700 years or so! The 12th-century housewife was, nevertheless, expected to cope with all such challenges and accordingly set about her task. After carefully spreading a little dried moss and soft down feathers on the centre of the thick stone slab forming the hearth, she took up the piece of sharp-edged stone which was kept at the fire-side and struck it against a piece of yellow "iron-stone" held in her other hand.

The proof that this primitive method actually worked was amply demonstrated by Mr S's reaction when, on the sixth strike of the stone, a fragment of metal flew off and landed on her already irritated husband's foot, which reacted with the speed of light to the "assault".

"Bloody 'ell woman, that was hot!"

Hardly able to contain herself, Mrs S stifled her laughter, uttered a brief apology and continued striking the stones until a hot fragment landed on the soft tinder patiently waiting to smoulder. A few quick puffs of breath soon aroused a small flame which hungrily devoured the straw and small dry twigs which were subsequently fed to it. Within minutes, spiralling twists of smoke searched inquisitively for the opening which would give them freedom whilst others spread their grimy hands around the clean walls of the little cottage intent on making their mark as soon as possible.

Mr S was rather anxious to get off as he had work to do in the fields of the Lord of the Manor this week along with all the other peasants in the village. This had to be done before continuing with work on their own land as part of the "services for land" deal which his Lordship had imposed on villagers.

Not everyone, of course, was a peasant (or villain as they were often called). Many were simply labourers who had no possessions, no home of their own and were in effect slaves. Take Thomas and Josh for instance. They worked for Mr S in return for a bed at night and a bit of food during the day. They'd proved to be particularly helpful whilst he was building his new home, doing much of the "leg work" whilst he provided the know-how.

However, our kindly Sheffield family struggled to make ends meet themselves and were wondering how to keep both men on. Letting them go was not a simple matter as the incident in the village last month had proved.

It had started simply enough. Mr Weaver's strip of land which he cultivated near to the forest had been trampled by wild game (possibly deer or boar, no one really knew for certain) and his crops had been destroyed. Since the Lord had brought in new laws punishable by death or torture for killing his game, this type of occurrence was becoming more common. However, the consequence of this action had necessitated Mr Weaver letting his labourer go as he simply couldn't afford to keep him. In desperation the poor fellow had wandered off and, coming upon the nearby home of a wealthy Yeoman, had broken in and stolen food and some personal possessions. His apprehension by the Lord's guard had been swift and the subsequent trial at the Manorial Court had led to his conviction and a subsequent death penalty being imposed.

The sight of his sad lifeless body hanging on the scaffold

was still fresh in the minds of Mr & Mrs S as they mulled over the problem of Thomas and Josh.

"Let's leave it for a few more days dear" pleaded Mrs S "I'm sure something will turn up".

Never had the lady said a truer word, for the very next day news came that Sheffield was to have a new Lord of the Manor who wanted to build himself a castle to live in.

Whilst locals were uncertain what to expect of this new Lord who went by the a fanciful name of William de Lovetot, they knew that building-work meant jobs and for this they were grateful.

Within a week or so, the new Lord sent his bailiff to the village to recruit teams of men to carry out the construction. There was no shortage of volunteers, evidenced by the fact that a large crowd had gathered on the banks of the river to listen to what he had to say.

"Listen here gentlemen. His Lordship has charged me with the responsibility of securing the services of both skilled and unskilled men to carry out this project in the quickest possible time. I shall require carpenters to construct the castle tower and other associated buildings, joiners to build fittings and furniture and strong, willing men for labouring work. Are there any takers?"

No response came from the crowd as the men shuffled and murmured amongst themselves.

"He's a bit "posh" this fellow isn't he. What's all this about "gentlemen". There's none of them sort here!"

"I've never built a castle before. I wouldn't know where to start, would you?"

"I hope this new Lord isn't expecting us to work for nowt. I've got a family to feed".

"Alright, alright, gentlemen. If you wish to know more, you've only to ask".

"Well sir," blurted out Mr S trying his best to be polite, "how about telling us what this 'ere castle looks like and how we're going to build it."

Pleased at last that someone had actually responded, the bailiff briefly explained that the castle would be what was known as a Motte and Bailey type, constructed entirely of timber. The main tower or keep would be constructed on a large mound (or motte) and would also have a large court-yard (or bailey) in which other buildings would be located for housing some of the soldiers, the horses, stores and food. Both the motte and the bailey would be surrounded by a wooden stockade and a wide ditch or moat.

"I will need 50 strong men to dig the ditch which forms the moat and 20 more to cart the excavated soil and rock to the site of the motte to be used for its construction. The carpenters, meantime, will construct bridges and buildings, and I require the whole project to be completed within three months."

"Three months! He must be mad" exclaimed Mr Weaver, unable to contain himself.

"And what about wages?"

"I'll pay master carpenters and joiners one and a half pennies a day (about ½p in today's money) and common carpenters a penny. Labourers will not of course be paid, but will be well fed and housed until the work is complete".

"This new Lord's not exactly chucking his money about is he?" muttered Mr S to his colleague as they all queued up to sign on. "At least Thomas and Josh will be looked after and the missus will welcome the penny or more I can earn every day."

Work was very hard during the next three months during which time many whippings were used to ensure that those who slacked in their duties did not do so a second time.

Mrs S hardly saw her husband as no sooner did he stagger home after six or seven hours at the castle, then he was off again to tend the animals or work in the fields until the light faded.

"I'll be pleased when this bloomin' castle's finished," she sighed. "Little S hardly recognises you these days. It's alright having extra money, but we need a life as well!"

Times hardly change, do they? How many times do you hear the same comments made today, 800 years or more later?

At last the work was finished. It had taken just over three months as several days of heavy rain had hampered progress considerably. The Lord's agent was, nevertheless, pleased

with the result and on the day of William de Lovetot's arrival the bright yellow sun was beaming in a clear blue sky as if to welcome him.

Those who had worked on the project had been invited to attend the castle's official opening and were assembled in the courtyard, whilst most of the remaining villagers congregated on the river bank, curious to see their new Lord.

An advance party of armour clad horsemen suddenly appeared, galloping swiftly towards the assembled crowd which dispersed in alarm at their intimidating arrival. Laughing loudly, they clattered over the newly-constructed bridge spanning the deep moat at the entrance to the courtyard and admired their new home.

A further flurry of activity heralded the Lord of the Manor's arrival at the head of his personal company of soldiers. Looking resplendent astride his magnificent white horse in his fine silks and green robe he nodded to the inquisitive Sheffielders who had regrouped at the castle entrance. It was really quite a spectacular scene as the greens, blues and reds of soldiers tunics contrasted with the whites and blacks of their prancing steeds, whilst their silver grey armour and shields reflected continuously changing bolts of sunlight in all directions.

The back cloth upon which this colourful scene was painted was equally breathtaking as the new castle tower sat majestically on its huge mound, cloaked by endless mountains of lush green trees which gave way to pasture and farmland in the meandering river valleys below.

"He doesn't look a bad sort of chap, does he?" voiced Mr S, acutely aware of the huge, sweating flank twitching perilously close to where he was standing as he was lightly brushed by its well groomed tail.

"I wasn't keen on the first bunch who came in mind you. They looked a right rowdy lot."

"Come on gentlemen" came the now familiar voice. "If you wish to eat, follow me."

The bailiff, looking nearly as well turned out as his Lord, led the hungry workers to the far side of the courtyard where a group of women from the village had just finished preparing

large quantities of cooked meats, vegetables and fruit. Two large tables of such food had been set aside for them, there being sufficient distance between these and the remainder of the tables to ensure that the soldiers did not have to mix with the common Sheffield villagers, even on an occasion such as this.

Not all the soldiers were hostile, however, as some were not of Norman origin. Although being in the service of the Norman Lord, several were of Anglo-Saxon or Danish background, having fought as professionals for their respective Kings. Time had brought the mixed races together and men were being chosen for their fighting ability rather than simply their nationality.

Language had also presented problems for some time as Danish speech had been totally foreign to the Angles, and Normandy French was likewise alien to them both.

"They don't talk proper them lot" exclaimed Mr S as he washed down a mouthful of chicken leg with a large beaker of ale. "I don't know why we always get foreigners in charge. It's just not right!"

The festivities carried on throughout the day until Mr S could eat and drink no more and by the time he arrived home he was most certainly the worse for wear.

"You can sleep over there and don't dare complain that you're feeling ill" came a voice from within as the lurching figure almost fell through the doorway of their new little home. "And don't wake up little S, she's not been well today".

A troubled night was in store for our unfortunate reveller as his feelings of nausea and dizziness were punctuated by cries of distress from his young daughter who complained of pains in her stomach.

No one had much sleep that night and as the gentle rays of the dawn sunlight reached through the small windows, Mrs S looked troubled and concerned. As she rekindled the warm embers of the fire she tried to recall the previous day's events which might account for little S's worsening illness.

"We went into the woods yesterday and gathered berries from the trees. A couple of charcoal burners were there, raking out their pit, and we shared the berries with them"

"But did you all eat them or was it just little S?"

"I didn't have any myself" responded his agitated wife," but the child and the two men did. In fact it was at their request that we shared them as they said they often ate them as a kind of delicacy."

Now Mrs S had an enquiring mind and there was something troubling her which she couldn't put her finger on. She recalled the large, black rooks which had edged forward to cheekily steal some of the discarded berries before scurrying back to the charcoal pit to peck amongst its contents. She also recalled the black stained fingers of the men as they gratefully received the soft berries and licked off the juice after eating.

"That could be it," she suddenly exclaimed. "It could be the charcoal. Don't you see?"

Mr S didn't see, but put it down to the gentle throbbing still echoing in his head.

"If those berries were poisonous then the men and even the birds should have been affected. But they all ate charcoal, the men from their fingers without knowing it, and the birds deliberately because they knew it would do them good".

Mr S had always thought that his wife was a perceptive woman but this was taking it too far. Little did he know, that over many years some birds had acquired the knowledge that charcoal was a natural antidote to some of nature's poisonous berries.

"But that's sheer guess-work dear. I think…"

"Never mind what you think", she retorted, "I want you to fetch me some charcoal straight away. A few pieces will do and the men will be only too happy to oblige. Off you go, now."

Not knowing where the charcoal pit was located in the vast woodland, the beleaguered husband carefully tip-toed round the question before establishing that "anyone with any sense would know where it was". He knew that Mrs Weaver had been with them on previous walks and decided it would make good sense to ask her instead of incurring further chastisement from the anxious mother.

This decision proved to be a good one as Mrs Weaver knew of two such pits, the nearest of which was about half an hour's good walk away.

It was less than an hour later when an out of breath Mr S returned with several pieces of the prized, blackened wood and presented them to his grateful wife. Not knowing the best way to give them to her still suffering daughter, she scraped the black surface with a knife and added the fine flakes to a small amount of chicken broth which the child had been sipping for the last hour or two.

"All we can do now is wait. It will work won't it?"

The large, tearful eyes gazing up from the tired but determined face reminded Mr S just how precious his wife was as he put a comforting arm around her.

"Of course it will my dear. Of course it will."

There was no one more surprised and relieved than Mr S later that day, when, after several doses of the "black medicine", a pale little figure emerged from her sick room and slowly walked over to the two wheeled wooden cart which he was busily repairing.

"I'm feeling much better daddy. Thank you for fetching the magic medicine for me."

* * * * * * * * * *

Life soon got back to normal in the village following the "excitement" of the Lord's arrival at his new castle, and the men worked hard cutting and storing wood for use during the months ahead. It would be haymaking time before long and the women busily removed the rust from the long bladed scythes using hard flat stones which also gave them a keen edge.

William do Lovetot had now settled in and was taking an active interest in his people. In particular he was concerned for their pastoral care and decided he would build them a church. He had come to respect Mr S's advice during the building of the castle, and he now requested his views on the suitability of the site he had chosen for the church's construction.

On a fine morning in late June, Mr S was summoned to accompany the Lord, together with his personal guard and advisers, on a visit to the site, commencing at the castle gates. Pointing to the ridge about 400 metres up the western valley-side, the small party made its way up the trodden pathway between the picturesque open fields and mature oak woods to their destination. Today, this route would follow the line of Haymarket, Castle Square and High Street.

The view from the ridge was magnificent as it took in the river valleys to the north and east and the wooded hills to the south and west. As a landmark, a church on this site would be seen for miles around and would be the focal point of the Sheffield Parish.

"Choose the best men, Mr S, and build me a small but sturdy church before the onset of winter. I'll pay you well but be sure to finish on time."

Without waiting for a response, his Lordship continued.

"Come next spring, we must build ourselves a corn mill at yonder bend in the river so that we may all benefit from bigger and better harvests. The little township sorely needs it."

"That's the briefest consultation I've ever had," thought Mr S as he followed the nodding, smiling group of men back down the valley side until politely taking his leave at the village entrance. The large hall in the centre was mainly used as a meeting place for the menfolk since the death of the head man in the last century, and it was to this building that he now make his way. Many were waiting for him on his arrival, and a runner soon told the rest that their presence was required if at all possible.

Addressing his friends and neighbours, Mr S explained the Lord of the Manor's proposals and emphasised the limited time scale which he had imposed.

"The church is the first priority, and we'll have to plan the work carefully to fit in with our other chores. His Lordship will still expect us to work in his fields and provide him with his quota of corn and other farm produce, otherwise he'll have us working for nothing!"

"It's them whip-wielding bully-boys of his I don't care for" came a shout from the back. "They expect blood for a penny a day."

Murmurs of agreement rippled round the room, and Mr S had to concede that the Norman soldiers who supervised the work had little or no feeling for those carrying it out. He also realised, nevertheless, that the villagers really had no choice in the matter and regardless of the hardships encountered, it meant food for many who would otherwise go without.

Despite the demands of haymaking and harvesting during the mid-summer months, labourers were sent to fell the trees and prepare the site for the new church. The long sunny evenings were used to the full by the team of carpenters, and although the first signs of frost had appeared before they put the finishing touches to their work, the church was completed on time.

Sheffield now had its Parish Church, and with this located at one extremity and the castle at the other, the village became a township as it grew along the new High Street which linked the two.

* * * * * * * * *

The corn mill which the ambitious Lord had spoken of was most certainly a good idea and the townsfolk had become used to the routine of combining their normal farm duties with those of building workers. There were, of course, several experienced men in the township whose main occupation was that of carpentry, although by far the majority were farmers with considerable DIY skills.

It was April before building work began, as the demands on time for soil preparation and the sowing of seed were considerable before then if the yearly crops were to succeed. The closeness of the site to the river had the considerable advantage that materials could be transported by boat if required, although much of the timber for the mill's construction was readily available in the forests nearby.

Whilst building work was in progress, it became evident that the land beyond the river was ideally suited for growing corn, although access to it was not possible except by boat. Mr S suggested to his Lordship that the construction of a wooden bridge (later to be called Lady's Bridge) would open up the area and be of benefit to everyone.

"It's a wonderful idea, Mr S, a wonderful idea. Tell your men to start as soon as they've completed the mill."

Both projects, of course, necessitated the assistance of the Lords soldiers, whose skills, strength and superior tools and equipment combined with those of the townsfolk to produce the best and quickest construction.

As with the castle, William de Furnival was pleased with his corn mill and the new bridge over the River Don, and he felt that a token of his appreciation would not go amiss. Despite the ruthlessness of his staff in enforcing law and order, he had a soft spot for the townsfolk and, being aware of the desperate plight of some of the poorer people, partic-

ularly the elderly and the sick, he decided to do something positive to help.

Summoning Mr S for yet another audience with him, he explained his proposals.

"I intend to build you all a hospital on the open valley side beyond the river in return for your help and support since my arrival. Access to it will be easy now that you have constructed the bridge and you can decide amongst yourselves how it is to be run and who may be admitted."

The townsfolk were delighted when Mr S broke the good news to them, and in what seemed no time at all, the little hospital of St Leonard stood proudly on the hillside surrounded by beautiful meadows.

Both the hospital and the corn mill provided additional and varied work for the people of the township, Mr and Mrs Weaver's daughter taking up residence as a nurse with several of her friends whilst the technically minded chose to operate the new-fangled grinding wheel in the water-driven mill.

Mr S had by now become the recognised spokesman for the township although all decisions were still taken collectively at meetings in the large hall. Many of the young men chose to join the armed forces of the Lord of the Manor and the way of life progressed steadily under three generations of de Lovetots.

Gerard de Furnival, the last incumbent of the post in this century, was far less popular than his predecessors, particularly with the mothers of the township. His enthusiasm for glory and excitement was understandable as his life had been spent fighting, much of it as a brave and capable knight in the service of his King. He had little interest in the township other than to encourage the strongest and bravest to join him and follow him to war.

Mrs S had given birth to a son 17 years earlier and the strapping young man was unhappy to follow the family tradition of farming.

"If it's been good enough for your father for all these years, then it's good enough for you".

"But mother," came the usual exasperated response, "I don't want to be a farmer. It would bore me to tears; I just want to do my own thing".

Mrs S stomped out of her neat little cottage muttering to herself.

"Kids, you can't tell them anything. You bring them into this world and what do you get? Ingratitude, that's what. It wasn't like that when I was young. You had to do as you were told and that was that."

She didn't notice her husband coming back from the mill as she hurried round to Mrs Weaver's to gain a bit of sympathy. "And you're no help," she shouted as they both collided. "You let him do just what he wants."

It wasn't the most difficult of tasks for Mr S to guess that mother and son had been having words again as he opened the door to his home.

"Look dad, this bloke Gerard de Furnival's having an "open day" at the castle tomorrow and I must go. He's going to explain about these crusades he goes on at the other side of the world, AND he's going to show us how to fight. All my mates are going and I just can't miss it."

"I know what you're going through son. Your mother's afraid of losing you, that's all. Just do what you think best, but make sure you do think hard before deciding. Fighting isn't as glamorous as you might think, you know".

It was a sombre evening at home as all three of them sat in silence, knowing what each other was thinking but daring to say nothing.

"Anything for supper love?" said dad, trying to relieve the tension.

"Is that all you can think about? I sometimes think you enjoy your food more than you do me," retorted his rather fed-up wife.

They glared at each other for a moment and then burst into laughter realising how funny that must have sounded. Before long the whole house was full of laughter and they eventually retired to their straw filled mattresses to see just what tomorrow would bring.

The following morning came to life in a blaze of sunshine, which quickly burnt away the mass of red and gold streaks painted so dramatically across the sky. Following a hurried breakfast of cheese, bread and a mug of ale, the excited teenager made his way to the castle courtyard where demonstrations of jousting, sword play and hand-to-hand physical combat had already commenced. The paddock in the shady corner of the simulated battlefield housed several well-groomed stallions which gained the admiration of everyone. The whole scene was a 17-year-old's dream which, even without the subsequent "sales-talk" from the armour clad knight who Lorded over the manor, had already convinced him of what decision to take.

The sun was beginning to sink behind the distant hills as the weary teenager returned home.

"Well son, how did it go?"

"Mum, its great. I've signed on."

Mrs S caught her breath and had all on to control her emotions.

"Don't worry mum. Hardly anyone gets hurt. I'll be home in no time."

Those words haunted Mrs S for the rest of the century as she heard nothing from her son who had departed that following month for Palestine to fight alongside his Lord and his King. We can only speculate when and if he returned home.

The Third Hundred Years (1200-1300 AD)

(a) Size and General Growth

THE population during the first half of this century probably grew at a fairly steady rate and is estimated at about 900 by the year 1250.

However, in 1266, barons opposing the way that King Henry II ruled his country marched through and plundered the Norman-controlled township of Sheffield, burning down both its castle and the parish church. Although the rebellion was short-lived, Sheffield had to almost start again and whilst many people would have fled to the hills for safety, many others were probably killed.

The burning down of such important buildings as the castle and the church inspired their replacement by bigger and more substantial buildings. The new stone castle was built in 1270 and was destined to last until halfway through the 17th century. Ten years later, in 1280, the church was also rebuilt and dedicated as the Church of Saints Peter and Paul, which, with very extensive alterations and improvements, was to eventually become the Sheffield Cathedral of today.

During this time, the small manors of **Ecclesall, Darnall, Owlerton, Wadsley** and **Shirecliffe** were created by the Lord of the Manor, although they were not part of Sheffield as we now know it and probably had very small populations.

By the end of this century, therefore, Sheffield had a fine stone castle linked by its narrow High Street to a small but beautiful church. A few wooden cottages had been built near to and between these new buildings which, together with the mill by the river and the almshouse on Spital Fields, set the scene for the growth yet to come.

(b) Local Rule and Government

Just as the de Lovetots ruled the area during most of the 12th century, the de Furnivals ruled for most of the next two.

Following the death of Gerard, the first de Furnival, his son Thomas took over in 1219. This family was, by all accounts, more interested in war than in looking after Sheffield's interests, and Thomas (the first) spent much time and money out of the country on costly crusades where, like his father before him, he was killed in battle.

There were five Thomas de Furnivals in all who ruled over Sheffield, and it was the second Thomas who actually secured the permission of the King to have the castle rebuilt in stone.

The third Thomas, who took over as Lord of the Manor in 1272, held the position for 60 years during which time, in 1297, he granted a famous "Charter" (a written grant of rights and privileges on the authority of the King) to the people of Sheffield which gave them a measure of self government. The Charter basically did the following:

(i)   It gave the Lord's free tenants, those occupying land and property on rent from the Lord under the feudal system, the ownership of such possessions for life.

(ii)   It discharged the tenants from their obligations to work for the Lord under the feudal system.

(iii)   It allowed the tenants to broadly run their own affairs (more or less on the principle of a small borough council) which resulted in their selection of a Town Collector to oversee such organisations.

(iv)   It established courts to be held every three weeks by the Lord's bailiffs, and any fines imposed on anyone convicted had to be determined by the tenants themselves. This court was known as the Court Leet and was held at Sheffield Castle.

Whilst this represented the first step on the road to local government in Sheffield, the conditions applied to such Charter were:

(a)   The Lord still demanded total loyalty and allegiance to himself.

(b)   An annual payment of £3 8s 9¼d must be paid to the Lord for the discharge of services and demands.

(c)   Property and land reverted to the Lord if the tenant owner had no legal heirs upon his death.

(d)   The Lord was still responsible for upholding the law.

(e)   No one was allowed to trespass on to the Lord's land upon which his game is preserved.

In effect the Lord of the Manor still ruled personally with ultimate power, but the benefits to the people were still considerable.

It must be remembered, however, that the labouring classes still had no rights and in effect were slaves who were still not very highly regarded by the aristocracy.

Indeed, laws were passed nationally prohibiting vagabondage (wandering without a fixed home) with cruel punishments for those convicted.

In general, the rule of the sword was still applied by the Normans although it is possible that Sheffield fared better than some areas in the light of the introduction of this limited degree of local rule now allowed in the township.

During this century one national event which impacted on the exercise of law and order locally was the signing of the famous Magna Carta (the Great Charter) by King John, under pressure from the country's barons, in 1215. It finally became the law of the land in 1225 and pledged the King to uphold the feudal system of the country. In particular it stated that no freeman should be imprisoned, exiled or deprived of property except by the law of the land, and that law and justice should apply to all, even the King.

Did You Know that during the reign of King John in the years 1199 to 1216, he was reputed to take a bath once every three weeks? Bathing by his subjects was much less frequent and took place in large, wooden communal tubs as long as the water stayed hot.

After Magna Carta, manorial courts were not able to deal with felonies (serious offences such as murder, rape, arson, burglary), such cases from Sheffield being heard at York Assizes or the West Riding Quarter Sessions.

Imprisonment in York Gaol was common, the conditions there being a horrific blend of starvation, disease, brutality and death. If the penalty of the York court was execution, this was usually carried out in Sheffield itself.

This century also saw the introduction of the country's first parliament convened by Simon de Montfort, a French knight who became the Earl of Leicester and a favourite of the King. De Montfort's parliament of 1265 included two knights from every shire and two burgesses from every town and in effect was the beginning of the House of Commons, although Sheffield township was far too small at this time to be included.

(c) Working Life

This period saw a gradual shift in Sheffield township from that of a farming community to its creation as a little market town, evidenced by the fact that in Thomas de Furnival's first Charter of 1296, he consolidated the trend by granting a

market in Sheffield every Tuesday as well as a fair to be held once a year.

The real beginning of the area as a potential industrial centre was also evident with little smithies operating in **Sheffield Park** and local woods.

Charcoal continued to be produced to feed the smithies, using raw material from the forests, whilst stone was available from the quarries of **Rivelin**.

By the end of the century there was also evidence of coal-working in the Manor of **Norton**, probably near to Hutcliffe Wood in the vicinity of the River Sheaf, and the monks of Beauchief Abbey were given permission to dig and use it.

(d) Domestic and Social Life

This must have been an unsettling time for the people of Sheffield as wars raged both at home and abroad for most of the century.

The Crusades in Palestine, wars with France and conflict with Wales and Scotland, all demanded the allegiance of the Lord's people at such times. Many a family would be temporarily or permanently without a husband or father during these 100 years. The civil strife which resulted in the destruction of much of Sheffield in the middle of the century was obviously catastrophic and life must have revolved around survival as much as anything.

The latter part of the century, however, saw better times, particularly with more independence given to the free tenants (but not the slave labourers) with Thomas de Lovetot's Charter.

Little time was probably available to other than the aristocracy for relaxation and leisure, and the very poor had an even harder time as wandering around begging for food became a heavily punishable offence.

Not surprisingly food continued to be held in importance,

particularly by the rich who enjoyed their lavish meals. Beef had developed as the country's favourite meat, whilst pork and ham were in some decline. Sausages and black puddings together with spices and onions also graced their tables, with a starter of oysters and a sweet of strawberries complementing the meal.

Affordability, of course, was the "name of the game" for the working classes, and oatmeal porridge, bread, cheese and stews could be washed down with ale which sold at only ½p for four gallons.

(e) Travelling and Communications

Whilst horseback and walking remained the only modes of travel, with written communication being entrusted to faithful servants, narrow pack horse tracks were being trodden along the valley bottoms and over the hilltops by a few travellers, some curious to see who these Sheffielders were and some desperate to leave the place behind. Soldiers who entered and destroyed much of the township in 1266 would have used such routes, although with much difficulty and discomfort.

Chapter Three
1200 to 1300

"IF WE"RE not fighting in those crusades then we're at war with that lot from France!" Mrs S was feeling very vexed as yet another directive from the castle instructed the prime of the township's youth to report forthwith to follow their lordship into battle.

"It's not as though we've anything to fight about. I know that many of those high and mighty barons don't like the way that our King John does things, but fancy inviting foreigners over to help them! They must be mad."

It was, of course, Mrs S who was mad; she was mad that her beloved son had not returned; she was mad that the Lord of the Manor demanded more and more taxes for war; she was mad that she couldn't feel settled. But this was life in the 13th century.

Her regular weekly stroll down to the market in the castle courtyard did, however, make her feel more relaxed. It was a welcome change from the monotony of household chores, cooking meals, sowing and weaving, making clothes and helping on the farm. Feeding the chickens, collecting the eggs and milking the goats were still routine tasks that the womenfolk had to carry out, although the men did help with milking the cows. Catching rabbits in the ever-increasing number of warrens was something that the youngsters enjoyed doing, although it did form part of their duties to provide a tasty meal or two for their families whenever they could.

The castle market was not really what it seemed, as the large tables covered in an array of cloth, grain, meats and vegetables, around which a few squawking hens and hissing geese made their protests, was really a collection point for the Lord.

The little tenant farmers were obliged to provide the Lord with both goods and service in lieu of rent, although selling and bartering did take place in this market environment.

Mrs S's little wooden cart which she pulled behind her was overflowing with a variety of items varying from woollen shawls and hoods to eggs, butter, cheese and vegetables. It also

included two iron sickles which her husband had been given by the smiths in the Park area which overlooked the castle.

It was only a month previously that Mr S had decided to venture into the distant western hills to see for himself whether there was any truth in the rumour that iron was being produced by the locals who lived there. He knew that smithies were operating in the huge wooded park behind the castle and, being a shrewd man, he thought that if he could broker a bit of trade between the two, he might make a bob or two out of it for himself.

Armed with his usual bread, cheese and ale, he set off on his trek into the unknown. Fields gave way to woods, which in turn gave way to meadow land and then more woods. The distance seemed endless, although the scenery was magnificent. Wildlife was in abundance, although the sight of the mutilated carcass of a large stag made the brave rambler wonder whether wolves had been responsible, or whether it could be that the odd native brown bear was still roaming the forest?

It must have been an hour or more before he stumbled across the iron smelters amidst the small cluster of thatched huts and smoking little furnaces.

"Mornin' folks."

There was no response to his cheerful greeting other than suspicious stares from the workers.

"I'm from the township over there in the valley bottom. Look, you can just make out the Church."

It was several minutes before the wary smelters spoke, and from the sound of their accent they were obviously of Danish origin. They were not used to strangers on this rather breezy hillside and were not in a particularly welcoming mood.

"Well, what do you want?"

"I've heard on the grapevine how skilled you all are at producing iron in your "state of the art" furnaces, and I'm interested in buying some from you".

Now there's nothing better when confronting a Yorkshireman for the first time than hitting him with a good dose of flattery and the promise of money. As a budding entrepreneur, Mr S was an expert at this and the sudden change in the attitude of the smelters was ample proof of his skills.

"Well, Mr Townshipman, what can we do for you? Would you like to see how we work?"

Trying hard not to cough as a gust of wind fanned puthering, smokey fumes into his face, he followed the now cheerful, expectant workmen to a furnace which was being prepared.

"Boy, fetch Mr Townshipman a drink" called out the boss-man before starting with his explanation of the process as they stood in front of the stone, beehive-shaped, flat-topped iron producer. Large piles of iron ore had been heaped up on the edge of the small settlement clearing (having been collected from nearby excavations) adjacent to which were also several piles of charcoal burnt from trees in the surrounding woods.

"All we do is put this charcoal in the bottom of the stone furnace and get it glowing really hot before we pack it up with a mixture of more charcoal and that iron ore over there. If a few scoops of these white stones gets shoved in with it, it doesn't really matter. We then slide this stone slab over the top and you've got the hottest little oven you could wish for."

"And how long does it take?"

"Well, that's the tricky bit. With a good wind blowing through the gaps in the stones it only takes three or four days, but it often takes longer. We keep adding more charcoal, of course, through the hole in the top."

The boss-man went on to explain that they could tell when the process was complete as molten iron began to seep out of the bottom joints in the stonework, after which they let the whole furnace cool down before removing the lump of warm, hard metal.

Although impressed with the process, Mr S wondered if it would not, perhaps, be better to have an arrangement whereby the molten metal could be allowed to run out of the bottom of the furnace into some sort of channel formed in the ground, thereby allowing the furnace to keep hot for further, more continuous production. Perhaps someone would think of that later on.

The next hour was one of discussion and negotiation over a pot of ale and a slice of venison, a rare luxury illegally obtained from the forest, following which he made his thankful return home feeling pleased with his days dealings.

The following day saw Mr S visiting the Park smithies where the workmen were busy heating up iron they had bought from the castle market, and hammering it into shape whilst it was still glowing hot. By repeating the process many times they were able to produce a variety of tools, including the sickles which Mrs S had taken to the market to sell.

An agreement with the smiths was made, and within a week Mr S had despatched a sturdy wooden wagon pulled by two oxen to the iron-smelters which returned the same day with a good, fresh iron delivery to the smithies in the Park.

"And what do you get out of this", quizzed Mrs S when her husband returned home. "I hope it's worth it."

"Don't worry lass, I've made a bit of brass on this transaction and there's more to come. I've even had a sickle or two thrown in with the loose change."

Money, of course, is only useful when you can spend it and up to this century little trading had taken place in Sheffield amongst the peasants, who had to be self sufficient. The small but steady growth of the population, together with the introduction of metal goods, the building of the corn mill and the greater involvement of the Lord of the Manor, began to put money into circulation. Silver pennies were the main coins used although gold was used by the rich.

* * * * * * * * *

As a sense of stability threatened to establish itself in the developing township, the inevitable happened.

"They're off again" chimed Mrs S as the family sat down to their supper of pea and rabbit stew. "Those stupid barons are fighting each other again." She paused while her husband dunked an enormous piece of semi-stale bread into his thick gravy and almost choked after ramming it into his mouth.

"Mrs Weaver was only saying the other day that this French fellow called Simon de something-or-other was trying to overthrow the King and that a lot of barons were supporting him. What a nerve they've got."

Before Mr S could explain the point of the confrontation, she went on. "You can bet that his Lordship will get involved and then where will we be? We'll be in a right pickle that's what. Just you mark my words."

As usual the perceptive lady was completely right, for as the sun rose high the following day, pandemonium down at the castle soon spread to the township as the news everyone feared spread like wild-fire.

"The barons are coming. The barons are coming!"

Men were streaming back from the fields and terrified women raced around collecting their children from the scattered locations where they were happily and peacefully playing.

"What did I tell you?" sobbed Mrs S as she stood shaking outside their precious home crushing little S to her body as any protective mother would. "What shall we do, where shall we go?"

Her grim-faced husband stood there for a moment embracing them both, recalling with trepidation the previous bloody assault on their village. But the township was bigger now and the extending fields had pushed the woods that bit further away. He knew that the relatively small company of soldiers at the castle would be heavily outnumbered and would probably not put up much of a fight, if any. There was little the towns folk could do and he viewed with anxiety the congregating crowd of shouting, excitable young men who, against the wishes of their screaming loved ones, were preparing to take on the intruders.

"We'll have to make a run for it before its too late, just like the rest of them. If they chase us we're done for but we'll just have to hope."

"What about the church? Let's go there. They'll never dare torch the…"

Mrs S wasn't able to finish her sentence as the sight of the vast column of armour clad fighting men advancing along the river bank towards the castle had tightened her throat in a grip of terror.

"Oh my God, there's hundreds of them! Quick lass, over there to the woods. It's the nearest."

Glancing to their right as they fled the township, running figures and billowing smoke signalled the rapid end to any resistance from the castle. The advance through the township was equally severe as both sword and flame destroyed all in their path as the soldiers marched relentlessly on.

It wasn't often that Mrs S was wrong, but as deep red flames chased angry grey clouds through the windows and rooftop of the distant church, she thanked God that they hadn't had time to go there.

It was several hours before the last of the soldiers left. As the townsfolk crept back to their smouldering homes, the burning castle tower shone like a beacon on its huge mound as it sent out shimmering signals of distress to the sad remains of the hilltop church, which was unable on this occasion to offer any comfort at all.

As Mr and Mrs S stood amongst the ashes of their once proud cottage and gazed up in disbelief at the blazing remnants of the castle and the church which had taken so much time and effort to build, the initial emotions of sadness and grief were slowly overtaken by determination and pride, qualities which were to remain with Sheffielders until the end of time.

"WE'LL BUILD IT ALL UP AGAIN" roared Mr S, his voice trembling with emotion. "What do you all say?" The vocal support from the men, women and children now assembled around him was immediate, and with grim determination the daunting task began.

* * * * * * * * *

The civil unrest which had destroyed much of the township and many of its sons only seemed like yesterday, but four years had passed as seemingly endless streams of oxen-drawn carts carried huge blocks of stone with which to re-build the castle.

Thomas de Furnival had survived as Lord of the Manor and had decided that he would like a more permanent and secure home for himself and his family. The massive stone structure which now rose above the Sheffield township on the banks of its two, meeting rivers was most certainly that, and was in stark contrast to the simple homes of the peasants.

"Now that our daughter's grown up and can look after the home for us, I've decided to do a bit of part-time work at the castle," said Mrs S as she and her husband stood admiring the remarkable building. "I fancy a nosey round anyway and this is the best way of getting it."

"It's news to me woman. What about my meal when I get in from work?"

"There you go again, always thinking of your stomach. She'll cook you as good a meal as I can you know. In any case, its only mornings to start with so it will hardly affect you at all."

It was a slightly damp, chilly morning about two weeks later when Mrs S made her way down to the castle entrance. She wasn't really sure whether she was shivering with cold or with first-day nerves, but whatever the reason she pulled her shawl tightly over her head and shoulders.

Arriving at the bridge which spanned over the deep moat surrounding the castle, she took a deep breath and marched over, determined to show strength and confidence regardless of how she felt inside. She was ushered down a dark corridor by a fussy little man, who obviously had responsibility for domestic staff, and eventually arrived at the kitchen. It was the largest room Mrs S had ever seen, with two huge fireplaces let into the grey stone walls which seemed to go on for ever before reaching the thick timbers of the roof. The cold stone floor upon which sat several large oak tables was almost a welcome relief as the roaring log fires threw waves of heat over anyone who ventured near them. Holes had been let into the side walls to form ovens for baking, whilst further on another formed a sink which drained to the moat below.

Whilst still trying to catch her breath at the scale and ultra modern design of the kitchen, she peered out of one of the rather small windows overlooking the enclosed courtyard, in a corner of which stood the granary and the dairy. In the opposite corner was stabling for the horses, servants quarters and a well.

"I may as well show you round" said the fussy little man, "as you'll have to know where to go when you're wanted."

The remainder of the tour was as interesting as the incredible kitchen and Mrs S was bursting to tell her family about it as she hurried home in the early afternoon.

"You've never seen anything like it," were the first words which bounced around Mr S's ears as he came in from work later that day. "I thought the kitchen was big, but the "Great Hall" next to it was enormous. And the bedrooms; you ought to see the bedrooms!"

"Calm down, wife, calm down, I've not got through the door yet."

"But they had this bed with a thick, soft base called a mattress to lay on and soft pillows for your head and sheets to put over you and…"

"WHERE IS MY SUPPER?"

Realising she might have gone on a bit, Mrs S thought it might be prudent to give the tired, albeit spoiled, worker some attention before continuing with her account of the castle tour. She'd managed to bring home a few delicacies which had been left over from the Lord's meal the previous day and, wishing to please her husband, she arranged them carefully in his bowl. Two fine red strawberries on one side were matched by a plum and a damson on the other, whilst the centre of the bowl carried a black pudding and two cold sausages. Three small radishes garnished with tender chopped carrot completed the colourful mixture which, with loving care, she placed before her husband.

It was several seconds before the stunned Mr S was able to speak, not having seen such unusual and expensive food before.

"Just what the "ell have we here? It's food I'm after woman, not colourful garbage like this. I don't know whether to eat it, roll it or kick it!"

Her ungrateful husband stormed off to next door's cottage to calm down over a "quick half", a not unusual occurrence since their neighbour had taken to making ale on a large scale and was selling it at six gallons for a silver penny or the equivalent in goods. She re-heated the boring evening stew and wondered if she'd ever be able to experience the joys of comfort, relaxation and something different to eat.

"Oh well, you can't win 'em all," she mused with a glint in her eyes as she calmly tipped the dish of "delicacies" into the hot, bubbling broth and stirred it with extra vigour.

* * * * * * * * * *

Life had certainly been a struggle this century for the Sheffielders and it was with some envy that they heard the stories of pleasure, games and sports which circulated from the castle. Mrs Weaver's daughter had told of laughter and music at the Lord's regular banquets where she sometimes worked as a serving wench, with harps and horns leading the after-dinner dancing. Jugglers entertained whilst guests gambled with dice, and on a fine evening some of the men took to hitting hard wooden balls with clubs. Others preferred to go hunting and hawking, and many a fine pair of stag's antlers adorned the great hall as proof of their skills with the lance and the bow.

The very poor, however, were still at the mercy of his Lordship and entourage who used them as slaves. In fact it was only last week that Mrs Weaver had confided in Mrs S that her cousin's brother, who lived many miles from here, had been sold, along with his wife and children, by the Abbot (of all people) for 13s 4d, about 67p in today's money.

"You just can't trust anybody these days, can you?"

The next Lord of the Manor did, in fact, provide a new stone church for the use of the townsfolk, and for this they were very grateful. It was probably the only place where the suffering and bereaved could truly find some comfort and peace.

There was, in fact, some excitement as the century drew to a close. Instructions had been given for the townsfolk to congregate on the new green area outside the castle as Lord Thomas had some announcement to make at 12 noon.

"What's all this about?" grumbled Mr S "I've got three cottages to repair and then there's the milking to do afterwards."

"Stop moaning husband. If his Lordship says we have to go down to Castle Green for a meeting then that's that. No amount of complaining will change anything."

"Have I got to go as well?" chirped their teenage daughter. A quick glance at mum's frowning face gave her the answer.

Quite a crowd had gathered by the time the S family arrived. A cool breeze was blowing even though the sun was trying to disperse the light cloud.

"I hope we don't have to stand here long. It's cold and I want to go for a walk with Mrs Weaver's son when I've finished making you that shawl," said daughter S.

"There's more to living than making shawls and going out with boys, my girl. There's plenty of work for both of you to do before nightfall. And another thing, there's no wonder you're feeling cold. That dress you are wearing if far too short. No decent girl would show her ankles like that."

"Alright, alright you two. That will do," grumbled Mr S "I've come here to listen to an important announcement, not to listen to you both arguing as usual."

"OYEZ! OYEZ! OYEZ!" boomed out the bailiff as he began to read out the declaration on behalf of the Lord in the name of the King.

"Good grief, what's he shouting at. Has he stubbed his toe or something?"

Both Mrs S and her daughter cringed with embarrassment at the outburst and pretended they weren't with him, as the bailiff went on to explain that the townsfolk were now allowed to hold a market every week at which they could buy and sell their goods. This was the real beginning of Sheffield as a little market town and, when combined with the provisions of a second more extensive charter announced a year later, paved the way for the people to be more involved in running the township's affairs themselves.

Thus, democracy was born, and perhaps the population as a whole could now expect to be treated more fairly, more equally and with some respect. At least we can hope!

The Fourth Hundred Years (1300-1400 AD)

(a) Size and General Growth

The population of Sheffield had reduced due to the destruction of the town in the middle of the previous century and the wars abroad had taken their toll.

To compound this problem, the first 20 years of the century saw harvest failure, sheep deaths due to infectious disease and cattle deaths due to a virulent plague. Indeed, it has been observed that harvest failures and livestock disasters were unparalleled in the history of English farming.

As if this were not enough, the middle of the century brought in the Great Plague (Bubonic Plague combined with other diseases), commonly known as the "Black Death".

Whilst only at its peak during 1349-50, it wiped out up to 50 per cent of the population in many areas.

Twelve years later, a second major epidemic known as the "Children's Plague" hit the area with many people, particularly children, succumbing to the killer disease.

The impact of these events had limited growth yet again with the population being estimated to have only recovered to about 800 by the end of the century.

Whilst only having one main street from the Castle to the Church, small lanes and pathways began to link the additional wooden houses and little workshops which slowly developed up the valley side.

(b) Local Rule and Government

The third Thomas de Furnival was Lord of the Manor until his death in 1332, at which time he was succeeded by his son Thomas, the fourth de Furnival. Within seven years he too had died and the last and fifth Thomas became the new Lord in 1339. As this last Thomas later died without any children, he was succeeded by his brother William de Furnival, the last male member of the family, who remained as Lord of the Manor until his death in 1383.

Thus, seven de Furnivals ruled as Lord over Sheffield and their memory is retained today by such locations as Furnival Street and Furnival Gate in the city centre.

The end of this century saw William de Furnival's daughter Joan marry Sir Thomas de Neville (a brother of the Earl of Westmorland) who became the 14th Lord of our ever-growing little town.

This century saw gradual improvements in the conditions of labouring classes who, whilst not being classed as free, were nevertheless given some freedom to follow their own devices. However, for those who chose to leave their place of servitude for a life of relative freedom, vagrancy was often the disappointing result which led to begging and the inevitable outcome of violence and reprisal.

Early in the century Edward I had established Justices of the Peace (JP's) and determined the extent of responsibility of the courts of the land. Combined with this, he had established power for the arrest and imprisonment of anyone acting suspiciously at night. This power was extended during the mid-1300s to the arrest of suspicious persons day or night, indicating the desire of the Crown and its advisors to clamp down on their perception of crime.

This perception was reinforced by the Statute of Labourers in 1349, designed to make "strong beggars" work instead of giving in to idleness, vice and theft. It was thus deemed an offence for anyone to help or pity them (punishable by imprisonment), and villages had to provide stocks and pillories for the detention and ridicule of runaway servants and labourers, classed as vagabonds and beggars in their search for freedom!

Not content with this, the law of the land in 1360 imposed a more permanent penalty on those absenting themselves from service by requiring that they be branded on the forehead with a letter F as an indication of falsity.

The last quarter of the century saw a greater push for freedom which was unfortunately being sought by violence and there was greater hostility between master and inferior classes.

Also, war and disease had killed large numbers of people, and those who were left became more valuable and important.

It was probably for this reason that the statute of Richard II was introduced in 1388, which prohibited servants and labourers from leaving their place of residence without the written permission of a justice of the peace. The punishment for any transgression of this ruling was an appropriate time spent in the stocks, complete with an enforced return to the place of origin.

This century was, therefore, notable for its attempts and progress made in the emancipation of ordinary people from forced servitude, and a degree of personal freedom and equality of civil rights was asserted. It was still, nevertheless, an uphill struggle as new laws were created on a regular basis to combat perceived immorality, laziness and crime which was always associated with the poor. A brief look in the mirror by the barons and associated aristocracy should have told such law-makers who the real culprits were for many of the indiscretions and crimes of the day!

(c) Working Life

Whilst farming was still carried out in the rural parts of the Sheffield area, the little town itself was slowly but surely growing.

During the first half of the century, the economy of the area had been savaged by the costly absence of the Lords and their followers at war, the destructive effects of harvest failure and farm animal deaths and last but not least the devastating effect of the "Black Death".

Nevertheless, by 1379, when England was at war again with France, the people of the country were assessed for Poll Tax, which necessitated the preparation of a list of people with enough money to come within its scope. Sheffield's contribution to the Poll Tax was assessed as the third highest in the West Riding at the time.
The assessment also clearly identified the types of occupation which included:

Sheffield: 1 Cattle Merchant, 6 Butchers, 9 Smiths and 1 Cutler.
Handsworth: 13 Smiths and 3 Cutlers.
Tinsley: 1 Cutler.
Ecclesall: 1 Cutler.

The making of Sheffield Cutlery and in particular knives was first identified in 1340 and also again in 1380.

Pitsmoor had also been identified by this time, taking its name from "orepitts" which had been dug early in the century.

It is interesting to note that our little township had six butchers amongst its workforce, a very high number for such

a small place. It is possible that the 14th-century butcher was also a producer of meat, having a farm to run as well as meat to sell. Demand would probably have been largely from the Lord of the Manor and his household who were resident in Sheffield Castle, as well as from his personal regiment of soldiers. Meat would also be sold at the outdoor market which was now regularly held every Tuesday.

(d) Domestic & Social Life

Times were still very hard for the Sheffielder as the 14th century came and went. Food was scarce at first and with farm wages fixed at between 6s and 10s per year, the possibility of such workers ever being able to afford the luxury of a roast chicken dinner was totally out of the question with fat hens costing just under one pence each. Even ale prices had increased to between ¼d and ½d a gallon so the poor man's table consisted of inferior quality home-brewed ale, milk and cheese from the farm animals and the relentlessly consistent diet of porridge, bread, eggs and vegetable stews.

Some of the townsfolk were, nevertheless, a little more affluent than their land-working neighbours and added the luxury of fruit, fish and fresh meat on occasions.

The aristocracy continued to benefit from unlimited supplies of delicacies and were now treated to the delights of sugar at 2d a pound, roast heron at 7½d each and the latest kitchen wizardry of pastry tarts.

Whilst fresh water had always been available to the growing population, it had to be collected either from the river or from wells in the little High Street, the area known as the Ponds (now the Pond Street bus station) or several other areas of the town. This task was usually carried out by children, who often managed to balance the water pots on their heads. Its main purpose was for cooking and washing, for although it was regularly drunk by the poor, it was not popular with those who could afford to buy a substitute. This

unpopularity was due to the "medical" opinion of the day which opposed the drinking of water on the grounds that it was cold, slow, and hard to digest.

Caring for children, preparing meals and the making of clothes continued to be the domestic chore of the women in families, and they probably fed the animals and collected the eggs from their geese and hens in addition.

It was considered important by those of influence, however, that class distinction was properly recognised and administered and that the less well off should not rise above their station. Laws were introduced in 1363, therefore, which regulated the clothes people could wear and the amount they could eat and drink.

For the working class (those with goods and possessions worth less than £2), no one was allowed to wear any cloth except blanket and russet (a course, home-spun cloth) costing no more than 5p a yard (metre). In addition, they had to eat and drink only in a manner befitting their station, and not excessively.

Whilst many people were not able to exceed the restrictions imposed even had they wished to do so, those relating to excessive drinking was regularly ignored and drunkenness became a serious problem in this century, and many more to follow.

As Sheffield grew as a little town, more communal entertainment developed, and on special days such as Easter, Whitsuntide (the seventh Sunday after Easter commemorating the descent of the Holy Spirit) and Christmas, its people made their way over the little wooden Lady's Bridge and assembled on the large green area there. At this location, which became known as Assembly or Sembley Green (now The Wicker), archery, wrestling, dancing and horse riding took place to celebrate the festival of the day.

(e) Travel and Communication

Little progress in this aspect of Medieval (middle-ages) life was able to be made whilst the almost continuous ring of heavily wooded hills made movement into and out of the area so difficult. Wheeled vehicles, which lumbered noisily to and from the market place and castle, carried food and supplies in simple horse-pulled carts.

Chapter Four
1300 to 1400

IT WAS pouring with rain outside and had been doing so almost continually for the last four months. Although it was August, neither hay-making nor harvesting had been able to be carried out. Food was scarce for everyone in the township and depression and despair had now set in.

"This is the third year running we've had weather like this. I just can't understand it," said Mr S.

Even Mrs S was unable to cheer up her husband.

"It's not just the corn. I decided to give up most of my pigs and change to sheep when the forests were cut back for charcoal and building. There was nowhere left nearby for them to forage. They almost lived on acorns and oak apples you know."

"I know dear, I know. Who would have guessed that this awful disease would have attacked the sheep like it did."

Five years of sheep deaths had decimated the flocks everywhere. There had been no respite from the unknown infectious disease and now we had the rains. The lack of corn meant no bread for the hungry or fodder for the animals, this in turn creating famine, weakness, disease and death. Sheffield township, like the rest of the country, was in crisis, and worse was to come!

It was like a quagmire outside as Mr S, wearing waterproof skins, squelched his way down the high street to the old lady's cottage. Granny, as she liked to be called, was a kindly soul who was a trouble to no one, so when a message was delivered asking for his help, he obliged immediately.

"She'll probably want that leaking roof fixing," he mused as he approached the somewhat dilapidated front door. "I'll see what I can do although half the township's in the same boat."

He knocked gently and went in but was rather taken aback by the cold, damp air which caressed his face with its clammy hands. There was no fire burning on the hearth and no cheerful welcome from granny. Only the constant tap-tap-tap of water dripping on to the rush covered floor broke the un-healthy silence of the dismal little room, and Mr S felt afraid.

"Are you there gran?" he whispered whilst peering into the shadowy corner of the room where she usually slept on sacks stuffed with straw. He could see the lamb fleece cover which Mrs S had made for her last Christmas, but there was no movement from the small huddled figure beneath it.

"Gran, are you all right?"

"I think so lad, I think so".

The feeble reply brought tears of relief which quietly rolled down Mr S's drawn, ashen face as she continued to speak.

"And I'll thank you to call me granny like everyone else. I've known you since you were knee high to a grasshopper and you've always had a mind to be different. Cussed, that's what you've always been. Cussed!"

This torrent of mild abuse was like music to his ears as he knelt by the frail but determined old lady and planted a kiss on her cheek.

"Don't be so soft, lad. I don't need molly-coddling you know. Mind you," she continued after a brief pause, "I'm glad you're here."

It was an hour or two before granny was sorted out that morning. Mr S had quickly popped back home to fetch his wife and between them they'd made her warm and comfortable. The bright yellow flames of newly set fire quickly devoured the skulking pockets of dampness which had made the cottage their home for the last few weeks, and the cheerful chatter of the burning twigs was a joy to hear.

The last remnants of food had long since been eaten by the ever-hungry mice which sought shelter from the ravages of the weather outside, and the soft, wrinkled face smiled gratefully for the bowl of hot broth that had been given to her.

"She can't go on like this," whispered Mrs S as she brushed hundreds of unwilling insects out into the torrential rain. "She's too weak".

There was, however, nothing wrong with granny's hearing. "You've got another think coming if you're considering putting me in that hospital place at the back of beyond. That young fellow from the Town Collector's Office made that suggestion a few weeks ago so I sent him away with a flea in his ear."

Granny's view was typical of that of many of the elderly at this or any other time, but she was probably more obstinate than most. Her family had offered her shelter and care on many occasions, but her desire for independence since the death of her husband during the civil uprising had resulted in her continuous and defiant rejection of all such help. But now she was tired, and she knew in her heart of hearts that her survival was only possible with the care and help of her family.

Things did work out for this lonely old lady, but many others were not so fortunate as the rains continued and food

prices soared. With the cost of wheat having risen eight-fold by the third harvest failure, no one could afford to make bread. Most went hungry and many a sad family made their way to the little church on the hillside to bury their loved ones.

There were some things to be grateful for during this difficult time. Not everyone, for example, took up farming and the upsurge in smithies for the making of tools had now extended to the township itself. These small iron workers could earn a few pence selling or exchanging their wares at the weekly market where at least poultry and dairy produce was still available.

* * * * * * * * *

It was now over a year since the rains had given way to a normal summer and the corn mill was grinding again.

"It seems an age since I last dunked some bread in my broth," commented Mr S as he sat down to supper that evening. " I shall enjoy this."

The warmth of the fire took the chill off the approaching winter as he trailed blobs of gravy up his coarse cloth tunic to match the many other stains which had lived there for months. "Working clothes are for working in," he would always say. "They don't need washing."

"I thought old Daisy looked a bit tired as she came in for milking," he mumbled, trying hard not to shower too many soggy crumbs into his wife's bowl of previously breadless broth.

"What do you think?"

"If I had wanted some bread I would have asked for it," came the curt reply. "As for Daisy, she's been a bit off for a day or two, as have several others. We'll have to keep an eye on them."

Little did they know then of the significance of their observations, for within four or five weeks a quarter of their herd had died. Cattle plague had hit Sheffield along with most other northern towns and once again the farming community was devastated. The terrible disease spread rapidly over its two year duration, during which time most of the cattle died.

"I can't even plough the land to grow corn," said a distraught Mr S as he viewed the silent carnage before him. "The oxen have gone, so the ploughs are useless. This is the end. We're all done for."

It was indeed a desperate time for everyone over this first 20 years or so of the century and it needed every ounce of grit and determination for the little Sheffield population to survive. Although horses were borrowed from the Lord of the Manor's stables to harness the ploughs, progress was slow and difficult as they were not used to working together and were built for speed and stamina rather than patience and strength. All trades suffered as the population declined; farmers were broke, food prices shot sky high and earnings plunged. This was a depression at its worst.

By the end of the 60-year rule of the third Thomas de Furnival as Lord of the Manor, the population and livestock was at such a low level that less than one eighth of the Lord's grazing land in the park was now rented and used. As a result, his income was also greatly reduced, and the £16.75 annual rent he would have normally expected to receive was now only a mere £2 in total.

Thus, the vicious circle had continued as lack of investment in maintenance rendered the castle in serious need of repair and the corn mill almost in ruins. No tenants occupied the forges in the Park and even the quarry at Rivelin had come to a standstill. Things just couldn't get worse, or so the Sheffielder thought!

Despite the enormity of the problems that Mr and Mrs S and all those around them had been asked to endure, they slowly but surely rose from the ashes of utter despair to face the ever changing challenges that life chose to throw at them. From somewhere came those reserves of strength that would be needed to carry them through seemingly impossibly difficult times, yet still have a smile at the end.

Mrs S had given birth to another boy and was busily tucking up her new baby in the wooden cradle which her ever handy husband had made for her, making sure she placed it behind the thick stone guard which shielded the direct heat of the fire as well as the bright dancing sparks which delighted in jumping as far out as they could.

"We've been more fortunate than most you know dear. We lost our farm but we kept each other and at least you've got a new job."

Mr S was more than ready to agree, for what could be more important than each other? It was the cattle plague that had been the "last straw" regarding his work and he'd now rented a little smithy right here in the township. They'd had to move house, unfortunately, as home and smithie came attached, but at least there was very little travelling involved.

He was in fact doing rather well and, being a man of initiative, was toying with the idea of trying to make a short-bladed knife which could be put to a variety of uses whilst at the same time not being too unwieldy.

"What's wrong with your hunting knife?" Mr Weaver had asked him. "It's done you well up to now, why change it?"

He had a point of course. Whether stabbing fruit, cutting meat or gutting a pig, it had always done its job. A smaller one, however, would be able to be used by his wife to better effect for jobs such as preparing food, particularly if it had a sharp, one-sided edge. They would also be easier to carry about and Mr S was certain he was on to a winner.

"If you can give 'em good sharp edges, Weaver my old pal, I'll make the blades and even provide you with the handles if you like."

"I'll give it some thought my friend, but I'm not convinced it will sell."

In the meantime, our multi-talented farmer-cum-carpenter-cum-soldier-cum-DIY expert was anxious to get working in his smithie although not everyone was as enthusiastic as he was.

"I'm sick and tired of that continual banging all day long. We've not had a minute's peace since you started this

new job and I can"t stand much more of it," complained Mrs S.

"But love, that's what forging is all about. I've got to hit the metal whilst its hot to knock it into shape. There's no other way of doing it."

Unfortunately, Mrs S just didn't want to know.

"And that's another thing, all that heat and smoke is driving me mad. It's bad enough with my own hearth blazing away just to cook your meals, but that one you've got is twice as big and that charcoal smells revolting. I've a good mind to take little S to my mother's for a while to give us a break."

It was understandable that the new, tired mother should be irritable. Who wouldn't be with a baby crying half the night and a husband banging all day? One or two of the smithies were in fact located in separate out-houses, but Mr S's was more of an "en-suite" and interference with the normal domestic running of the home was inevitable.

* * * * * * * * * *

Life did, nevertheless, carry on with some reasonable degree of normality for the next decade or so until that fateful day in June almost halfway through the century. There had been an unusual amount of activity at the castle and word had got out that a killer epidemic called bubonic plague had struck in London and people were dying everywhere. A hastily called meeting of the township's ruling group of tenants was chaired by the Town Collector, who subsequently requested an audience with the Lord of the Manor to clarify the situation as it related to Sheffield.

"We're assured that there is no need to worry as the disease is highly unlikely to spread to such a remote township as ours," the chairman told the re-convened meeting a few hours later.

"But what is it?" asked Mr S, "And what precautions can we take?"

"They say its highly contagious and starts with a swelling in the groin or armpit. There doesn't seem to be much anyone can actually do to prevent it."

"Well none of us ever get off to London, but his Lordship does. We'll just have to stop mixing with the likes of him, won't we?"

It was, of course, easier said than done to avoid contact with people at the castle. Some of the township's girls were dating the fellas and many actually worked there. In addition, the Tuesday market was always attended by the bailiff or his assistant, an ideal location for transferring a disease.

Whilst the plague raged on in London with ever-increasing ferocity, Sheffield managed to keep free and the worried residents began to relax a little. Mrs S had banned her daughter from seeing the dashing young knight she had been dating and an uneasy calm settled over everywhere.

Autumn came and went and winter was now giving way to spring as a visit by her daughter caught Mrs S by surprise.

"I thought you were still at work love," she said affectionately, leaning forward for the kiss that never came. "Is everything alright, you look at bit pasty."

"Well, I've got this swelling mum and I'm a bit concerned".

"You're not pregnant are you love? You're dad'll kill him if he finds out."

"No, no mum. It's nothing like that. It's under my arm."

The smile suddenly froze on Mrs S's face which had now turned a greyish-white. For a few seconds she was gripped with a sense of panic and it dawned on her why her daughter had not wanted to kiss her on arrival. But, as most mothers do, she managed to convey an air of composure and hold back her tears.

"Oh, it's probably nothing to worry about my dear. I had plenty of those when I was your age and they soon come and go."

"I think you'd better look at it mum." She slowly slipped the russet gown off her slender shoulders and raised her left arm to reveal an angry swelling, the like of which Mrs S had never seen before. "What do you think mum?" she whispered, gazing up into the tear-filled eyes which lovingly caressed her. There was no need for words as with racking sobs mother and daughter embraced as the world fell apart for them both.

The market had been packed that morning where Mr S had taken and successfully sold his forged iron goods. A disturbing rumour was, nevertheless, circulating that an officer of the Lord's guard had died and no one would confirm how this had come about. As he made his way home he was troubled by the news as the tragedies in London were still at the back of everyone's mind.

The solid wooden door was closed when he arrived home, which was unusual, so he made his way round the back where he entered through the doorway to the smithie.

"What are you doing in here?" he asked with surprise as Mrs S backed slightly away from him. She wanted to rush forward into the comfort of those strong arms; she wanted reassurance; she desperately needed his love. But she had to hold back for fear of what might be. Hardly able to speak, she had to force out her words.

"Our daughter has the swelling. It could be the plague."

"Please God, no. But how? Where is she? I must see her." He felt Mrs S pushing him away and didn't know why. "You must keep away," she screamed "you must keep away!"

His mind was now searching and he cursed the young knight in the Lord's guard, not that the poor soul would ever hear him.

"We must get some help. Mrs Weaver will know what to do, you'll see."

His quivering voice trailed off into the distance as he staggered down to her cottage, hoping for a miracle and wondering why.

There were no doctors in Sheffield but Mrs Weaver had as much experience as anyone regarding illness and health. Her herbal remedies were well respected by everyone and she could splint a broken limb better than most. Unbeknown to Mr S, or anyone else for that matter, she'd been summoned by Lord Thomas to give an opinion regarding a young knight who had recently returned from the capital and who, it had been reported to her, was sorely ill. Her arrival had been too late, but the large blackened swellings under his arms had confirmed the worst. His Lordship had sworn her to secrecy for fear of panic amongst the household and the township, but now she was being consulted again.

"You must calm down Mr S," she said kindly, taking hold of his strong, shaking arm. "Let's go and see how she is. We must never assume the worst. I'll just collect my things."

The slow walk up the rough, cobbled high street seemed an age to Mr S as they carefully avoided the open sewer which ran down its centre, smelling somewhat in the summer sun. Piles of rubbish were building up outside the cottages and rats darted amongst them, scavenging for anything they fancied to eat. It was little wonder that disease was on the increase, and this was just the beginning!

A small group of neighbours had gathered outside the cottage by the time they arrived, having heard the commotion and seen Mr S running off.

"Is everything all right my friend? Can we help?"

Mrs Weaver disappeared inside whilst the brave father tried to cope with the well-meaning townsfolk, realising that they would all have to know sooner or later if his fears were founded.

The little room was quiet as the gentle flames of the fire flickered over the two pale faces huddled beside it. "We're so glad you're here," said the tearful mother, embracing her old friend. "I hope you can help."

It was a difficult time for the kindly old lady with her bag of "medicines" and "cures". An examination of the frightened patient identified further small swellings in her groin and, despite her complaints of feeling cold, her head felt hot. The fever had begun and the symptoms were chillingly recognisable.

"Now you just relax dear. You'll be as right as rain in a few days. I've just got to make this little cut then you can have a rest."

The letting of blood to rid the body of poisons was still the first treatment for many illnesses, but this one was special and needed something extra. The knowledgeable lady was already prepared for an eventuality such as this, having established through her contacts at the castle what was being used in London as the most effective treatment for the dreadful disease.

"I want you to make sure that you lay these on the swellings as best you can for as long as you can," she said, handing Mrs S two dried toads which she had taken from her bag. "Their skin has special qualities which will do her the world of good."

It was with a heavy heart that Mrs Weaver came out of the

cottage. She had done her best but she feared the worst. As she approached Mr S, not quite knowing what to say, the look in her eyes said it all.

"I'm afraid so," she told the stunned group of neighbours who were still reassuring him. "The "Black Death" has arrived".

It was not until a week later that the desperate hopes of the tormented parents were finally dashed. As Mr S carried the shroud covered body of his beloved daughter at the head of the sad little group which made its way up to the township's already much used churchyard, little did he realise that this would set the scene for many months to come.

Once again the little township of Sheffield had to cope with tragedy and loss on a huge scale. Once again its people had to rise from the ashes of despair. On this occasion they shared their grief with the rest of the country but surely they could take no more.

* * * * * * * * *

The tragic loss of life which accompanied this epidemic was not only a human disaster, it also created a shortage of labour on a large scale. The poorly paid workers tried to demand higher wages from the Lord of the Manor as landlord, but this was prevented by new legislation which attempted to fix wages and food prices for the benefit of the rich.

If sympathy and understanding had been expected by the decimated population, then they were to be sadly disappointed as more laws were introduced to make sure that the poorer workers stayed at their jobs.

This was made very evident when early one Monday morning, those living in the cottages adjacent to the high street were awakened to the rattling and rumbling of a small horse-drawn cart making its way laboriously up the cobbled street to the church. The yapping of dogs and the squawking of geese added to the unwelcome five o'clock call as Mr S tried to open his eyes.

"What's all that racket out there? A chap can't even get a few hours sleep these days."

He noticed, when he eventually struggled to the door, that the cart was loaded with several large pieces of timber and dragged behind it a slouching, stumbling figure. A chain was attached around his neck which tightened if he fell behind the pace of the cart whilst three guards who accompanied him laughed at his dilemma.

"This will teach you to try and run away," one guffawed, oblivious to the still sleeping township around him.

"It looks like young Josh," said the quiet, concerned voice at Mr S's shoulder. "He said only last week that he couldn't stay any longer now that his family was gone."

Josh had been a good friend to them and found plenty of work over the past 18 months since the plague was at its peak. The early loss of both parents had been devastating enough for him, but the sudden recent loss of his son had been almost too much to bear. He hadn't been seen for several days and had obviously left to start a new life away from the memories which tortured him. But, he'd been caught, and for that he was to be punished.

Hammering and banging announced the arrival of the small party at their destination as town stocks were erected at the corner of the Churchyard.

"What are those for?" came a shout from the small crowd which had decided to come and watch. Mrs S was trying to talk to Josh but the guard would have none of it. He roughly turned him away and the deep red cuts and weal's to be seen on his back were plain evidence of the "gentle persuasion" used by his apprehenders to make him confess. Perhaps he'd taken some vegetables from a garden or some bread from a table. Who knows?

It was the first time that the townsfolk had seen stocks which cruelly trapped the legs of its victims as they sat on a make-shift seat. This was public punishment and was here to stay. A day in the sun without food or water or perhaps in the driving rain, wind or snow without warmth had to be endured to be appreciated.

"It's the law of the land," snarled the guard as he padlocked the leather straps forming their vice-like grip. "Let it be a lesson to you all."

So this was the law. This was justice. I wonder what Josh thought as he sat there for hours staring in anguish at the three mounds of earth which lay silently before him, only a few paces away. Did he give in do you think or did he resolve to fight even harder. I think we all know the answer.

We could, of course, take a stroll ten years later when another epidemic of plague ravished the country. This time it concentrated its destructive effort on children who were particularly vulnerable to the deadly disease. The tragedy and sorrow endured by everyone can be imagined but let us leave the Sheffielder's to their private grief on this occasion. Suffice to say that once again, in the face of seemingly impossible odds, their stubborn refusal to submit or give in got them through.

* * * * * * * * *

As the years progressed and life was re-built, the township developed more as a market town with a slowly increasing number of smithies and shops. New farms were being let out to rent by the Lord of the Manor in the ever growing areas which would one day be part of Sheffield.

The government of the day was as always trying to squeeze more money from those who could not afford it and even imposed a poll tax of a groat a head on every person of 14 years upwards. As this was almost a week's wages for servants and labourers, many of whom still worked only for food and lodging, it caused massive disruption and protest all over the country.

Many of the poor sought the hospitality of Monasteries and Abbeys where lodging, food and drink was usually available. Beauchief Abbey was a regular calling place for any poor wandering Sheffielders who had nothing to call their own.

"Well lass," said our dear Mr S as he sampled the latest invention of toast and butter with his afternoon ale, "Its been a hard one this century. It can only get better in the next".

The Fifth Hundred Years (1400-1500 AD)

(a) Size and General Growth

By the year 1400, Sheffield had been in existence for about 600 years or so and its growth could probably be likened to that of the well-known story of the "hare and the tortoise" in which the determination and steady resolve of the latter led him to win the race between the two of them. Sheffield is without doubt the "tortoise" of the story and remained so until the 18th century, when progress began its unprecedented acceleration.

The population by the end of this 100 years, however, had only risen to an estimated 1,200, during which time new streets had emerged, more thatched cottages had been built, and workshops and smiths' forges became a common sight. Windmills were also gracing the landscape, three such locations being at Weston Park (not yet in existence), Herdings and Attercliffe Common.

The track to Sembly Green (The Wicker) had now developed into a street and the old wooden structure over the River Don was replaced by a far superior one in stone at Lady's Bridge.

(b) Local Rule and Government

It is probably very obvious by now that England, probably along with most other countries at the time, was a warlike nation and this century was no exception to the rule. Wars with France and Scotland occurred with regular monotony but in particular the so called "Wars of the Roses" between the Duke of York and his successors (who had a white rose as an emblem) and the Duke of Lancaster and his successors (who had a red rose as an emblem) were fought over a period of 30 years (1455 to 1485) and culminated with Henry VII succeeding to the throne. This continuous strife, which as

always was about property and power, involved much of the nobility in the country and the new Lords of Sheffield gave their support to the Lancastrian army.

At the beginning of this century Thomas de Neville was still the Lord of the Manor, but upon his death his daughter married John Talbot, the first Earl of Shrewsbury, whose family held the lordship for the next 200 years.

The first three Earls of Shrewsbury, all by the name of John Talbot, were fighting men. The first John spent much of his time fighting for the King in France where he became a hero and was killed in battle in 1453. The second John, who was Lord for seven years, died during the Battle of the Roses in 1460 and was succeeded by the third John, who suffered a similar fate in 1473.

The demise of three generations of Talbots in a relatively short time resulted in George, the fourth Earl of Shrewsbury, being only five years old when he took office. When he became of age, unlike most of his predecessors before him, he decided to live in the castle which had been built within his township 200 years earlier by Thomas de Furnival.

In the absence of the Lords from their manor, which had been common practice for centuries, the ruling knights probably exercised their power and authority with usual Norman forcefulness. The Burgery of Free Tenants (the organisation set up by Thomas de Furnival's Charter 100 years earlier) still continued to function as a small "Borough Council" (in practice although not in name) with its chief citizen still being the Town Collector.

During the early 1400s, many more people were freeing themselves from slavery and personal bondage, and by the end of the century freedom was more or less complete.

The feudal system introduced by William the Conqueror 400 years earlier was beginning to crumble, this being exacerbated by the high death toll of the nobility during the devastating wars which had taken place.

Freedom, however, was only a word to many labourers as the number of people without work increased, and they became a new society of begging poor.

Punishment for crime continued to be severely executed with offences such as horse-stealing attracting the death penalty. Minor offences such as fishing in the Lord's waters attracted a fine of 1 pence whilst, surprisingly, attacks with a deadly weapon only resulted in fines in the order of 15 to 30 pence.

The persistence of punishing vagabonds and beggars also continued unabated with laws in 1495 providing for such offenders to be put in stocks for three days and nights with only bread and water for sustenance. This law also applied to idle and suspected persons living suspiciously.

(c) Working Life

Slow though progress was, Sheffield now boasted a number of craftsmen working at their forges, some producing the beginnings of what was to become the world famous Sheffield cutlery industry. Farmhouses were still producing grain crops as well as breeding animals for meat, milk and hides on the outskirts of the township.

Wages had increased significantly over the last half century, with the average farm worker earning about £1 a year plus 20 pence clothing allowance, with food and drink thrown in. Craftsmen were able to earn about 1½ pence a day plus meat and drink when work was available, whilst the common labourer had to make do with about ½pence a day.

Even though these represented an improvement on previous wages, this new level of income was still pitifully low.

So, although Sheffield was increasing in numbers, with new trades beginning to flourish, its remoteness as a little town with no roads other than tortuous pack-horse tracks leading in and out created a real obstacle to trade. Without such trade and the subsequent creation of wealth which good access to outside markets would give, the majority of people in Sheffield remained virtually in a state of poverty.

(d) Domestic and Social Life

The little timber cottages which had gradually increased in number along with the township's population had not changed significantly since the early days of the Norman Invasion about 400 years earlier. They all had thatched roofs and timber walls although most now had the luxury of one or two narrow open windows and a front door. A central hearth of stone was provided for cooking although with the absence of chimneys, the provision of windows was essential for ventilation.

Straw was still the main material upon which to sleep, either bundled up in its natural state or stuffed into a course woven cover to form a mattress.

Other than for the aristocracy, who had the benefit of fine linens and silks and a bed and bedroom in which to sleep,

changing into night clothes at bedtime was still a pleasure of the distant future for the average Sheffielder. Day and night clothes were one and the same, and with few facilities to adequately wash, personal hygiene left a lot be desired.

Laws relating to the type and quality of clothing for differing classes of the population were still being made, and in 1463 it was the gentry who were being targeted. Knights, gentlemen and any other person were banned from wearing any gown, jacket or coat unless it was of such a length as to cover his buttocks! Even the pikes (pointed toes) of his boots and shoes were restricted to 2in (5cm) in length. By 1482, servants and common labourers were allowed to use cloth (for their clothes) costing up to 10d a yard, an improvement on the 5p a yard limit of 100 years earlier.

Food for Sheffield's working class was still very basic, although lettuce was now available as a stew ingredient rather than a salad. Honey was still used as a sweetener, as the extremely high cost of sugar was only able to be afforded by the rich. Toast had also appeared on the scene during this century and has proved to be popular with all classes of people to this day. The traditional English breakfast of fried bacon and eggs, or even scrambled eggs with herbs, cheese and milk was now appearing on the tables of the gentry, and by the end of the century marmalade was available as a very expensive luxury.

Whilst ale at ¼pence a gallon was still widely drunk, those who could afford it tried a tot or two of Madeira Malmsay, a fortified white wine imported from the island of Madeira off the north coast of Africa.

(e) Travel and Communications

As the township grew, one or two of the better-off members

of the community acquired a horse for their personal use, although only the packhorses could slowly tread their way out of the area carrying a few goods and possessions.

Chapter Five
1400 to 1500

IT HAD been a long hard week for the S family, with Mr S working well into the summer evening at his smithie and his wife doing her usual domestic chores, as well as caring for the animals which pottered contentedly in their back garden. Little Elsa, their milking cow, was the only one to have survived the ravages of the cattle plague and she welcomed the company of the noisy young goat, the dozen or so hens and the family of pigs. During the cold winter nights they were fortunate enough to share the comfort of the still warm smithie with Tom, the labourer-cum-servant who was employed by Mr & Mrs S. Although able to turn his hand to anything when asked, he only earned five pennies a week (2½ pence nowadays), as Mrs S threw in board and lodgings was well. He enjoyed his work, however, particularly helping in the forge, where he was becoming quite skilled.

Mrs S was pregnant again and easily tired. Although it was Saturday morning with much work to be done, she fancied a change. A good steady walk had always done her a world of good during the last two months of pregnancy, and she felt that today was as good a day as any for a day off with her husband.

"Well my dearest, how about letting me fry you two big brown eggs and a rasher or two of bacon for breakfast. You deserve it after working so hard."

Now Mr S had been given thick, lumpy porridge for breakfast for as long as he could remember, except for the time when he had helped himself to three chunky slices of bread and butter to the horror and disbelief of his wife. "We're not made of money you know," still rang round his head when he recalled the liberty he'd taken that morning, but here she was, now offering him fried bacon and eggs!

"It must be the baby," he thought to himself. "Perhaps its turning her mind."

"I would sit down and have a rest if I were you love," he said patronisingly. "You've probably been over doing things a bit."

It was transparently obvious that this conversation was not going to get anywhere, so, forgetting the smooth talk she tried the direct approach.

"Look, husband, we hardly ever go anywhere together these days and all I want is a walk. Surely that's not too much to ask for!"

"A walk? On a Saturday? You must be mad woman. It's one of my busiest days."

Now you don't live as long as Mrs S without knowing a few tricks of the trade and it was time, therefore, for her to play her trump card.

"You never do what I want do you," she sobbed with real tears in her eyes. "You just don't care. I've got pains in my back and my stomach feels like lead but you still expect your food on the table. You're downright unfeeling, that's what you are."

The sight of tears had always been Mr S's "Achilles heel", so after instructing Tom on the work which had to be done that day, they both set off for a stroll.

It was a warm, pleasant day and Mr S rolled up the sleeves of his tunic to let the gentle breeze cool down his sore arms. Working with iron was a hazardous job and many a sore was caused from a cut or a burn as the handling and forging of the heavy metal took its toll.

"You need some balm on those sores," grimaced his now happy wife, recalling that Mrs Weaver had told her where this medicinal herb grew nearby. "It grows on the large open green near Mr Barker's farmhouse, just above where those coal workers have dug that small pit. It can't be more than half a mile and its beautiful countryside up there."

The walk to the green took the couple up the little cobbled high street, which was still smelling foul, past the quaint stone church with its hundreds of graves, to a narrow country lane,

the far end of which opened like a gateway to the huge orchards and endless fields beyond.

"This is beautiful," exclaimed Mrs S "I'm going to call this far-gate so that it stays in my memory for ever".

Being a romantic at heart, the happy mother-to-be was always making up names to remind her of the few pleasures and joys that could still be found, and nature was usually the best provider.

A hundred yards further on, the pleasant, soothing aroma of the balm plants drifted over its rich green carpet as though enticing the couple to their destination. A blue-grey pool shimmered in the sunlight alongside them and for a few precious moments all the cares of the world were forgotten.

The pool had, in fact, been dug by Mr Barker who, as well as being a farmer, also prepared oak tree bark in water for tanning leather. He had tapped into several small streams and springs in the hillside above which provided him with a plentiful supply of clear pure water for his work.

"The oak bark and the growths often produced on it by insects or fungus," Mr S carefully explained "provide a yellowish tannic acid when prepared in water. The resulting tannin rich liquid is then used for the tanning process in which raw animal skins are converted into leather by soaking them in the liquid, which both cleanses the skin and seals all its tissues."

"Thank you dear, that's a wonderful explanation," remarked Mrs S, trying not to sound too bored and wondering why when she wanted a simple answer to a simple question, he always gave her a book!

"The townsfolk sometimes pop up here to collect water for themselves if there's a queue at the wells," continued Mr S "There's even talk of the pool being enlarged by building a wall round it if water becomes scarce. We'll have to wait and see."

With the talking over and little baby S doing its best to pummel its way out well ahead of time, the pair settled down in their peaceful surroundings for a bite to eat. Bread, cheese and ale tasted much better up here, but when her loving husband produced the secret desert which he'd acquired from the castle two days earlier, she couldn't believe her eyes.

"But only the rich buy these as a treat for their pregnant wives," she sobbed as she gratefully grasped the large fresh orange in her hands. "You do care after all."

They'd enjoyed their stroll to the balm on the green that morning, and as she gathered a few bunches of sweet smelling herb, she had little doubt what she would call the beautiful picnic area at the side of Mr Barker's pool.

* * * * * * * * * * *

Mrs S had a rather difficult birth with her latest child and it had taken all Mrs Weaver's experience and skill to ensure a safe delivery. Not content with kicking and thumping its way around its warm, cosy resting place, baby S had decided it wanted to come out feet first. A bit of gentle persuasion by the firm hands of the equally determined "mid-wife" had at least turned it halfway but the rest was really a struggle. Persistence nevertheless brought success, and the lusty "blast" by the outraged addition to Sheffield's ever growing population was evidence of her success.

Sadly, the end result was not always as successful as this one was. Many a birth ended in tragedy for both mother and child during these times of negligible medical aids, no anaesthetics, no antiseptics and a high dependency on faith.

"You know, we really ought to get better organised regarding this health issue" remarked Mrs S whilst sharing a beaker of fresh goat's milk with her good friend at "elevenses" one morning. "We can't just rely on you for ever you know."

Mrs S recalled the old tribal days of yester-year when everyone hunted, fished or gathered their food. They lived a different lifestyle, of course, and didn't stay in one place long enough to pollute water with human wastes that transmit diseases or pile up refuse that attracts disease-carrying insects. Being on the move most of the time also restricted the population to small groups which reduced the probability of viral and bacterial infections. Contagious illnesses such as measles or smallpox, for example, need large, dense populations for their disease-causing agents to survive.

"And then there's the wild plant food," she recalled. "There was never any shortage of that. What with the wild game and the fish as well, we must have eaten a huge variety of foodstuffs. I bet there was no shortage of vitamins and minerals in those days."

"So why has it changed so much?" asked the amazed Mrs Weaver, never realising how knowledgeable her friend really was.

"Well, we only caught most of our present diseases when we became farmers," she explained. "Do you know, we've caught poxes from cattle, influenza from pigs, birds and horses and even measles probably comes from cattle and dogs. And, of course," she continued trying to emphasise the point, "we scatter all the farm animals" bodily wastes all over the land (along with our own very often) which attracts disease-spreading insects as well as probably "feeding" those that are already there."

Mrs Weaver was by now feeling a bit squeamish and politely refused the offer of a cold chicken wing to nibble on.

"And then there's the mice and rats. They've learned to live with us and even enjoy eating our food in comfortable warm surroundings. There's many a flea that's bitten a rat and then jumped on to your leg for a nice bit of "afters"."

The now slightly distraught listener shuddered at such a thought, spilling her milk as she involuntarily leaned down to scratch her itching leg.

"Of course, houseflies feed on faeces you know and they don't mind whose food they walk over as long as they create as many diarrhoeal diseases and dysentery as possible. What with that, those awful lice that the kids had last month and those hook worms and ring worms that the men keep on catching, we're like a living disaster, aren't we?"

"Well, I certainly feel like one after listening to that lot," croaked the now desperate lady. "But what can we do?"

There was certainly no easy answer to this question as the ever-increasing population meant ever-increasing squalor and better opportunities for diseases to spread. The Church advocated good Christian living and plenty of prayer which in itself was good advice. Unfortunately, it also suggested that illness or pain may be God's way of punishing the wicked, and a certain degree of lack of sympathy and understanding obviously accompanied that view.

Whilst some degree of knowledge relating to the causes of illness and the way the body actually works had been achieved as long ago as 410 BC by a Greek physician by the name of Hypocrites (after whom the still used Hippocratic Oath was named) and later in the year 145 AD, by the equally famous doctor and surgeon by the name of Galen, little advancement had been achieved to date. Doctors, of whom there were none in Sheffield at this time, still followed the Greek view that the body contained four types of fluid, namely blood (which did NOT circulate around the body), phlegm (cold and moist which was often associated with an apathetic temperament), yellow bile (associated with bad temper and anger) and black bile (associated with melancholy). It was considered that if the fluids were not correctly balanced, then illness would occur.

This system of four fluids was thus considered to determine a person's physical and mental qualities and was extended by the experts of the day to also represent the four elements earth, air, fire and water; the four qualities hot, cold, wet and dry; the four ages of man; and the four mental states of happiness, sadness, anger and calm. In effect, it offered an explanation for understanding man and his relationship with his surroundings.

But this was really heavy stuff, and by this time Mrs Weaver had nodded off.

"Oi! I thought you wanted to know what we could do," exclaimed our host, prodding the poor sleeping lady with the remains of her unwanted chicken wing, "We can train up some volunteers, that's what we can do."

Responding to the bleary-eyed nod of approval, Mrs S carefully outlined her plan.

"First of all, I think one or two of the farming menfolk could do a bit of bone-setting. They're used to dealing with animals so they only need to learn the finer points. Then there's delivering babies. Some of the barmaids at the new little Ale Houses often have time on their hands and I'm sure they'd be pleased if you could teach them how to carry on. The barber, of course, could easily manage to pull out a bad tooth or two. They're used to dealing with people's faces, so that shouldn't be any problem should it?"

"Well, I suppose not," responded the now wide awake listener.

"It would also be a good idea if a few people knew how to do the blood-letting cure," she continued. "It's not difficult if you know how, is it?"

"It might be safer to leave that to me actually. There's plenty of blood suckers in the ponds which will do the job just as well. We'd just have to make sure that we've got lots handy."

At last, the point had got home. Some real organisation was needed if progress was to be made and lives saved. It's a pity that better hygiene never entered the discussion as far as solutions were concerned!

* * * * * * * * * *

It was Easter Tuesday and everyone in the township was getting excited at the thought of the annual event which was to be held on Assembly Green, just as it had done for the last 200 years.

Sunday and Monday had been days of celebration and Mr S had won second prize in the archery competition, whilst his more discerning wife had paid her respects at the little Chapel of Our Blessed Lady on the opposite side of the newly-constructed bridge. The old timber structure had virtually

collapsed and access to the large open meadow was now much improved up the new small steps which led the would be revellers over the four stone arches of the narrow little bridge.

> **Did You Know that Lady's Bridge in Sheffield was originally known as The Bridge of Our Lady in recognition of the small chapel which stood nearby? The chapel was later converted to almshouses for four poor widows and was demolished in 1767.**

Flushed with success at the archery, Mr S had also tried his hand at fishing in the adjacent waters of the River Don, in which salmon, trout, chub and eels were in abundance. Fishing in the Lord's waters was, of course, forbidden but on this occasion consent had been given as long as all that was caught was put back.

Young master S loved Easter Tuesday as it always started off with two baked eggs and a thick slice of bread. It would be another hundred years, however, before anyone would discover the joys of cutting off a "soldier" of bread and dipping it into a soft, yellow yolk, which would ooze over the edge and down the side of the shell. The poor boy just didn't know what he was missing!

"I want you to wear your best "bib and tucker" today young man. It's your father's special day and we must look smart for him."

Yes, this was the day that the Earl of Shrewsbury, as Lord of the Manor, chose to review the "Dad's Army" of the Sheffield township who would line up in their fighting uniforms complete with spears, long bows and swords. The few that could afford to own a horse brought them along and the whole colourful sight was greeted with rapturous applause from the large crowd which gathered to watch.

"Come on dad!" yelled young master S proudly as the Earl shook hands with the tall, powerful figure standing before him. "I pity anyone getting in my dad's way if war breaks out, and that's a fact."

Waiting and shouting had made the proud pair thirsty and hungry so they decided to avail themselves of the refreshments which the Earl had kindly provided. The aroma of barbecued pork and lamb which had been drifting tantalisingly over their heads for an hour or more soon led them to its source, and within minutes they were tucking into what was probably the best hot pork and lamb "sandwiches" they had ever tasted.

"You'd better get one for your dad before they all go. You know what he's like with his food," said Mrs S.

They needn't have worried, however, as further down the green a huge iron pot of his favourite stew was simmering merrily over the dull red embers of a previously blazing fire. This rich entrail pottage of liver, heart, kidney, lung, spleen and gut with lashings of seasoning thrown in, was probably the medieval equivalent of today's liver and onion delight and, to quote Mr S as he dunked his in bread, "It'll put hairs on yer chest this will lad."

The edge of this green meadowland ran down to meet the river where the firm green pasture gradually gave way to soft, wet marshland. Mrs S had noticed that large quantities of bulrushes and reeds were growing there and, being quite a handy lady, decided that she could usefully use some

herself. She already had a good collection of willow and twigs which she intertwined to make fine baskets, stools and mats to sell at the market. These softer, pliable reeds would, she decided, compliment their design and result in a better quality product for which she could obviously ask a higher price.

"You know, I could develop quite a good wicker work business from this," she mused as she sent master S scampering off to collect as many reeds as he could. "How about "Mrs S's Riverside Wicker Goods" with a logo saying "Make your Wicker Work", or something like that? I could even set up a stall here in due course and the place could be famous. You never know, do you?"

The Sixth Hundred Years (1500-1600 AD)

(a) Size and Growth

The 6th century was really the springboard from which growth and development eventually launched itself.

Whilst the population only rose to 2,000 over this 100 years, it nevertheless represented the greatest rate of increase of any century since the town's formation.

Within the town itself, new streets and cottages continued to appear together with many more little workshops for the expanding number of cutlers and other metalwork craftsmen. Retail shops had also begun to trade by the end of the century.

Farms grew on the outskirts of town as a few of the more successful cutlers moved residence to attractive locations and took up farming as a second occupation. Such people were probably the beginning of what we might call the "middle classes", as they invested some of their earnings back into their

trades and some into land, and eventually acquired wealth and position midway between the gentry and the working classes.

A number of residences belonging to the aristocracy and the gentry were also built during this period including a large stone mansion, known as Manor Lodge, located in the huge enclosed deer park above and to the south and east of the little town. The Lord of the Manor had built this residence (often wrongly referred to as Manor Castle) to escape the cold and damp conditions of his present abode at Sheffield Castle. He spent many a fine summer enjoying the magnificent panoramic views of the hills of Sheffield which extended to every point of the compass over the tops of the walnut and oak trees which covered most of the park.

In contrast to this mansion, a timber-framed house was

A RECONSTRUCTION OF
SHEFFIELD
MANOR HOUSE
AS IT APPEARED ABOUT 1580

built at Norton Lees by the Blythe family who farmed their own land and rented out smithies and grinding wheels for scythe making. The two sons of the owner, William Blythe, became the Bishops of Salisbury and Coventry and the house, now standing at the top side of Meersbrook Park, became known as Bishops' House.

Other residences of note include Hazelbarrow Hall (now the site of Hazelbarrow Farm) which was built by Lord Frecheville, and "The Oakes" in Oakes Park at Norton. This latter residence was, in fact, demolished and replaced by the present building about 80 years later, in 1672.

(b) Local Rule and Government

George Talbot, the fourth Earl of Shrewsbury and Lord of the Manor, was 32 years old when his son Francis and eventual heir was born at Sheffield Castle in the year 1500. Being permanent residents of Sheffield, the Talbot family showed more interest in the township than their predecessors and became involved in local affairs.

Having built his country mansion in Sheffield Park, George was visited by the famous Cardinal Wolsey, who was not only Archbishop of York and Lord Chancellor of England, but the Pope's special representative in this country also. This powerful man, who had virtually taken over the governing of the country on behalf of King Henry VIII, was not, however, on a social visit as, having fallen out of favour with the King, he was being taken from York to London where he was to be tried for treason. His 18-day stay at Manor Lodge, where he was entertained with kindness by Earl George, were to be his last days of comfort as he died at Leicester Abbey within a

week of leaving, being too ill and weak to complete his journey to the Tower.

In 1538, the fourth Earl died, being laid to rest in the Shrewsbury Chapel which he had built for himself and his family 18 years earlier in the Parish Church.

His son Francis subsequently became the fifth Earl and acquired many of his father's qualities (George having reached the powerful status of Lord Steward of the King's Household and Lieutenant-General of the North) and became President of the Council of the North in 1549.

Francis's lordship lasted for 22 years and actually extended over the reign of four monarchs (Henry VIII, Edward VI, Mary I and Elizabeth I). He proved to be very popular with his people, who turned out in great numbers to support his grand public funeral after his death in 1560.

It was now the turn of yet another George Talbot to take the reins of responsibility for Sheffield. As the sixth Earl of Shrewsbury, George had what might be called a "colourful" life. Following the early death of his first wife he married the notorious "Bess of Hardwick" who was purported to be very fond of money, rather selfish and more than a little unfeeling.

> **Did You Know that George Talbot, the 6th Earl of Shrewsbury and Lord of the Manor of Sheffield wrote to Queen Elizabeth on 26 February 1575, mentioning that the walls of his Sheffield Castle had been shaken by an earthquake?**

Bess had three husbands in quick succession and George was her fourth. He had to finance her extravagant hobby of building large mansions, which included both Hardwick Hall and Chatsworth House (the predecessor of the present mansion).

George, like his father, was a popular Lord but had to spend much of his time and money carrying out the pleasures of Queen Elizabeth, in particular looking after Mary Queen of Scots at Sheffield Castle and Manor Lodge.

Mary (who claimed she was the rightful heir to the English Throne) was, in fact, a prisoner of Queen Elizabeth, who had charged George with the responsibility of her safe-keeping for nearly 14 years in a lifestyle befitting her status. This responsibility broke his marriage and his health and was certainly no help to any political advancement. Whilst Mary's main place of imprisonment was at Sheffield Castle, she spent much time at Manor Lodge, where the Turret House (outside the gates of the Lodge) was also adapted for her needs and stricter security.

The Turret House in the grounds of Manor Lodge.

The last and seventh Earl of Shrewsbury was Gilbert, who took over the Lordship of Sheffield in 1590 following the death of his father, George. He was not particularly liked and was reputed to be of ill-tempered disposition with a tendency to live beyond his means. As such, he was unable to provide for the town in the same manner as his predecessors. The only thing that he was remembered for was that he was the last Lord of Sheffield to have influence over the township and its government.

Whilst the Lord was still responsible for the main policy decisions affecting Sheffield, and so held ultimate authority, the Town Burgery of Free Tenants (today's local councillors)

continued to be responsible for its day-to-day running. These responsibilities included the maintenance of the streets, the Barker's Pool and Lady's Bridge, together with the provision and repair of the town's means of punishment. These included the gibbet (an upright post with an arm upon which executed criminals were hung up), the local stocks (a timber frame with holes for feet in which offenders were locked for public ridicule), a ducking stool (a chair fastened to the end of a pole which is plunged into a pond) and the pinfold (a pound for stray animals).

The Tennants were also responsible for maintaining the archery butts in the Wicker (Sembly Green) and the running of the Court of Sembly Quest (previously called the Court Leet) at the same location.

Although police forces did not exist until the 19th century, law enforcement had always been the responsibility of the Lord of the Manor and it is during this period that constables emerged. Their area of responsibility related to the whole area of the Lord's ownership which, in the case of the Earls of Shrewsbury, was covered by the Parish of Sheffield, this having been divided earlier into the townships of Sheffield, Upper Hallam, Nether Hallam, Heeley, Attercliffe/Darnall, Ecclesall Bierlow and Brightside Bierlow (meaning "administrative area").

The constables, two of whom served Sheffield township at this time, had to carry out the punishments imposed by the courts such as locking vagrants in the stocks, flogging or even branding them. They were also responsible for conveying poor convicted beggars to the constable of the next parish, as well as for the unusual task of collecting taxes and fines.

Their income was based on the duties actually carried out rather than on a weekly wage. Arresting a wrong-doer and putting him in the town cage, whipping a sturdy beggar or taking a vagabond to the next parish all generated different payments, and an enthusiastic officer could easily earn himself enough to live reasonably well.

In the middle of this century, a further body was created by Queen Mary called the "Twelve Capital Burgesses" of Sheffield (later to become the Church Burgesses) who were provided with funds of £17.47 to maintain three priests to assist the vicar of Sheffield in his ministry of all the townships, and to maintain and repair as and when necessary the Parish Church and the footpaths and little bridges of the parish. The poor were also to be helped from this fund. This left the Burgery of Free Tenants only £9.53 to carry out all its functions.

Thus, a rather complex system of Local Government developed, involving the Lord of the Manor, the Free Tenants, the Church Burgesses and Justices of the Peace (who had been in existence from the early 1300s), as well as the constables and the vicar, who had considerable authority in their own right.

This century continued as the previous one finished, with an ever-increasing amount of legislation relating to the poor – some of it being of assistance but most of it imposing severe penalties and punishment on the unfortunate beggars and wandering vagabonds. These laws were of considerable significance to Sheffield as many of its population were very poor, the better off usually living outside the then township boundary.

Legislation which was designed to help the poor included their registration for charity, finding appropriate work for them and latterly, relief of the destitute being recognised as a public duty and charge, with accommodation for such people being provided.

The appointment of Overseers of the Poor in every parish was also established, which gave those appointed (Church Wardens and four householders) power to raise taxes on the inhabitants and distribute the income for the relief of the poor as they thought fit. This added yet another ingredient to the already overflowing pot of authority.

The negative aspects of the legislation (albeit not in the eyes of the lawmakers) were the unnecessarily severe and degrading aspects of the punishment for various indiscretions. These included begging outside prescribed limits (punished by stocks and whippings), beggars and idle persons not turning up for work (punished by whippings, prison, cutting off one ear and even death), and loitering and idle wanderers refusing to work (punished by branding with a letter V on the breast, beatings and hard labour, branding with a letter S on the cheek as proof of now being made a slave for life, or even death). Further legislation towards the end of the century reversed some of these laws, but imposed grievous whippings and burning through the right ear with a hot iron for simply being convicted of being a rogue or vagabond, with the possibility of death for further indiscretions.

Government, power, authority, law and order thus became complex and interrelated during this century with the very poor suffering, the poor obtaining some help and the rich getting richer.

(c) Working Life

The number of cutlers working in the township continued to grow, and rose to about 100 by the end of this century. Such was the importance now attached to this thriving little industry that the exclusive use of the cutlers' own marks was granted by the Lord of the Manor as an indication of the individual quality of their products. The first such mark (the

forerunner of the later and jealously guarded "Made in Sheffield" Trade Mark) was granted in 1554 to a cutler by the name of William Ellis for exclusive use on his iron knives. Anyone else using such a mark had to pay the Lord a fine of 10d (about a week's wages) and also recompense the cutler.

Within four years, 60 marks had been registered and sufficient trade was now generated to make the slow and perilous journey to outside markets worthwhile. Such journeys, by packhorse trains over steep unmade tracks exposed to the perils of treacherous weather and highway robbers, took many days before arriving at the fairs and markets held periodically in locations such as the Peak District. Cutlery even found its way to Ireland via Chester during the latter part of the century, and a determined packman from Attercliffe actually managed to reach Worcester and Hertfordshire to make his sales.

Water wheels for grinding were now springing up, the first in this area being for grinding scythes at Holbrooke in about the year 1500. During the next 50 years, similar wheels were built at Ecclesfield, Wisewood, Millsands, Little Sheffield (bottom of London Road), Heeley, Sharrowvale, Wadsley Bridge and Greystones. By 1581, Sheffield's Lord was renting out 15 wheels, having provided the money for their construction on land in his ownership.

Coal mining was also becoming more common as many forest trees were felled for farming and charcoal production, and collieries existed at Handsworth and Ecclesfield to add to the ever-growing diversity of employment in the area.

Farming was still a major industry outside Sheffield township, although harvest failures due to appalling weather conditions were common. The 1580s and 1590s were the worst years and resulted in major famines. Sheffield Parish registered its highest-ever level of deaths, being 178 in 1592, only to exceed this unwanted record again in 1597 when 253 deaths were registered.

However, many outlying farmers were reasonably wealthy,

and the inventory of the widow of a Dore farmer in 1591 identified an estate value of £57.62, comprising 50p in cash, £35.13 in farm animals (65 in all including cattle, pigs and sheep), £9.30 in crops (wheat, corn, oats and hay), £4.80p in tools, equipment and cooking pots, £5.98 in beds, bedding and other cloth, 71p in honey and food making utensils and £1.10 for 5½ swarms of bees.

The inventory did not include any land or property, so it is concluded that the farm was rented off the Lord of the Manor. With the value of money at this time being 150 times less than that of the present day, the farmer's total wealth can be equated to nearly £9,000 at today's prices.

(d) Domestic and Social Life

Although the life of those living outside the limited Sheffield boundary was difficult – particularly for the very poor labouring classes who tended to drift into town in search of work – the lives of those within the township bordered on desperation.

Survival for the skilled craftsmen and their assistants in the industrial township depended on their ability to sell their goods and obtain a living wage. This was rarely possible as although demand for knives and cutting tools appeared to be high, the remoteness of the market and the low prices probably paid, resulted in very poor incomes for such workers.

These low incomes, combined with food shortages and consequent high prices, created an environment of extreme poverty, with more than half the adult population being classed as "begging poor" by the end of the century.

Living conditions were dire and many still slept on beds of straw scattered on the stone or wooden floors of their cottages. Clothes were all home-made in the poorest households and shoes were probably rarely provided for the children.

The Laws of the land, however, continued to introduce rules and regulations relating to the wearing of clothes, and in 1571 required that every person over the age of six must wear a woollen cap or hat every Sunday, subject to a fine of 16½ pence (double the weekly wage of many people).

The simple act of socialising during the evening (the most common activity of present day society) was also banned in case this led to the hatching of conspiracies and plots! To prevent this, a curfew was introduced between the hours of 9pm and 6am (which were classed as unlawful hours) and fines imposed for anyone transgressing. This law must obviously have had some effect on the Inns and Alehouses which had sprung up all over the country and Sheffield was probably no exception. Imagine telling today's Sheffielders to "sup-up" and get home by nine o'clock!

Not content with preventing the visiting of one's friends in the evening after 9pm, the law also frowned on the playing of games for entertainment. Playing dice in the evening was already an offence, and when

Henry VIII introduced further laws banning games such as cards, tennis and bowls to prevent people wasting their time (with a fine of 33 pence for each transgression), there was little else to do except work and sleep.

This, then, was the 16th century for the working population of Sheffield. But what about the rich?

Fireplaces were appearing in the side walls of their large houses and turkeys were being bought at 30p each for roasting. Marzipan proved to be a popular after-dinner dessert and oysters were often in demand. Sugar at 5p a pound was still extremely expensive and represented one or two day's wages for the town craftsman.

The emerging middle classes found boiled suet pudding very nourishing and this meal eventually found favour generally by the end of the century.

Whilst religion has caused, and probably always will cause, unrest, disagreement and wars, it was particularly evident during this century as the English monarchs supported opposing Roman Catholic or Protestant beliefs in succession.

Henry VIII, who ruled for the first 50 years or so, initially supported the Church of Rome, although halfway through his reign he decided to separate the Church in England from the authority of the Pope. He ordered the dissolution of the country's monasteries during this time and took over their funds for himself. Beauchief Abbey was one of those which thus ceased to function in 1537, such action having a significant impact on the poor who had up to this time depended on charity from monks in the absence of help from elsewhere.

After Henry's death, there was a move towards Protestant beliefs; altars were removed from churches and the English language Prayer Book was introduced and made compulsory. This period, which extended from 1547 to 1553, was known as the "Reformation".

When Mary I came to the throne in 1553 as a strong supporter of the Church of Rome, she crushed opposition to her beliefs very harshly and became known as "Bloody Mary". During her five year reign, which became known as the "Restoration", 300 Protestants were put to death for opposing her views, 45 of whom were tried at York.

Heresy laws had been introduced during both Henry's and Mary's reigns, and even though Elizabeth I tried to calm matters down with a more gentle return to Protestant beliefs from 1558 to the end of the century, opposition to the beliefs held by the Monarch still brought with it prosecution and punishment.

The people of Sheffield, like the rest of the country's population, had to keep a fairly low profile with regard to their religious opinions if they were to avoid confrontation and possible punishment during these sensitive times.

(e) Travel and Communication

It is interesting to note that the earliest known correspondence was communicated just before and during the time of Mary Queen of Scots' imprisonment in Sheffield, although the birth of the postal system did not take place until the 1600s.

> **Did You Know** that for hundreds of years, people spelt names as they sounded at the time? In 1643, for example, a letter being sent started off: "10 a klok in the morninge, Sheaf-feild". An even earlier communication to the Earl of Shrewsbury was addressed in 1563 to "Therle of Shresbury, Sheffeld Castell".

The earliest letter sent was one from London to the Earl of Shrewsbury at Sheffield Castle in 1563, whilst Mary herself sent many letters to her cousin and her Ambassador in France in the same period.

Chapter Six
1500 to 1600

LIFE, as we all know, is a very strange experience. One minute you're enjoying it, the next minute you're down in the dumps. It would, of course, be boring if it plodded along in the same old way without challenge or change, and although we all like stability, there must always be something to look forward to.

Mr S considered himself to be fortunate in this respect because although he'd had his share of downs, he was excited at the thought of developing his smithie and expanding more into cutlery production.

There were those, however, who had nothing but worry and despair to keep them company. The best they could look forward to was the possibility of a few scraps of food to eat and an occasional shelter at night. Poverty was rife and Sheffield had its fair share.

The law, so they say, was doing its best. Justices of the Peace were charged with seeking out and distinguishing between the poor who were unable to help themselves by virtue of illness or disability, those who were old and weak and those who were able-bodied. The ill, the disabled, the elderly and the weak were not only poor, they were fortunate! Their names were put on a register and the JP then gave them a letter of authorisation to beg within prescribed limits, usually the boundary of their own parish.

Such generosity hardly brought tears of joy to Mr S's eyes, however, as many of these poor souls hardly had the strength to stand up, let along being allowed to wander around the little townships and villages in search of food. But what of the able-bodied poor, those who were fortunate enough to be strong and able to work, even though there was little or no spare work to be had? For them, being poor was a crime!

"I'm not really sure," mused Mr S as he noticed the tragic procession trundling along the High Street, "whether it's better to be poor and infirm but able to beg, or poor and strong and die of starvation!"

A crowd had gathered now as the overcast sky looked down angrily on the spectacle unfolding beneath it. Jeering and shouting was accompanied by cries of distress and the crack of a well-aimed whip as the degraded, naked figure of a thick-bearded man stumbled into view. He was unable to escape the knotted leather strands which tore into his flesh at any sign of resistance or delay. Not that any was possible, as

the thick rope which securely bound his hands in front of him was equally securely bound to the back of the old wooden cart being reluctantly pulled by the skinny old packhorse in front.

This, of course, was justice. Unable to find work, the poor man had been caught begging, and the cruel and degrading spectacle now being witnessed was his punishment. Perhaps he should have given in; perhaps he should have sifted through the vermin ridden scraps and rubbish on the sides of the street; perhaps he should have been more careful when he begged. But when your belly is craving for food and your mind is tormented with despair, perhaps you have no choice!

"Don't give in son, don't give in," whispered Mr S as the wild, desperate eyes of the tortured man met those of the angry observer in a hidden cry for help. "Never give in," he repeated. "You'll get there in the end, I promise."

The vicious, flailing leather wielded by the high-handed constable, who was escorting his charge to the next village, abruptly stopped their silent conversation as the abused man jerked back to reality. Mr S was sure, as he watched him depart, that his back was straighter, his stature was taller and just possibly his determination was stronger!

"I can't believe I made that promise" muttered the puzzled cutler as he strolled back to work. "What can I do about it?" Perhaps he could do nothing, but let's wait and see.

It is reasonable to ask ourselves whether this incident is typical of the little town of Sheffield which, after all, was beginning to thrive. Sadly the answer is yes, as over a third of the adult population could be classed as "begging poor" at this time.

Take Mrs Weaver's neighbour for example. She was a poor sickly lady, but proud with it. There was no way she was going to have her name on this list of people needing charity and she most certainly didn't want the letter allowing her to beg. She didn't want any of it!

But times change, and as her needs became desperate she knew she had to ask for food.

"I'm not going to show myself up by asking Mrs Weaver," she thought as she hobbled off to the green outside the castle where one or two people in similar circumstances were begging for food.

It is with considerable regret that we have to observe the consequences of this lady's actions, but this is where our stroll had taken us.

Today of all days the Justice of the Peace was visiting the castle and he was in no mind to tolerate the "whining" of the beggars.

"Check their papers," he ordered the constable who accompanied him. "Bring anyone to me who has no letter."

We could, of course, guess what happens next but perhaps we should continue just to see how life was lived by some.

"I could have you whipped for this," retorted the JP as he glared at the poor cringing figure who had been brought roughly before him. "Mind you, I don't think you would survive."

The frightened but brave little lady said nothing as her tormentor ordered three days and nights in the stocks instead, with only bread and water to be given for sustenance. This was his kinder alternative! Sadly she only survived two days but justice had been done! At least her pride won through. Her name never did go on that "charity list".

"Well at least things can't get worse," said a bitter and very troubled Mr S as he discussed last weeks tragedy with his equally bitter and upset wife.

"Don't you believe it, husband. Do you remember when poor Mrs Psychs decided to leave the town a couple of years ago to do a bit of fortune telling and palm reading around the parish to make ends meet? Well, now they've gone and brought in this new law which makes such things illegal."

"She's not been caught and fined has she? She's a lovely lady and people really get a buzz when she tells them they're going to be rich, marry a dark man or have 17 kids. It's harmless really."

It wasn't easy for Mrs S to talk about her friend. They'd grown up together and it had been a sad day when the high-spirited, albeit very poor, lady of enterprise had left to seek her "fortune".

"She's been caught twice, actually," she responded with a break in her voice. "She was publicly whipped for two days the first time but the second was even worse".

Mr S leaned forward and put his comforting hand on his distressed wife's shoulder. "Now, now dear, how do you mean it was worse?"

"Well," she sobbed (as Mrs S often did), "they not only gave her two days whipping again, they put her in the pillory for two hours and cut off her ear."

They both sat there feeling shame, anger and frustration. They were ashamed that the society of which they were a part could allow such cruelty to those less fortunate than themselves; they were angry that the law makers could impose and enforce such barbaric punishments, and they were frustrated that they were unable to do anything about it. But this was life at this time. Punishment was still the solution for most things and not only was there no provision for sustaining the weak, there was equally none for helping the strong to find employment.

Now whether it was people-pressure or whether, perhaps, Mr S and his "councillor" colleagues had spoken with the Lord of the Manor about their concerns, or whether the government actually had a conscience we don't really know, but changes did come.

Poor people, vagrants and beggars were given charity through voluntary collections taken in the little church, with books of payments being kept by the church wardens. Work was to be found for these people until such time as they could work for themselves and an atmosphere of optimism briefly reigned in the town.

Unfortunately it was not to last as more and more unemployed people wandered from village to village, town to town, parish to parish in seek of work. Ex-soldiers, now released from service after the many years of civil wars, swelled the ranks of the homeless, and Sheffield, like most other towns, attracted its share of such unfortunates. The monasteries had also been dissolved by order of Henry VIII and a hitherto important source of food and shelter ceased overnight for hundreds of destitute people.

"Sheffield's getting like a cattle market these days" commented Mr S one day. "There'll be more wanderers than residents if we're not careful. Something will have to be done about it."

Sadly, something was done, and the sight of young begging children being "given away" to masters as little more than slaves, older children being publicly whipped with rods if they ran away, or wandering idle men and women screaming as they were being branded on the breast or cheek with hot, sizzling irons was a vivid reminder to Mr and Mrs S that there was a long way to go before society was to become more humanised!

* * * * * * * * *

We said at the beginning of this century that life had its ups and downs, and bearing in mind all we have come across so far, a stroll through some better times wouldn't go amiss.

A "better time", you might say, was when Mrs S's daughter, born 15 years previously, successfully applied for a job as chambermaid at the Earl of Shrewsbury's posh new residence called Manor Lodge in the Park.

"It's a fantastic place mum," she said excitedly on her first visit home, "and I can't believe the size. It looks more like a castle than a manor house and the rooms are simply enormous." Pausing only to gulp down some fresh milk, she continued. "There's this really long room called a gallery with beautiful windows and hundreds of little glass panes. And it's got oak floors, oak panelled walls and loads of pictures, cabinets and books. That's not to mention the beautiful coloured tapestries and thick red carpets all over the place."

"Well it sounds very grand my love. What about…?"

"Oh, and I must mention the tables and chairs. They're absolutely magnificent. This great big oak table's got these lovely carved legs and even the chairs are carved all over. Our dad could have done that type of work if they'd asked him, couldn't he?"

"Of course he could love, but what about your work? Are the bedrooms nice?"

"Mum, that's the understatement of the year. Her ladyship's room has this massive four-poster bed with this lovely silk canopy and curtains all round. Mind you," she said in a slightly more sedate voice, "they've also got hinged lid chamber pots under the beds and these closed stools with padded seats in most rooms. Just guess who has to empty these every day?"

> **Did You Know that the 16th century "Close Stool" was a chamber pot enclosed in a wooden stool where the natural evacuation of human waste took place? The reference to stool was gradually changed to that of the waste product rather than the furniture upon which the person sat, especially in reference to the faeces of babies and young children.**
>
> **Did you also know that a "stool-pigeon" was originally a decoy of a pigeon fixed to a stool? It is now accepted to be either a person acting as a decoy or, more usually, a police informer.**

"Yes, but I bet you enjoy sleeping in nice soft beds don't you. That must be a change for the better."

"Well, you'll never guess mum. I have to sleep in the passage-way outside her ladyship's room, while some of the others sleep in the window seats nearby. It might be posh for them but its not very posh for us. Mind you, I've not told you the best bit yet."

What, thought Mrs S, could the "best bit" actually be. Had she met some handsome servant or had she been given a pay rise? She was dying to know.

"Well, don't keep me in suspense then. Just what is it?"

Her lovely, mischievous daughter leaned a little closer and smiled tantalisingly, pausing before she spoke.

"I've met her."

"What do you mean, you've met her? Explain yourself girl."

"I've actually met Queen Mary, you know, Mary Queen of Scots."

Whatever the 16th-century equivalent is of the 20th-century expression "gob-smacked", well that's what Mrs S was. It transpired that Queen Mary was staying there as part of her term of imprisonment by the Earl at the wishes of Queen Elizabeth. Part of her time was spent at the Lodge and part at the Turret House which was located near to the Lodge Gates.

"Do you know mum, she's a beautiful lady, just like you. She loves animals and she's rearing some baby partridges and pigeons. But you must see the lovely litter of little white puppies that she's got. They're absolutely gorgeous.

"But where does she get them from? Surely the Earl doesn't buy them for her."

"Oh, no. I think he has to tread carefully because his wife's rather jealous. From what she told me, she writes to her Ambassador, the Archbishop of Glasgow, who's living in Paris at present. He gets the animals for her. These puppies look rather like tiny poodles to me but I think they could be a similar kind of dog called a Bichon Frisé. Anyway, whatever they're called, they're lovely. I don't suppose we can have one can we?"

Her mother's glare said it all, so daughter S quickly changed the subject.

"She showed me inside the turret house last week. It's really quaint. You have to walk up two narrow winding staircases to get to the top floor where her rooms are. The main one has the most beautiful plaster ceiling and fireplace you could ever imagine with the most incredible moulded design. She even let me sit in her chain because she thought I might be tired after climbing the stairs."

"You must have had a good view from up there. What could you see?" asked her mother with genuine interest.

"Well you couldn't see much from the room itself because the windows are quite small and built from those tiny pieces of glass, some with patterns on them. But you can climb one flight of steps further and them you're on the flat roof. You can see the whole town from there, the castle, the church, the houses and everything."

"Everything", of course, was the growing Sheffield township surrounded by open fields, woodlands and moors which extended to the far horizons to form the Sheffield of tomorrow. For now, its narrow little streets were lined with houses and shops, behind which lay dilapidated old cottages occupied by the poor, cutlery workshops operated by many of the menfolk, swine hulls, cowhouses, stables, bakehouses and the inevitable malt houses for making ale. Beautiful orchards, gardens and new little farms linked this urban setting with the fields and woodlands beyond and from the elevated eye of the young beholder, this must have looked like paradise.

"It's very wrong though mum, isn't it?"

"What is?" questioned the exasperated mother, recalling that her daughter always came out with statements which assumed that the listener was a mind reader.

"The Queen's been imprisoned for years and there seems

There were no facilities such as refuse collection or street cleaning in these times of course, although towards the end of the following century a "town scavenger" was appointed to try and keep rotting carcasses down to a minimum.

But today was a special day and everyone was looking forward to it, especially the children who viewed it as their monthly treat. Mrs S's youngest, along with his mates, loved to watch the whole process, particularly the beginning when the water surged from the pool to the cheers of the surrounding crowd which always congregated there.

There were, even in these days, rules and regulations which had to be complied with, for each householder was responsible for getting rid of his or her own rubbish and sewage. As much as possible was stored for this "once a month clear out", whilst human wastes, along with those of pigs, cows and goats, were taken and spread on the fields or commons. Mrs S recalled with regret the time that she and several of her neighbours had been too tired to dispose of their sewage during one particular busy period and had simply dumped it into the open drain running down the centre of the street to await the monthly wash. A spell of dry, hot weather at that time had brought the offence to the town's authorities who subsequently fined each householder four silver pennies, a sum they could ill afford to pay.

to be no chance of her getting out. Do you know, she sits for hours in her chair doing nothing but embroider cushion covers. I know she's unhappy most of the time and she's really not too well."

"Such is life," thought Mrs S to herself. "Many a poor beggar would gladly exchange places with her and its anybody's guess who would live the longer."

* * * * * * * * * *

It was street cleaning day in the busy little town and as the warm sun shone down on the rubbish-filled streets, the stench alone justified the occasion.

The town had much to thank Mr Barker for when he first built his pool at the side of Balm Green. It had since been enclosed by a stone wall and fitted with sluice gates and now provided the means of flushing the streets once a month.

It was about 11 o'clock when master S and his gang began their "tour of inspection" of the streets en route to Barker's Pool. The Bellman had just rung his warning, which meant that the sluice gates were be opened at noon, giving ample time for everyone to get prepared. Pigs were happily roaming about, foraging amongst the piles of refuse which lined the streets everywhere, whilst others were feeding at the troughs which stood outside the doors of many of the houses. Their grunting and squealing was accompanied by the barking of the slightly more discerning dogs and the cackling laughter of the multi-coloured hens as they too looked eagerly for an early lunch.

It was not a good idea to have animals on the street at cleaning time, however, and the group of helpful lads delighted in catching and penning the pigs for their grateful owners before the deluge began. The dogs and the hens could take care of themselves, but the loss of a valuable pig was serious.

The open drain set in the middle of the cobbled streets was now quite full of accumulated rubbish and filth and the lads always enjoyed betting each other how many dead rats, fowl or dogs they would spot rotting on their walk to the pool. Despite the main purpose of the open drain being to take away daily household slops, collect any rainfall and dispose of any rubbish and refuse at the monthly wash, it was regularly used to dispose of much, if not most of the town's sewage and was a constant source of disease and illness.

The time was approaching noon and the townswomen were now standing outside their homes with brooms and buckets at the ready, awaiting the drain being in full flow at which time they could brush or rake in all their garbage and rubbish so that it could be washed away. The buckets could then be used to scoop up fresh water with which to wash their house frontages and at least have a day or two free from smells and the sight of heaped up rubbish.

"Five, four, three, two, one, open!"

The cheers rang out as the water burst out of its gates, eager to get to work. It poured down Balm Green before beginning its gentler descent down Fargate, waving carelessly to Pepper Alley as it passed. The children were racing beside it, but the torrent was leading by far, pushing forward all in its path. A careless dog was flung off its feet as the surge overflowed at High Street and no more would Mrs Weaver have boiled eggs from her favourite hen now lifelessly riding the waves.

The Market Place was its next port of call where it lurched to the left to charge down the street before "splitting in two" down Water Lane and Truelove's Gutter to its final resting place at Under-the-Water and the River Don.

For those who were not born at the time, the route of this great cleansing surge, which lasted about half an hour or so, may seem unfamiliar in parts as Pepper Alley is now known as Norfolk Row, whilst Market Place has become Angel Street. Truelove's Gutter has also acquired the less romantic title of Castle Street, which is rather sad as the popular belief that its name derived from a tragic event relating to two young lovers, cries out for remembrance.

To help those who may not be aware, it is worth recalling the story of the loving couple who sat one evening on the rails of the small bridge which had been built over the drain (or gutter) in this street. They were, without warning, washed away by the sudden flood water of a late summer storm which raged down the gutter whilst they were gazing into each others eyes, oblivious to everything around them. Surely we should remember a tragedy of love as much as the many tragedies of hate and war which occupy history. You may, of course, prefer to remember that a local resident called Mr Truelove owned some property nearby and the name may actually relate to him. Who knows? At least we know that True Love's Gutter Bridge existed for at least another 100 years and I would suggest that its memory should last for ever.

As for Under-the-Water, this low-lying street leading to Lady's Bridge took its original name from the fact that it was often flooded, eventually changing its name to Bridge Street when drainage improved.

> **Did You Know that the Old Queen's Head pub in Pond Hill was previously called the Hall in the Ponds and is thought to have been built in the late 15th century? Whilst some historians were of the view that it was originally the old laundry of Sheffield Castle, more recent investigations have indicated that it was more likely to have been a sporting lodge for use by the Lord of the Manor. It is often referred to as "Sheffield's oldest pub" which is not strictly true. Whilst being Sheffield's oldest commercial building still in use, it did not become a beerhouse until about 1841. The Nailmakers' Arms at Norton was built in 1627, and it is this pub which can rightfully claim to be the oldest in Sheffield.**

Whilst washing the streets was the "pleasure" of the poor, coupled of course, with much drinking in the ever-increasing number of ale houses, the Lord of the Manor preferred shooting wildfowl with crossbows and fishing on his lands in The Ponds.

This land has now become a large, thriving bus station (or "interchange" as its operators prefer to call it), but it was originally a large flat marshy area by the side of the River Sheaf with artificial ponds stocked with fish for consumption by the Lord and his household.

A good morning's fishing or fowling was usually followed by the partaking of food and drink in the grand dining room

The Old Queen's Head pub in Pond Hill. It was originally a 16th-century sporting lodge called the Hall in the Ponds.

of the Hall in the Ponds, a fine lodge built adjacent to the ponds to allow the sporting gentlemen to enjoy rest and refreshment after their activities.

Meantime, Mr S and his wife were standing at the back of their little workshop on High Street taking in the beautiful view of the valley which stretched out below them. The fields of corn and those pastured with sheep gave way to the wild beauty of the marshes, alongside which the clear blue waters of the Sheaf twisted and turned as it burbled its way towards the Castle.

"It doesn't seem fair to me," said Mr S. "Not only has the Earl got his huge castle to live in over there, and his great fancy Manor House on the top of that hill surrounded by gardens and trees, he's even got himself his posh little Lodge to rest in when he and his mates have worn themselves out fishing."

"Now, now" chided his wife. "Jealousy and sarcasm just don't suit you. He's not a bad chap, this Earl George. He's had a lot to put up with looking after Queen Mary all those years and he's not getting any younger you know. He deserves a bit of pleasure while he can."

Mrs S never said a truer word, for within a few weeks of her defence of this Lord, George Talbot, the sixth Earl of Shrewsbury died. If she had ever doubted his popularity, then his funeral on 13 January, 1590, was to remove all such doubt forever.

It was the day before when it became clear that it was to be something out of the ordinary. Mr and Mrs S were awakened in the early hours of the morning by the sound of trundling wheels, the snorting of horses and a hubbub of voices.

"Go and see what all that noise is about lass, I'm tired this morning."

"You'd better come and have a look love. I can hardly believe my eyes," came the somewhat startled response after opening the shutter of the small window directly above her bed.

It was with disbelief that the sleepy couple viewed the  amazing scene unfolding before them in the eerie moonlight of what seemed like a pre-dawn invasion. They came out of the woods and over the hills; they crossed the fields and walked the streets; some were on horseback and some were in carts, but most were on foot, and they continued coming.

"But who are they, what are they?" questioned the now wide awake but frightened housewife. "Surely we're not being attacked again."

"God rest his soul" shouted a lone voice. "Long live Gilbert."

It was several seconds before Mr S decided to respond. It didn't seem possible but it must be true.

"They've all come for tomorrow's funeral. There's

hundreds of them, possibly thousands. We'll be swamped!"

Sheffield had never seen anything like it. They came all day in droves, choking the streets, filling the taverns, trampling the crops and raiding the orchards. By nightfall, camp fires were burning like a star-studded tapestry which had been draped over the landscape, but still they came.

As daylight dawned on the day of the funeral, the steady beat of drums drifted slowly over the early wakening little town. Its 2,000 inhabitants had now been completely overtaken by an estimated 15,000 others and yet more were still on the way. A steady stream of nobility and gentry made their way to the castle as preparations for the funeral parade were finalised and the drums went on beating. No one had anticipated such vast numbers and by the time the horse-drawn cortège clattered noisily over the wide castle drawbridge it was dark, and the huge, jostling, impatient crowd had grown to 20,000.

It was a sight that would never be repeated that evening as the magnificently clad guard of honour flanked the large oak coffin as it made its way on its open topped carriage to Church on the hill. The four pure white stallions which pulled the carriage pranced nervously as they slowly made their way up the High Street in the flickering light of torches and fires, acutely aware of the semi-hushed crowd which now lined the route. As if to reveal the extent of the spectacle, the moon appeared in full light for a few minutes to paint the long twisting procession of mourners which seemed endless as it edged out of the castle gates to the beat of the drum. This was a night to remember!

The funeral was an amazing event for the townsfolk of Sheffield, and they were proud that their Lord received such recognition and respect at his departing. But with it had come chaos and death. Fires had been started, trees were burned down, fighting was everywhere and the taverns were dry. Buildings had been damaged and at least three people died with many more being injured.

Mr S was rather cynical of the whole affair as he watched the vast numbers of people queuing up the next day for their traditional funeral dole which was handed out to an estimated 8,000 begging poor.

"That's what they're here for, you know. Most of these come from Derbyshire and had probably never even heard of the Earl before his funeral was announced."

Our shrewd Sheffielder was probably right to some extent, but the 30-mile radius from within which the mourners came is a long way to travel just for dole. And there were still about 12,000 people who came simply to pay their respects or perhaps to enjoy the spectacle.

Well, my advice on the matter is simple. If in doubt, assume the best. Most people are genuine, you know, even as long ago as this. Let's carry that thought forward with us as we enter the next century.

The Seventh Hundred Year (1600-1700 AD)

(a) Size and Growth

This new century, whilst being one of significant growth and development for Sheffield and its neighbouring areas in terms of population and industry, did not bring with it the improved standard of living so desperately needed.

A survey carried out in 1615 for the Lord of the Manor identified a pitiful situation in the little township whose population had now risen to 2,207. Of these inhabitants, 725 were described as begging poor, 100 householders were poor craftsmen who could possibly help others, 160 were householders on the verge of being driven to beggary and the remaining 1,222 were children and servants, the latter working extremely long hours for very small wages.

In effect, about two thirds of the adult population were beggars and only ten per cent of adults had enough money to be self sufficient and possibly give a little charity to their neighbours. About ten of this latter category had a small amount of land on which to keep a cow.

Although more streets continued to be built to accommodate the steady growth of population and industry, the township itself had not changed its boundaries for the last 200 years or so, these still being the River Don to the north as far as Lady's Bridge, the low-lying area of the Ponds to the east (now occupied by the Pond Street bus station), Barker's Pool and Coal Pit Lane (now Cambridge Street) to the south and West Bar to the east.

Beyond these boundaries lay the common land of the Wicker to the north, the Lord's vast park to the east in which he had built Manor Lodge, the large open area of the Moor to the south and the common land of Shalesmoor to the west.

By the end of the century, Sheffield's population had risen to about 5,000 with a further 3,000 or so people living in the other five townships of the parish. Even though classed as townships, Attercliffe and Heeley were still small villages and along with Darnall and Crookes, were still farmed by most of their residents.

Building had continued to expand and about 200 cutlers' smithies formed the built-up area by the mid century. Some of these were still timber framed, although by 1700 many were of stone. Attercliffe, Darnall and Brightside also hosted smithies, and Sheffield's first charcoal "blast furnace" was established at Wadsley with associated forges for the reworking of the iron into bar-form being established in Attercliffe.

Unfortunately, the ravages of Civil War had once again affected our growing township and in 1648 resulted in the eventual demolition of Sheffield Castle, the last remnants of which can be viewed in the Castle Market building which exists today between Castlegate and Exchange Street.

On the brighter side, a large Almshouse, known as the Shrewsbury Hospital, was built in 1665 on the site now forming the Park Square Roundabout and existed there for 162 years giving help and sustenance to those in need.

This century also saw the formation of the "Company of Cutlers in Hallamshire" in 1624 followed by the building of their first Cutlers Hall in Church Street in 1638.

Education was now beginning to be available

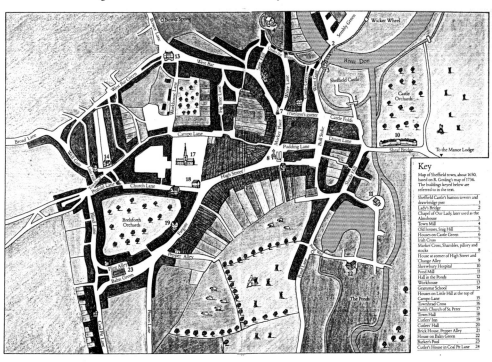

Key

Map of Sheffield town, about 1650, based on R. Gosling's map of 1736. The buildings keyed below are referred to in the text.

Sheffield Castle's bastion tower and drawbridge pier	1
Lady's Bridge	2
Chapel of Our Lady, later used as the Almshouse	3
Town Mill	4
Old houses, Snig Hill	5
Houses on Castle Green	6
Irish Cross	7
Market Cross, Shambles, pillory and stocks	8
House at corner of High Street and Change Alley	9
Shrewsbury Hospital	10
Pond Mill	11
Hall in the Ponds	12
Workhouse	13
Grammar School	14
Houses on Little Hill at the top of Campo Lane	15
Townhead Cross	16
Parish Church of St. Peter	17
Town Hall	18
Cutlers' Inn	19
Cutlers' Hall	20
Brick House, Pepper Alley	21
House on Balm Green	22
Barker's Pool	23
Cutler's House in Coal Pit Lane	24

to more of the community, and schools provided during this period included The Free Grammar School of King James at Town Head (a large house with a slated roof, a coal house and an orchard) which was established in 1604 and re-built in 1645-48 using some stone "borrowed" from the Sheffield Castle ruins and some quarried in Crookesmoor. Others which appeared at this time included Norton School in School Lane, built in 1654, Sharrow Moor School at Sharrow Vale, built in 1668, Mosborough School, built in 1680 and Hackenthorpe School, built in 1699.

(b) Local Rule and Government

This 7th century saw the end of direct rule by the Lord of the Manor in Sheffield as Gilbert Talbot, the seventh Earl of Shrewsbury, died in 1616 without a son. Although the Talbot estates passed to Gilbert's brother Edward, the eighth Earl, he died within nine months and Sheffield ended up belonging to Thomas, the Earl of Arundel and Surrey through his marriage to Edward's daughter Alethea.

Thomas later inherited the title of the Duke of Norfolk from his famous forefathers and this important family still hold rich estates in the Sheffield area today. However, Thomas and his successors became Lords of Sheffield in name only as they had little interest in the affairs of the township, and were content to let their affairs be managed by an agent who set up residence in Fargate.

This was the real beginning of Sheffield's self government, complicated though it was, and paved the way to its eventual incorporation into a Borough about 200 years later.

The local Government system which existed at this time was a body of Free Tenants elected by householders, the Capital Burgesses elected by the Church, Overseers of the Poor elected by the Church and Constables elected by the Lord. In addition, the Free Tenants created a body of 13 Town Trustees in whom the control and proper administration of the Township's public property was entrusted. One significant act performed by this body, which was established in 1682, was the shared funding with the Duke of Norfolk of a new Town Hall (in which the basement was also used as the towns first gaol), this being erected in 1700 at the south-east corner of the Parish Churchyard.

Sheffield's very first Town Hall is reputed to have been built at 10 Pinstone Street in 1637, the outer wall of which contained chains in which prisoners were detained.

Both the Manorial Court (dealing with matters such as small debts) and the Court of Sembly Quest (dealing with minor offences) continued in their present form whilst serious crimes continued to be heard in York or the West Riding.

The ducking stool, introduced in 1580, was still in use for ducking cheats and "nagging women", whilst the stocks continued to publicly imprison petty offenders.

Stealing deer from the Lord's forests was considered to be a serious offence and carried with it a three-month gaol sentence which could extend to life imprisonment if either damages to the owner were not able to be made or sureties for seven years' good behaviour could not be found.

Thefts of personal property or goods valued at more than 5p even carried a death penalty, whilst the punishment for thefts under 5p only generated a good whipping!

Women had long been considered as inferior to men (this notion still being held today by some ill-advised men), and the law was certainly no protector of their rights.

The early 1600s saw the introduction of laws against witchcraft with those "predicting the whereabouts of buried gold or silver" being given one years' imprisonment coupled with six hours on the pillory every three months. Conviction of a second offence automatically resulted in the death penalty. The practice of witchcraft by enchantment or sorcery or the calling up of any evil or wicked spirits which results in anyone being lamed or killed was again punishable by death.

Did You Know that the last execution for witchcraft took place in this country in 1712?

Suspicion of being a witch was an agonising time for the accused as there was little or no defence if the accuser could generate enough support against the poor woman. The fact of being different to others, the existence of unusual birth marks, the possibility of some mental disability or simply the action of some irrationality (possibly PMT?) could all spark off vindictive accusations if blame had to be apportioned for some normal phenomenon like premature death, unaccountable illness or disability (which could never be attributed to an act of God in those days).

Probably even more serious and demeaning during these difficult times was that relating to women having children out of wedlock. Whilst today it is quite normal for such an occurrence, with many people having partners rather than husbands or wives, law invoked in the early 1600s treated unmarried mothers as lewd and shameful.

Whilst this stigma applied to all such women, it was far worse for the poor than for the rich who could at least afford to maintain the child. If the mother was poor and was receiving charity herself, then the child became a burden on the parish in which she lived and as such the mother was sent to gaol for a year. Should she repeat the "offence", she was sent to gaol until such time as someone could act as surety for her and take responsibility for guaranteeing no such offence happened again. Such surety was often unable to be obtained

and resulted in the unfortunate mother having to stay in prison for life!

To avoid this dreadful punishment, some women took to killing their new-born children to conceal their birth, such action precipitating a new Act in 1623 which imposed the death penalty for any convicted mother. Still-births, of which there were probably many in those days of negligible medical assistance, had to be proven by a witness to escape this ultimate punishment of the law.

It is of interest to note at this stage that the Act of Habeas Corpus was introduced in this century (1679), which established the still-held principle that no person may be tried more than once for the same offence.

(c) Working Life

The cutlery trades were expanding rapidly in Sheffield and included not only the manufacture of knives and forks, but also scissors, shears, files, buttons, snuffboxes and awl blades (pointed tools for piercing holes). The surrounding villages and townships also produced metal goods such as scythes, sickles, forks and nails. These were often made by people who continued to work on the land as part-time farmers.

From 1624, the cutlery and associated iron and steel trades were governed by the "Company of Cutlers" without interference from anyone outside the trade. The company was headed by the Master Cutler and produced rules relating to apprenticeship and general working conditions. It also consolidated the previous ruling of the Manorial Court made in 1614 that only steel should be used for cutting edges instead of iron. The Company's area of jurisdiction was considerable and covered the Township itself and all within a six mile radius.

The smithies themselves were small buildings, initially wooden framed but latterly constructed of stone. They were often built on to the house in which the cutler and his family lived, although sometimes they stood in their back yard. Travelling to work was obviously no problem, although the proximity of the workplace with its associated noise, heat, fumes and smoke made living conditions rather unpleasant.

By the year 1700 the almost continuous working of the forges had resulted in the township's little stone cottages being blackened by the relentless attack of the smoke and the truly industrial town had emerged.

In the first quarter of the century 32 water wheels were operating along the rivers in the Sheffield area, providing power for the hammering (forging) of the metals into shape or the grinding of edges to form blades. It was estimated that about 400 master workmen were employed for the grinding of knives alone, many others being apprentices or employed in other grinding or forging activities.

Norton Parish, not part of Sheffield for many years, was famous for its scythe makers (although it also had iron smithies and wood colliers), who were selling scythes to Scotland and north-eastern market towns by the 1620s. The distribution of this trade was handled by the Blythe family of Bishops' House who, in their capacity as "wholesalers" or "middle-men", kept stocks of up to 2,000 at a time.

A similar example of the combined farming and metal working activities which took place in the outer areas was Bell Hagg Farm in the Rivelin Valley which, in 1637, supported a smithie alongside its dwelling house and barn set in 50 acres of arable, pasture and meadow land.

In contrast, a poor craftsman in Ecclesfield had a combined dwelling house and smithie alongside his beast house, all set in one acre of land.

The busy little township of Sheffield had also, by the late 1600s, developed the embryo of what might loosely be called its "tourist industry", for in 1686 the War Office Returns for Yorkshire showed that it contained 119 guest beds together with stabling for 270 horses. This adequate facility may not have had the glamour and glitz associated with today's Posthouse-Forte, Grosvenor House or Stakis hotels, but its "parking provision" was better and it was almost pollution free!

71

Wages continued to increase very slowly over this 100-year period with a labourer's daily wage in 1661 being between 5p and 6p. By 1682 a Chief Husbandman (foreman farmer) was able to earn £5 a year, whilst the farm labourer earned £3.50. A dairymaid or cook had to rely on £2.50 a year, which works out at about 1p a day during a working week.

An important piece of legislation was also introduced during this century which had a significant impact on the working life of the population. The Act of 1662 for the betterment of the Poor provided that all poor people (which included the whole of the labouring classes rather than just the idle and impotent poor as previously was the case) were obliged to stay in their own parish and not move around looking for work in other areas. This was a bad law which prevented labourers moving to better themselves.

(d) Domestic and Social Life

The improvements in housing over this century were very welcome as the thatched wooden framed cottages gave way to stone with tiled roofs and even the use of brick by the year 1700. Fireplaces with chimneys replaced the old central hearth and cooking became possible without the ever-lingering taste of smoke in the air.

Water from wells was still the main source of supply although little was spared for personal cleanliness in the slowly deteriorating environment of dirt and grime which menacingly spread over the township.

Whilst schooling had become available within the parish area of Sheffield, its main priority centred around religious teaching. The original Grammar School, established by the Church Burgesses in 1559, was fee-paying and admitted more "middle-class" pupils from the ages of seven or eight wishing to prepare for university entrance (Oxford or Cambridge). When it was re-established as a Free Grammar School in 1604, up to 50 pupils were taught without charge from all areas of the parish, some boarding at the school and others staying with friends or family in the township due to the difficulties of travelling. School days were long and extended from seven o'clock in the morning to five o'clock in the late afternoon, with a two hour break from 11am.

The poor in the area, which included all those within the central township, were not, however, able to avail themselves of such luxury because their parents preferred to put them to work between the ages of eight and ten, their learning only coming from experience. A workhouse had, however, been erected at West Bar in 1628 for vagrants and the very poor unemployed, and this incorporated a school of industry for 20 young paupers which lasted for about 30 years.

Illness is, of course, something that continues to afflict us all, regardless of age, sex or position in life. The year 1650 saw the first resident doctor in Sheffield (Dr Thomas Moreton), previous medical assistance having been sought from Doncaster in 1639 and Barnsley in 1643. It is unlikely that the poor could have afforded to pay his fees and the continuation of prayer, blood-letting and herbal remedies remained the order of the day.

Drinking was (and always will be) still a favourite pastime of many, despite the constraints which had been put upon evening activities during the last century. The year 1604 saw legislation introduced to "restrain the inordinate Haunting and Tippling in Inns and Alehouses" as Inns were not meant "for the entertainment of lewd and idle people to spend their money and their time in a lewd and drunken manner." As such, Inn keepers had to limit drinking to 1 hour at lunchtime for the town's workmen, longer drinking hours only being allowed to residents and their guests. The price of ale and beer was also fixed at ½p a quart (two pints) for best quality and ¼p a quart for lesser quality.

Not content with this legislation, a further Act was introduced against the "odious sin of drunkenness" in 1606 which described such condition as the root and foundation of the sins of bloodshed, stabbing, murder, swearing, fornication and adultery. This obsession with preventing drunkenness, which carried a penalty of 25p (a workman's weekly wage) or six hours in the stocks, may have had some justification for its introduction but it is highly unlikely that the aristocratic rich suffered the same restrictions as they partook of their similar social delights.

Entertainment still took place on Assembly Green (The Wicker) with horse riding, wrestling, dancing and archery being very popular. However, religion reared its head once again in the form of the Puritans who sought not only to simplify and regulate forms of worship, but also to practise and impose extreme strictness in both the religious and moral activities of the people. There were many supporters of these extreme views and these people were not only in positions of authority in the Sheffield area, they also held power in Parliament during the early and mid-1600s, during which time they introduced new laws against sinful activities such as dancing, games and sport, particularly on Sundays.

In 1644, this well-meaning body even banned Christmas, and by 1647 had removed all festivals and holy days from the calendar! Can you imagine today's society doing without Christmas dinner, presents and Easter eggs?

There was, however, some light at the end of the tunnel for the long-suffering, hard-working residents of our township, as the benevolent government decided that recreation was to be allowed on the second Tuesday of each month! Fortunately, a change of government late in the century re-established many of the old traditions and festivals (including Christmas), and dancing round the Maypole at

Whitsuntide was carried out with extra vigour on Assembly Green.

(e) Travel and Communication

The first references to a postal service in Sheffield were in the 1640s when private post was sent to outside destinations on horseback by personal servants or friends. A letter sent from Sheffield to London in 1648 by this method actually cost its sender 2½p (about £1.60 at today's prices).

The first official postal deliveries and collections in Sheffield were in 1663 and by 1688 the township had a Post Master by the name of George Carr with the post office being located at Carr's Coffee House, roughly where Boots the Chemist now exists at the junction of High Street and Fargate.

The mail was still carried by men on horseback (known as post boys) who, like the old Pony-Express riders of the wild west, galloped from town to town to make their deliveries. The London to Sheffield route at that time had stops at Towcester, Northampton, Harborough, Leicester, Loughborough, Derby and Chesterfield before arriving three

days later in Sheffield at 2pm. The post left town for its return journeys on Wednesdays and Saturdays at nine o'clock in the morning.

Postmen and women had not arrived on the scene at this early stage of the service so letters had to be collected and paid for at the post office, the charge for a letter from Sheffield to London being 3d (1p).

Chapter Seven
1600 to 1700

IT WAS a slightly overcast morning and young master S was feeling rather bored. His father had wanted him to help in the workshop as he had a backlog of orders to complete for more knives, but the onset of a "rather painful" stomach ache had conveniently got him out of doing such chores.

Last week, his parents had discussed with him the possibility of going to school, although Mr S could not really afford to lose such valuable help with his own work.

"Well at least we can go and see what it's like," his mother had proclaimed, "and he really could do with an education you know."

"Look, we've managed without any schooling all these years and I think we've turned out all right. What's so special about the youngsters these days that they've got to have this education lark? I'll learn him well enough, never you fear."

Needless to say, mother decided that they would "pop over for ten minutes just to have a look round," at this Free Grammar School at Town Head which taught pupils living within the parish for no charge.

"You rarely get owt for nowt these days," grumbled Mr S as he reluctantly made his way to the school with his determined wife and dubious son. Turning out of Pepper Alley, they made their way down Fargate past several rather nice, stone-built town houses on the left, one of which had been turned into an Inn.

"That's where the Cutler's Company used to hold their meetings son," said dad proudly, being one of the first assistants to the Company to attend. "I bet you didn't know that did you?"

"No dad, I'd never have guessed," came the somewhat sarcastic reply as his son glanced up at the huge sign swinging gently in the breeze which read the "Cutlers Inn".

As they turned into Church Lane at its junction with High

> **Did You Know that the cost of the first Cutlers' Feast held in 1648 was £1 13s 2d (£1.66)? By 1762, the allowance for the feast was £40, and today (1999) it costs in the order of £20,000.**

Street, the large stone building on the left complimented that of the Church which stood proudly opposite. "And this my son, is the present Cutlers' Hall. Do you know, it cost the grand sum of £155 15s 10d when it was built and it's worth every penny."

Now that, as you can imagine, was certainly a matter of opinion as there is little doubt about Master S's feeling on the matter.

"One hundred and fifty-five pounds!" he mumbled to himself. "I didn't think that much existed. Why, with money like that, I could buy myself some of those new "rich persons" drinks that I've heard about such as tea, coffee and hot chocolate. And then there's this sweet stuff called treacle which you can make biscuits and parkin from, whatever that is."

"Stop day-dreaming lad and listen to what I'm saying. Do you know, when I went to that first Cutlers' Feast in '48, the wine and ale never stopped flowing, and even with the food thrown in the bill for the lot of us was a few bob short of two quid."

"Have you two finished?" said the now exasperated Mrs S "I thought we were going to the school."

The "happy" trio strolled on to the end of Church Lane where the Townhead Cross and the Townhead Well stood near to the enclosed piece of ground which was known as the Pinfold. Master S liked coming up here as there were nearly always a number of grunting pigs snuffling around inside awaiting collection by their owners on payment of a small fine to the Pinder.

"Hi, Mr Pinder," he shouted, "where did you pick these strays up from?"

"Oh, they were foraging around the refuse in High Street, lad. I'll get four pennies a piece for them when they're returned to their careless owners a bit later on."

Once the now completely cured young man had met up with his pals, they decided they would like a bit of excitement. A stroll down to the corn mill didn't seem a bad idea, and they could take in one or two events en route.

Arriving at the Market Place, in the centre of which stood the Market Cross, the Pillory and the stocks, they decided to pop down Pudding Land to the Bakehouse to buy an assortment of fruit pies and tarts with Master S's "nest-egg". Hard bread was still the best they could manage at home, and fruit pies were something you only had at Christmas if you were lucky. "But what the heck, you only live once," he said as he exchanged his precious savings for a huge bagful of goodies.

Mr S, in common with most of the townsfolk, wasn't keen on the Pinder as he was employed to find the strays and charge for their return. He was only doing his job of course, but there was many a dark night when the Pinfold gate was smashed down and the impounded animals retrieved without payment.

A row of quaint, stone-built cottages signified their arrival at Little Hill at the top end of Campo Lane, round the corner from which was the school. Their first impressions were quite good as the school was set in a large three-bayed house with a slated roof which stood in its own grounds comprising a garden, an orchard and an area set aside for home-grown crops and vegetables. On closer examination however, it became obvious that the building was in quite a dilapidated state and as they carefully climbed down the steps to the rickety old doorway well below street level, they all had some doubts.

None of them were sure, as they made their way home later, what it was that had finally decided them not to pursue the idea of attending this school further. Perhaps it was the emphasis on a classical curriculum of Latin and Greek that had swayed them ("absolutely barmy" as Mr S had delicately put it), or it could have been the attitude of the lady showing them round: "Seven am prompt we start," she had shrilled, "with no excuses." Perhaps it was its dilapidated condition or probably it was everything combined. Whichever it was, they had now decided, and their relieved young son would continue helping his dad.

Master S was sitting there feeling bored that morning. He was thankful that any ideas of schooling had now been put on ice, but he longed for a bit of excitement. He'd managed to save three silver farthings over the last few weeks unbeknown to his parents and he felt like "blowing" them all at once.

"I'll go on a binge," he decided, "and I'll take my pals with me."

"I thought you'd got stomach-ache" cried a voice as he furtively crept out of the house.

"Well, its like this mum. I thought a walk would do me good so that when I get back, I can help you both."

"He must think I was born yesterday," she thought as she sent him packing. "And don't fall in the gutter again. You smelt like a sewer last time."

Did You Know that "treacle", which was introduced as a food in the 17th century, originated in the ancient Greek "theriaca antidotes", meaning antidote for the bite of wild beasts? It took the form of an "electuary" which is a medicinal powder (consisting of many drugs and spices) mixed with honey. It was used as an antidote for many poisons right up to the 14th century under the name "theriaca" or "triacle".

If it was excitement that the lads wanted, then the spectacle which was taking place in the broad open area opposite the Castle Folds, where the Lord of the Manor's sheep were kept, was probably just what they were looking for. As they strolled down Pudding Lane munching their tarts and licking the sweet sticky fruit juices off their grubby fingers, the deep throated snorts of an angry bull could be heard above the continuous barks of several dogs.

The area, known as Bull Stake, was normally used as an extension to the market place for the selling of beasts at the Tuesday Market. Today, sadly, it was the turn of those wishing to see some sport as they set their semi-wild dogs on to the powerful beast to taunt and to bait him. The odds were not fair, of course, as the bull was securely tethered to a stout stake knocked firmly into the ground, and the extent of his movement was controlled by the length of the thick rope by which he was tethered. A roar of approval met each successful strike at the enraged beast but it was with some degree of satisfaction that young Master S watched its creamy white horn lunge like lightening into the neck of one of its cowardly attackers.

"Come on everybody, let's go. I've had enough of this. I'll race you to the Irish Cross."

Dodging past the shouting, cursing dog handlers, they raced down towards the castle before nipping up Truelove's Gutter to their destination. The Irish Cross stood at the junction of Market Place and Snig Hill and denoted that part of the market in which foreigners could sell their goods, as well as acting as the boundary markers for the district in which they lived. It seems strange that in such a small community as Sheffield's, discrimination by race had reared its head so early.

"Mind your backs, lads," roared the voice of the burly grain wagon driver as he drew his team of horses to a halt. "This

'ere hill is a bit steep for my heavy load, so I'm going to have to put a brake on these back wheels with my snig."

The intrigued group watched with interest as he grasped a length of sturdy timber and thrust it through the back wheels of the wagon, effectively locking them.

"That should do it lads. If you don't snig your wheels at this point on the hill, the wagon'll take off with the horses and then we'd be in a fine pickle, wouldn't we?"

It was a stroke of luck that the grain wagon en route to the town corn mill at Millsands, had arrived at that moment, for the kindly driver agreed to take the merry band with him. He even let Master S, the youngest and smallest of them, sit on the buckboard and hold the reins whilst he walked beside the lead horses reassuring them on their slow descent. "I'd always wondered why they called this Snig Hill," mused the proud young driver. "Now I know why."

"It's been a great day mum," enthused the now tired adventurer as his "stomach-ache" began to return. You want to see that great big water wheel down at the mill and the huge round stones which it turns to grind the corn. It's really good

and they even gave us a small bag of flour each to bring home."

* * * * * * * * * *

Mrs S was, of course, grateful for the flour but her mind was on other things. There were grave concerns in the country regarding the disagreements which existed between Parliament and the King who, it appeared, seemed to disregard all advice except his own. There was even talk that Civil War might break out which, inevitably, would involve Sheffield!

"I don't know why son, but men always seem to be wanting to fight. If it's not the French or the Spanish or anyone else abroad for that matter, then they're at each other's throats at home. And what's the cause? You can bet that religion or power is usually involved, you mark my words."

"It won't affect us will it mum?"

"I'm afraid so son. It looks to me as though the vicar's in favour of parliament in this argument, and most people seem to be behind him."

"What about dad, mum, what does he think?"

"Well your dad reckons that the three big "noises" in the area, Richard Jessop of Broom Hall, William Spencer of Attercliffe Hall and Stephen Bright of Carbrook Hall are all supporting parliament and we'd best follow their example if we want what's best for the town. In fact young John Bright, Stephen's son, is already recruiting volunteers to fight for parliament if necessary, so things don't look good, do they?"

Things, unfortunately, were not good as Civil War broke out a few months later. Although the Castle was still in the hands of supporters of the King, the Sheffield volunteers managed to seize it without much problem as its main defences, four brass cannons, had been sent to Doncaster some months earlier to help out there. John Bright then took his men to other parts of the country to fight, this proving to be an unwise decision in the course of time.

"We've no one left to protect us now," complained Mr S after returning home from a committee meeting that afternoon. "We'll just have to hope they return before any of the King's men decide to attack us."

This hope was, unfortunately, futile and within a short time the King's forces had marched on the castle and re-taken it with virtually no opposition.

"Well, we're back where we started now, aren't we?" remarked Mrs Weaver, having popped round to try this new-fangled tea that Mrs S's daughter had managed to "borrow" from Manor Lodge.

"He's a bit impulsive that young Bright lad but I see they've made him up to Colonel and he's only 23 you know," said Mrs S.

"Yes, but have you heard about young William Spencer?" responded her friend. "They've made him a Lieutenant Colonel. They're not doing bad between them, are they?"

"I know, but have you heard the latest about Earl of Newcastle, the Commander in Chief of the Kings forces? He's gone and taken over all the iron works and forges in the area and he's forcing everyone to make armaments for his army."

"What a nerve!" exclaimed Mrs Weaver. "Mind you, and this is strictly between the two of us, I have heard that at least

one iron works is managing to supply cannonballs to both sides at once. That's initiative for you, isn't it?"

The course of the war was, however, slowly becoming clear and within a year the parliamentary army, nicknamed the "Ironsides" and led by Oliver Cromwell, defeated the King's army in the north. The taking of Sheffield Castle was next on their agenda but this was not as simple as they had imagined.

"They've got at least 200 foot soldiers in there plus a troop of horse soldiers and eight cannons," commented Mr S knowledgeably as he waited with the large crowd of townsfolk on Castle Green to welcome the parliamentary army on its arrival.

"Here they come".

A shout from the crowd immediately prompted a cheer which then changed to a roar as a 1,200-strong column of foot soldiers led by a regiment on horseback advanced to the intimidating throb of beating drums.

The next few hours were spent by the townsfolk in helping the troops to set up their camp on the bottom side of Sheffield Park near to the river, in preparation for the intended siege of the castle. Cannons were positioned behind a carefully constructed protective wall of stones and firing commenced to the delight of the crowd.

"They're bouncing off like peas!" roared Mr S in disgust as the salvo made no impression on the huge castle walls. "And they'll soon run out of ammunition by the look of things."

True to his forecast, hostilities came to a stop and for several days local ironworkers were instructed to make a new stock of cannon balls for the embarrassed army whilst volunteers from local mines tried unsuccessfully to dig a tunnel under the castle moat.

"It's going to be a long siege this one" said Mr Weaver as he viewed the now rather boring scene below him. "It's not more cannon balls they need, its a bigger cannon."

"Look its Colonel Bright and his regiment and he's brought two large cannons".

The sharp-eyed observer from the now much reduced crowd of townsfolk could hardly have heard Mr Weaver's remarks, but if he didn't perhaps someone else did. Suffice to say, the new, more destructive weapons did the trick and in the face of several breaches of the strong stone walls, the King's forces surrendered and Colonel John Bright was installed as governor of the new parliamentary stronghold.

That wasn't the end of the story for Sheffield, however, as four years later the Earl of Arundel, as Lord of the Manor, was given permission to buy back his estate.

"You'll never believe it lass," gurgled Mr S whilst trying to achieve the impossible of talking and drinking his supper time ale at the same time. "Parliament's let him buy his castle back for 6,000 smackers but he's got to demolish it first! There's no sense nor reason to it lass. I'm devastated."

Parliament had made it's decision that the castle must go as it wanted to ensure that never again would a pro-Royalist Lord be able to defend himself in such a stronghold.

It was with a heavy heart, however, that the townsfolk watched and even took part in it's demise over the next few months. Many chose to buy its materials and fittings for their own use whilst others "borrowed" the stone at night, but the loss of its magnificent heritage was a truly sad day for Sheffield.

* * * * * * * * *

Times had improved somewhat for the S family because of the continuing success of Mr S's cutlery workshop. His hard work, initiative and natural resourcefulness had enabled them to move to a slightly more up-market property built of stone with a tiled roof and even a fireplace with a chimney.

Christmas was approaching and Mrs S was looking forward to a cooking-spree to celebrate the occasion, particularly after the long spell of harsh rule by the Puritan controlled Parliament earlier in the century which frowned on entertainment, pleasure, celebrations and any form of such excesses. The banning of Christmas festivities had been the last straw and Mrs S now intended to make up for lost time.

One of her husband's customers, a fairly wealthy merchant called Mr Posh who lived out of town in the Broomhall area, had invited them both round one evening to coincide with a special delivery of knives which Mr S had produced for him. She had marvelled at the magnificent kitchen in her host's stone "mansion" which had a wonderfully large fireplace complete with wood surround, a chimney crane fixed to the back of the hearth to carry a cauldron for boiling, a spit driven by a mechanical weight jack, a salt container built into the chimney wall and a host of pans and utensils. It even had one of those new fangled grates which could burn coal, which only the rich could afford to buy.

The kitchen itself had plenty of light through its two sash windows, with shelves and cupboards for food-preparing equipment and containers lining one wall. Proudly standing in one corner was a tall wooden unit which combined shelves, two cupboards and a wooden working surface which, according to Mrs Posh, was the "very first and totally exclusive kitchen dresser in the area."

It was, however, the long stone trough shaped sink which took Mrs S's eye, particularly the short pipe which projected through the wall just above it. Through this miracle of modern living, cold water was able to be hand pumped from outside when required, thus saving the housewife the arduous task of collecting water in containers and buckets.

"My kitchen might not be as good as hers," Mrs S explained to her 14-year-old daughter a few days later as they set about the task of selecting all the equipment and ingredients they needed for the whole day's food preparation. "Mind you, it's much better than we had before."

Her much smaller but fairly well equipped fireplace stood proudly in the centre of the dining-kitchen wall with its merrily burning log fire supported by two ornate andirons which her husband had made for her. She had a small supply of coal at the side of the log pile in the corner of the room which she'd managed to acquire from the workings of Coal Pit Lane, but it wasn't really suitable without a proper grate so she only used it on special occasions.

The cast-iron fireback at the rear of the hearth, which protected the stone work from the heat of the flames, also reflected the heat forward and the two eager cooks were grateful for its warmth. A large cauldron of water was simmering gently as it hung over the flames, whilst its gentle white wisps of steam intermingled happily with grey clouds of smoke as they excitedly explored the new chimney.

"At least we can breath while we cook now that we've got a chimney, can't we love?" said Mrs S "Anyway, let's get started or we'll not be finished before your father gets home. You know how he likes his food on time."

Moving over to the corner of the room where Mr S had fixed the stout wooden shelves on which to store her kitchen accessories, she recalled how grateful she was to be married to a metal worker, particularly one who made sure she was never short of things which were necessary to provide him with food.

On the bottom shelf stood the brandreth, the long-handled iron tripod which could easily be placed over the fire to support the earthenware pipkin in which smaller quantities of food could be cooked. He had also bought her a skillet, the three-legged "saucepan" which could be used for the same purpose. The porridge cauldron with its large round lid and detachable handle, always brought back happy memories as she recalled the hundreds of times she had sprinkled oatmeal into boiling water and stirred vigorously to the tune of her husband's impatient demands for breakfast. Last but not least in her bottom row stood the long-handled frying pan on its three stubby legs in which she could cook the occasional bacon and eggs or the new-fangled pancakes without getting splashed from the fat.

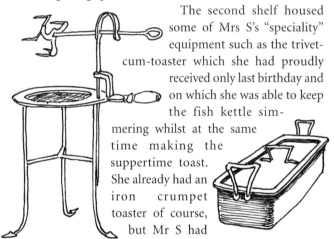

The second shelf housed some of Mrs S's "speciality" equipment such as the trivet-cum-toaster which she had proudly received only last birthday and on which she was able to keep the fish kettle simmering whilst at the same time making the suppertime toast. She already had an iron crumpet toaster of course, but Mr S had decided that this "two-in-one" invention was a must.

"But dad likes his food grilled sometimes doesn't he mum, particularly when he's on one of his "weight-watching" weeks."

"Don't worry love, the gridiron's on the end of the shelf next to the backstone so he can have his grilled sausage and his fresh bread cakes at the same time."

"I've never heard of a backstone mum. It looks like a circular iron baking sheet to me!"

"Actually, love, it's really called a girdle but we call it backstone round here after the time that baking was done on a hot stone many years ago. It's amazing how these names stick isn't it?"

"You've got a lot of equipment in here, haven't you" observed Mrs S's rather impressed daughter. "Did dad make it all?"

"No dear, not all of it. But he did make those iron posset dogs over there with the notches in them which support those spits in the rack over the fireplace. Mind you, I wouldn't fancy one of those new dog turnspits which Mrs Posh was showing me the other week; they shouldn't be allowed."

Mrs S had a good point of course. The usual way of roasting meat was to skewer it with a spit, suspend it on the fire dogs in front of the fire and slowly turn it with a handle attached to the end. In large houses, where servants were common, a "boy turnspit" was often used for this purpose where he knelt by the side of the roaring fire and was protected from its heat by a circular "wheel" of wet straw placed in front of him.

Mrs Posh, as we know, had already acquired a weighted pulley and chain device for her own use, but she was now in the process of selling her faithful old dog turnspit to her neighbour. This wonderful invention of man was like a giant golden hamster wheel, except that the hamster was replaced

by a golden, long-haired, long bodied, short-legged dog, specifically bred for this purpose. The poor dog was obliged to "tread the wheel" which, as it rotated, turned the wheel of the spit via a system of pulleys and chains.

"That's awful" cried young Miss S. "I can't believe anyone would do that."

"Well its very common nowadays dear, although you could say Mrs Posh has been a caring sort of person really."

"How's that mum? I don't understand."

"Well", she continued with more than a hint of sarcasm in her voice, "She did buy a pair of little dogs so that they could take it in turn to tread the wheel when the other one got tired!"

When the talking was over, the work then began. Oatcakes were the first and in no time at all Mrs S had mixed the oatmeal with water, buttermilk and yeast to make a firm dough. After leaving them to rise a little, she shaped the cakes on a wooden riddleboard which was scored with diagonal lines to give a pattern on the oatcake after rolling. The rolling pin itself was covered with ridges along its entire length so as to create a "ridged" cake which enabled air to circulate underneath it as it was baking, thus making it lighter. A quick turn with the heart-shaped iron bannock when the cake was half cooked, enabled it to be finished off on the sizzling iron baking sheet, cooked to perfection and ready for eating.

"We'll have to cook dad some of your special patterned

biscuits mum. He's anybody's after three or four of those, isn't he?"

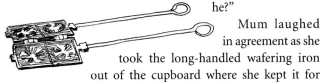

Mum laughed in agreement as she took the long-handled wafering iron out of the cupboard where she kept it for safety. This cooking utensil, which was the forerunner to the waffle iron, had two hinged pan blades and resembled a pair of tongues when closed. After pouring a batter of cream, eggs, flour and sugar into the pre-heated and greased pans, they were quickly closed and its contents cooked over the hot fire. The crisp, sweet biscuits were delicious for "afters", but Mrs S knew that they would be gone long before then once her husband and daughter had got their hands on them.

It was late afternoon by the time that the tired but satisfied cooks had finished their task. The wooden trestle table was almost groaning under the pile of wonderful food which sat tantalisingly on it. The chunky, crusty loaves sat next to the pies, pastries and tarts whilst the suet apple pudding leaned gently towards the two piles of gingerbread and parkin. Egg and milk custard was cooling in the black leather jug whilst the little pots of sausage meat lined up smartly at the front of the table.

"I hope supper's ready, I'm starving," came the all-too familiar voice. "Some of us have to work for a living you know!"

Not knowing whether to kiss him or kill him, the easy-going mother and housewife decided to let things ride and offered him her usual platitudes. "Coming dear. Have we had a hard day then? Just sit down and take it easy and I'll be with you in a minute."

"By gum lass, that was a grand meal tonight. I don't know what I'd do without you."

Such a glowing tribute from Mr S was more than she dared expect, and she felt pleased with herself as she drew the ashes over the fire's embers to dampen it down before placing the bell-shaped iron curfew over the top. This would enable it to keep on burning safely until morning, and the beginning of another day.

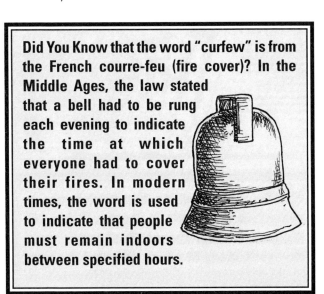

Did You Know that the word "curfew" is from the French courre-feu (fire cover)? In the Middle Ages, the law stated that a bell had to be rung each evening to indicate the time at which everyone had to cover their fires. In modern times, the word is used to indicate that people must remain indoors between specified hours.

The Eighth Hundred Years (1700-1800 AD)

(A) Size and Growth

In 1736, the Duke of Norfolk commissioned a geographical survey of Sheffield which established its population as being 9,695, with another 4,400 people making up the rest of the parish. By the end of the century, these figures had risen to 30,000 and 15,000 respectively with the Sheffield Parish (comprising the townships of Sheffield, Upper Hallam, Nether Hallam, Brightside, Ecclesall and Attercliffe) thus reaching 45,000.

This growth had been accompanied by the use of bricks for building houses in the town for the first time, a practice which became widely adopted by 1750. Most of the few remaining timber-framed buildings had fallen into disrepair (these always presenting a fire risk as they lined the narrow streets) whilst the more recent stone cottages survived for many years to come. Sliding sash windows were also being used from about 1750 onwards, and with the general use of tiled roofs, the town took on a different image.

It was not, however, a change for the better as working and living conditions became more cramped, smoke and grime continued to spread their cloaks of darkness and despair over everything in their path, and sickness and disease emanated from an almost total lack of sanitation.

The network of streets, lanes and passageways had increased significantly by the beginning of this century and numbered over 30. New buildings appeared which included a Workhouse on West Bar in 1722, a re-built Cutlers Hall in Church Street in 1725 at a cost of £442, a Debtors Prison in Pudding Lane (now King Street) in 1756, and St Paul's Church on the site of the now altered Peace Gardens in 1740 (although its dome was not added until 29 years later).

Industry continued its rapid expansion throughout the whole of the Sheffield area with cutlery manufacturing dominating the lives of the majority of the working population. Grinding was the most arduous of the cutlery trades and was carried out at water wheels up and down the river valleys. These were mostly rented from the Duke of Norfolk and by the year 1770 there were 133 grinding wheels and 28 rolling-mills, tilt hammers and forges worked by water power.

By the end of the century steam power was introduced which would result in much larger works and factories being built. This was aided by the ready supply of cheap coal from new collieries which had been developed in the once proud Park, now denuded of its many thousands of magnificent trees in the name of progress. Mining had also taken place in the township itself.

> **Did You Know** that the first brick house in Sheffield was built in Pepper Alley, off Fargate, in 1696? Thousands of people went to see it, many of whom ridiculed the new material suggesting that it would never last.

Perhaps the most significant change of this century was the introduction and implementation of the Enclosure Acts relating to the Manors of Ecclesall (1779), Ecclesfield and Southey (1784), Brightside (1788) and Sheffield (1791). These Enclosures, which were later followed by those of Handsworth (1802), Attercliffe cum Darnall (1810), Bradfield (1812), Wisewood (1815), Holmesfield (1816) and Totley (1839) represented probably the greatest injustice that the Sheffield working people have ever had to tolerate and accept.

From the very earliest days of the "feudal system" way of life which had been introduced by William the Conqueror in 1066, the subservient farming tenants and labourers who had little or no rights or privileges for many centuries still retained the enjoyment and use of the large areas of Common Lands in and around Sheffield (so called because they were open to and belonged to the whole community). As the value and benefit of land ownership became more apparent, the Lords of Manors, the large freeholders and the Church sought after this public land for themselves and, by the generosity of Parliament (of which they themselves were either part or had great influence), they succeeded in obtaining their selfish desires. Indeed, the House of Commons might more accurately have been described as the "House of Landowners" at this time, with the representatives of the very limited number of voting public being county aristocrats known as Knights of the Shire.

Rural Attercliffe.

Although several land owners, including the Lord of the Manor, claimed ownership of the commons, such claims appear to have no legal or moral justification. There was, of course, some argument in support of the Lord's claim of being the owner of all the original land of the manor. However, he and all those before him (the Talbots, the de Furnivals, the de Lovetots and back as far as Earl Waltheof at the turn of the last millennium) had raised no objection to the use of such land for hundreds of years by the whole community, and as such had acquiesced to its dedication to public use. Indeed, if such use and possession of land had taken place today, only 12 years needs to elapse before legal ownership by the user is granted.

However, in view of its importance in the history of Sheffield's growth and development, it is worth having a brief look at how the common land was established and how its

enclosure into private ownership affected Sheffield's residents. This can best be shown in the following diagram:

> *The King granted land and property (the Manor) to warriors or knights who had found his favour in battle.*

> *This warrior or knight was called Lord of the Manor and he divided up his land.*

> *He selected a portion for himself as his personal home, hunting grounds, farming land etc.*

> *He identified portions for his nobles, knights and lesser tenants (feudal system).*

> *The surplus of uncultivated land was called the Lord's Wastes as he had no need of it.*

> *People living near the wastes decided to squat on them. Eventually the wastes were used for pasture or simple recreation. The lands eventually acquired "rights of common".*

> *Applications were made to Parliament by major land owners for commons and waste land to be enclosed and distributed to land owners in the Manor, including the Lord of the Manor, other owners of land and property (which includes the Church) plus owners of ancient enclosed land.*

> *Parliament Agreed.*

Thus, those unfortunate people who had used the land, cultivated it or built on it for centuries but did not own it were left with no rights at all. In addition, village greens disappeared, many public footpaths were closed and most recreational use was eliminated.

The shape of Sheffield's open spaces now became a patchwork of ever changing scenery as miles of drystone walls were built together with roads to service the new developments contained within them. Thus, when Ecclesall Bierlow was enclosed in 1788, houses and workshops were built along The Moor, with similar buildings being provided in The Wicker in 1795 when Brightside Bierlow was enclosed.

This was, of course, progress and we cannot deny its inevitability. It would, nevertheless, have been to the considerable benefit of society, both at this time and at the present, if such progress could have been made without the poor having been so unjustly relieved of their heritage!

(b) Local Rule and Government

The Town Trustees and the Church Burgesses formed the continued basis of local government, although considerable influence was undoubtedly held by the vicar of the Parish Church, this being John Dossie for the first half century and James Wilkinson for the remainder.

> **Did You Know that for nearly 600 years between 1155 and 1751, New Year's Day had always been recognised and accepted as the 25 March? By an Act of Parliament made in 1751, the government decided it should be changed to 1 January from 1751 onwards, and it has remained so ever since.**

Of particular significance was that James Wilkinson was also a Justice of the Peace, a position of great authority during this century as the law of the land left much to their discretion and control. In his capacity as a Magistrate he enforced the law with harshness and was unpopular with many Sheffielders for some time. Such was the concern and outrage of his "flock" in 1791, that a rioting crowd, unhappy with the proposed enclosure of the commons of Crookes Moor and Little Sheffield Moor (of which the vicar was a beneficiary), attacked his home, Broom Hall, with the intention of burning it down.

Although armed soldiers were called out from Nottingham to quell the riots, parts of the property were damaged and the alleged ring leader, a person with reputed learning difficulties, was subsequently tried, convicted and hung. We thus have the perpetuation of the centuries old perception of justice: ignore the reason behind unrest whilst ensuring that the powerful and the strong are protected and the weakest and poorest take the blame. Needless to say, the Magistrate received about £600 compensation (about £30,000 in today's money) for the limited damage done to his magnificent home.

It is interesting at this time to compare the ultimate punishment imposed on the so called "ring leader" of this disturbance to that of a similar riot 40 years later during Parliamentary election unrest when a magistrate was struck on the head by a stone being thrown. Troops opened fire on the crowd and five people were killed, with many more being injured. The subsequent coroner's inquest returned a verdict of "justifiable homicide" and the whole matter was conveniently forgotten, with no possibility of a trial in a court of law being held which might embarrass those in power or authority!

One effect of the riot of 1791 was to make the Town's authorities realise that Sheffield had no local means of forcefully dealing with incidents of this type, which would inevitably arise again in the future. Police forces had not yet been introduced into society, and with the passing of time, the old military rule which once reigned supreme from Sheffield Castle had given way to a few special Constables, a Town Hall Beadle to carry out whippings, and the occasional recruitment of thugs (albeit referred to as additional constables) to break up riots and beat up ringleaders. This latter arrangement was in fact adopted in 1756 after four days of rioting took place in Sheffield in protest against further rises in the essential cost of living.

As a result of these concerns, a decision was taken to build a barracks at Hillsborough to accommodate 200 cavalry, thus establishing an effective method of law enforcement for the town, albeit without any proper form of democratic control.

The legislation which was introduced to prevent the

congregating of disorderly crowds, angry demonstrations and riotous assemblies was The Riot Act of 1714. It provided that if such assemblies of 12 or more people refused to stop their activities when requested to do so in the name of the King, then the death penalty may be imposed. Whilst the Act allowed force to be used to disperse crowds (with those carrying it out not being classed as responsible for the consequences of their actions), it did not allow for indiscriminate shooting. It is of interest to note that the expression "read them the Riot Act" is commonly used in the workforce and society of today in the context of, for example, an employer annoyed with his workers or a father angry with his children. This stems from the provisions of this almost 300 years old legislation which requires a Justice of the Peace to read out the requirements of the Act to the riotous crowd in a loud voice before ordering any action to be taken to suppress them. This Act was not actually repealed until 1967.

> **Did You Know** that a debtor's gaol with two cells existed in Pudding Lane (now King Street) in the 18th century? Each cell contained "criminals" who had failed to pay their debts. One cell was used for women and the other for men. Sheffield folk were often imprisoned there for owing as little as sixpence (2½ p).

There were, of course, many other Acts of Parliament introduced during this century which reinforced the strict control of crime in society. Harsh punishments continued to be imposed, including transportation to American colonies for seven to 14 years for theft of personal property, gaol for minor debts (often incurred in ale houses), execution for theft associated with house breaking and the usual fines, stocks and whippings for many minor offences.

Highway Robbery was still common, and the theft of a small amount of money, a breast of mutton and ½lb butter from a victim walking in the street near the Blue Ball public house in Attercliffe, plus a similar robbery nearby the same evening, resulted in the offender being hung on the gallows.

Perhaps the most famous of all Sheffield's highway robbers was Spence Broughton (probably the only criminal to have a road named after him) who, with an accomplice, robbed a post boy on horseback carrying the Sheffield to Rotherham mail in February of 1791. Whilst both men were caught and convicted of the crime, it was only Spence Broughton who was executed in York, following which his body was brought

back to Sheffield and hung in chains on a gibbet near to where the crime had been committed on what is now called Broughton Lane, just off Attercliffe Common. The highwayman's bones, and for many years the tattered remains of his clothes, hung there for 36 years until the gibbet was taken down in 1827.

> **Did You Know** that when Julius Caesar decided to organise the calendar nearly 2,000 years ago, he didn't get it quite right? His 12-monthly year was slightly longer than the solar year which, being the time taken for the earth to travel once round the sun, is equal to 365 days, 5 hours, 48 minutes and 46 seconds. We account for the extra hours, minutes and seconds by having a "leap" year once every four years which is 366 days instead of 365, the extra day being added to February. However, by the year 1751, Caesar's calendar and the solar year were out of step by 11 days, so Parliament decreed that the day immediately following 2 September 1752, should become 14 September 1752, and NOT the 3rd. Thus, 11 days were omitted from the calendar to get in step with the solar year. There were many protests and requests for extra money as people thought (wrongly of course) that they had lost 11 days of their lives! It is also interesting to note that even leap years have to be adjusted occasionally as the extra 24-hour day added is not exactly 4 times the 5 hours, 48 minutes and 46 seconds over 365 days

It is evident that this century brought with it a considerable amount of unrest which was to continue for some time. Working conditions and income were very poor, with strikes for better wages taking place in the 1770s, '80s and '90s. In addition, the continued expansion of the cutlery and associated industries began to create an ever-widening split between workmen and bosses as the size and diversity of business grew. Poverty and uncertainty created tensions and stress, with the only steadying influence being force rather than understanding.

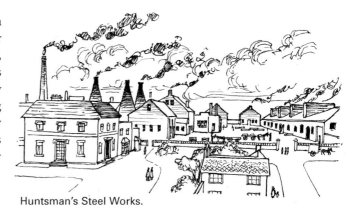
Huntsman's Steel Works.

(c) Working Life

As the population grew over this restless period of Sheffield's history, the diversity of work and people grew with it.

The "high" society at this time included professional people such as doctors, lawyers, bankers, senior clergy, wealthy merchants and the landed gentry, who still occupied large homes in the more rural areas.

Fastly approaching these were the newly-rich manufacturers in the cutlery and silver trades, which were growing in size at a fairly rapid pace. By 1743, Thomas Boulsover had invented silver plate (a process of fusing silver on to a copper base) which was subsequently developed by his apprentice Joseph Hancock in 1758. By applying the processes to a variety of luxury articles such as tankards, candlesticks, tea-urns etc. he successfully sold them to the growing middle-class market at home and abroad.

By 1773, there were 16 firms of silversmiths in the town and Assay Offices for the testing and hallmarking of silver goods were established both in Sheffield and Birmingham.

The hallmark is the stamp applied to an article of precious metal such as silver or gold after testing (assaying) of the metal for fineness of quality. No town is allowed the same mark and as Sheffield and Birmingham were opening their offices at the same time, the representatives of each met at the Crown and Anchor to decide their respective marks. The "Crown" and the "Anchor" were chosen as appropriate marks and, after winning the toss of a coin, Sheffield chose the crown which it has used ever since.

Of even more importance to Sheffield, however, was the invention in 1742 of crucible steel by a clock-maker called Benjamin Huntsman. At the beginning of the century, crude "blister steel" was made in the town from long thin strips of iron and basketfuls of charcoal heated together in cementation furnaces which looked like huge brick bottles rising above the rooftops of the township. The resulting steel, which was produced from this process of heating iron and charcoal together at very high temperatures for about ten days, had "blisters" or imperfections on its surface and was still fairly brittle. Whilst it was good enough for knives, shears and scythes, it was not suitable for more reliable mechanical parts and such delicate items as springs.

Huntsman's invention revolutionised the manufacture of steel which, for the next hundred years, was the best in the world, with most of it being made in Sheffield. The process itself was simply one of refining and was carried out by reheating broken up pieces of blister steel together with lime in clay pots or crucibles. After several hours, the molten crucible steel was manually teemed into ingot moulds and allowed to cool before it was removed and ready for use in forging shops where it was reheated, hammered, cut and shaped as required.

Working conditions for the town's cutlery workers were still very poor with smoke, stone and metal dust ensuring short life-spans for many. The grinders, who worked at "wheels" on the river banks usually earned the highest wages because this was the most arduous and damaging work of the industry. Lung diseases caused by the dust inhaled were almost inevitable and life expectancy for these workers varied between about 30 and 40 years.

Before the arrival of steam power at the end of the century, working hours were irregular and many tried to find additional work on the farms which now covered most of the Sheffield Park. They often met with little success, and under-employment was common.

In order to combat the problems of unemployment, rising food prices, sickness and fluctuating wages, the working population formed sick clubs and benefit societies which catered for the needs of the cutlers, tailors, file smiths, carpenters, grinders, braziers and masons. These organisations were the forerunners of the trade unions and often helped the poorest labourers and farmers at times when exploitation by the rich was threatened.

Wages identified for various trades in 1725 give some indication of the enormous difficulties encountered in simply existing at such time. The best farm labourer could expect to receive a maximum daily wage of 5p, the same also applying to masons, carpenters, joiners, plumbers, tilers and bricklayers. Whilst no such figures are available for the cutlers, their wages would likely be very similar.

(d) Domestic and Social Life

Conditions at home reflected the uncertainties of the time with food shortages, sickness and squalor affecting many of the working classes.

Poverty was rife and debt was common with drinking in the alehouse being the most popular form of recreation. This created even more poverty, and resulted in family tensions and even some wife and child abuse when the deadly cocktail of alcohol and frustration took effect.

The need to drink was not simply born out of any uncontrollable desire for alcohol, although alcoholism was probably not unusual. It related more to the working conditions and limited alternative recreational facilities available at this time. In particular, the continuous daily breathing in of smoke and dust particles by the many cutlery workers necessitated the availability of liquid refreshment, and relatively cheap ale was the first choice. It was in fact estimated that by 1787, there were 161 licensed victuallers in the little town itself.

With restrictions now having been lifted relating to the nine o'clock evening curfew, and with no control of opening hours applying at this time, public houses and beer shops served their willing customers for about 16 hours a day, the last "punter" usually being thrown out about two o'clock in the morning!

For those not wishing to venture out along the dark filthy streets and gennils at night, the drinking of crude, home distilled spirits had become very popular and had created a huge social problem following parliamentary legislation being introduced in 1703 to allow anyone to carry out this activity.

Earlier, in 1673, a Royal Edict had declared that brewing was forbidden by alehouse keepers, taverns and individuals and was only to be carried out by common brewers from whom all ale must be bought, this was introduced to make the levying and collecting of tax easier. This led to some of the large breweries such as Bass Charrington, Courage, Tetley, Whitbread and Worthington being formed and a system of "tied" public houses being introduced, although the only brewery (and therefore Sheffield's oldest) existing in the town during this century was "Thomas Rawson's", founded in 1758 and located in Pond Street on the site of the current Hallam University.

There was also much heavy drinking amongst the middle and upper classes with the latter being able to afford imported brandy from Cognac in western France. Dark stouts were available which had been produced using soft water (for which Sheffield was later to become well-known) and these also became very popular in thes 18th century. An Irish version of this drink later became known as Guinness after its "inventor", Arthur Guinness of Dublin.

The very poor had no access to any such luxuries as alcohol, being unable to even feed themselves or their families, and the workhouse was their only option for survival. Conditions in these were notoriously strict, with the West Bar workhouse being a typical example. Punishment for two women residents caught stealing some linen here in 1746 was confinement in a small underground room with no light (known locally as the "Black Hole") followed by a whipping on their eventual release. The order for this unreasonable punishment was issued by the Overseers of the Poor and the Church Wardens (the protectors of the poor!) in their capacity of having overall responsibility for the workhouse.

The Poor Law Act of 1601 had been the foundation upon which help for the poor had been based including the levying of a tax on all inhabitants of the parish and the setting of poor children and adults to work. Workhouses had stemmed from this and it had been their intention to make a profit from their activities. This had not been successful, and the uncaring and brutal attitudes of the establishment only added to the poor health and low esteem of the poor who worked there. Starvation was also common as money set aside for food often found its way into the pockets of the management.

By 1789, the West Bar workhouse accommodated 137 paupers, with one room having eight beds and 13 women living in it. Ten chained lunatics were identified amongst the inmates with ten others mixing freely with the rest. Chaining of so-called lunatics (who we now know to be people with inherited mental impairment or simply a learning disability requiring care rather than abuse and semi-torture) was allowed under an act of 1744 designed to make laws against Rogues, Vagabonds and Idle Persons more effective. Better known as the "Vagabond Act' it introduced or consolidated punishments of hard labour, houses of correction, whippings

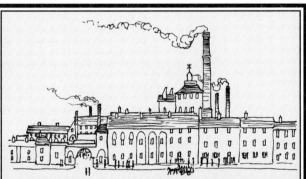

Did You Know that Sheffield's oldest brewery company was the Pond Street Brewery of Thomas Rawson, founded in 1758? A 17-year-old junior clerk called Samuel Plimsoll worked there for £1 a week in 1841. He later became famous as the inventor of the "Plimsoll Line", which is marked on the side of ships to regulate their loading. As if that wasn't enough, a soft shoe used in the gym and on sports days by many Sheffield children was also named after him.

or transportation to those who refused to work, or ran away and deserted their family or became minstrels, jugglers, actors, fortune tellers, peddlers or general wanderers. These days, many such people are paid handsomely for carrying out such "criminal activities".

Although later legislation (Gilbert's Act of 1782) changed the rules and regulations of Workhouses for the better, such establishments continued to be a huge drain on the parish's resources to the minimal benefit of those in care.

With the gradual increase of the middle classes such as shop keepers, small employers and merchants, plus the steady rise in professional classes, the standard of living rose. More people were able to enjoy the delights of drinks such as coffee, hot chocolate and tea, delicacies such as fruit pies, fruit jellies and ice cream, cheeses such as Stilton, Gloucester and Cheddar, and the continued partaking of sugar. Their indulgence in these delectable foods could easily be measured by the rapidly deteriorating condition of their teeth, at least one aspect of their lifestyle not envied by the poor.

Earlier in the century, a batter baked in dripping from roast meats had been developed in the Yorkshire area and gravy made from meat juices had taken over from broth. By the 1750s the culinary magic was complete and Roast Beef and Yorkshire Pudding became the country's favourite meal. Even though many labouring classes continued to live on dried bread and cheese interspersed with porridge and vegetable stews, the thought of such a luxury once a month was incentive enough for them to try and put a little money aside, particularly as boiled and mashed potatoes were now making themselves known as a tasty addition and filler.

The 1700s were not particularly good years in terms of human behaviour, and whatever suffering the working class took from the rich, they in turn were just as cruel in their choices of entertainment and pleasure. This manifested itself in blood sports which were popular with the Sheffielders. Bull baiting still took place on the street renamed Beast Market (now Haymarket), terrier dogs were encouraged to kill as many rats as possible in a given time in rat-worrying pits on the Moor (still open moorland at this time), and cock-fights were the culmination of an owners dedication and skill in

training his bird to tear its opponent to pieces with steel points fitted to its claws. Betting was the natural pleasure for the onlookers of these "sports" although the usual consequence was fighting and despair for all concerned.

Dancing and card playing in halls of church or chapel halls were the chosen activities of the more affluent members of society who, from 1785 onwards, also frequented the new and majestic Tontine Inn which was built on the site of the present Wilkinson's building between Dixon Lane and Castle Folds (now Exchange Street).

Local theatre was also becoming popular with "theatrical pieces" performed by touring companies in the yard of the Angel Inn in 1726. By 1760, a small theatre had been built in Norfolk Street attracting the leading actors and actresses of the day, and this was followed in 1773 by the opening of the Theatre Royal at the corner of Tudor Street and Arundel Street.

Whilst illness was a natural consequence of living in difficult times, medical advances had been very slow. Hollis Hospital had been founded in 1703 in a former Chapel at the junction of Snig Hill and "Under the Water" (now Bridge Street) but, like the Shrewsbury Hospital, was basically an almshouse.

Sheffield's first real hospital was in fact the General Infirmary and this was opened on 4 October 1797. This impressive stone-building, with beds for at least 100 patients, was located in pleasant country surroundings known as Upperthorpe Meadows and would later be known as the Royal Infirmary on its site bounded by Montgomery Terrace, Upperthorpe Road, Albert Terrace and Infirmary Road. The current use of this site as a Tesco Supermarket is a far cry from the original rural setting of the late 18th century.

Although water for the town was beginning to be provided by a number of dams built in Crookesmoor (albeit tap water would not be available for a century or more), the main supply for the hospital was the local Spring Vale stream which provided clean, pure water for all necessary uses.

The Waiting Room at the General Infirmary.

The new General Infirmary was, of course, a considerable advancement in terms of caring for the sick, although in common with most other hospitals, it could only provide relatively primitive care. Despite the progress in anatomy studies having developed nationally during this century, with the centre for medical education in Europe being located in Edinburgh in 1726, surgery was rare and dangerous and took place without the aid of painkillers or antiseptics. When such a drastic step was unavoidable, strong saws and sharp knives were used whilst patients were restrained.

The usual reasons for hospitalisation were consumption (similar to tuberculosis), fever, diarrhoea, ulcers, tumours and fractures. Conditions were usually poor with crowded wards, limited ventilation, wooden beds and often straw mattresses. Washing of patients and bedding was a rare event and buckets were used in the absence of flush lavatories. The spread of infection was common and most of the aristocracy preferred to engage a doctor to tend to them at home, even for the most serious of illnesses (though with little more success).

Health care was not the only improvement to be seen in Sheffield at this time. Educational facilities for the poor began to be provided in Charity Schools which were established by subscriptions from those who could afford it, usually a combination of the gentry, merchants, tradesmen and similar classes. The initiative for such provision came from an organisation called the Society for Promoting Christian Knowledge who felt that Godly learning was the antidote to the ignorance of the common people, especially the poor. Along with Religious instruction, both reading and writing were taught at such schools, the first of which was established for orphans, the fatherless and the destitute within the existing Shrewsbury Hospital (almshouse). This temporary school had 12 boarders, who were clothed and schooled, and up to 25 day pupils, all of whom wore distinctive blue uniforms and were referred to as the "Blue Coats", a name unfortunately associated with that of low status and being in receipt of charity.

In addition to building new Charity Schools, some existing schools were similarly funded, and were able to give free education to a limited number of poor children. Examples of these Charity Schools are the Fulwood Endowed School built in 1730, the City Charity School adjacent to the Grammar School, the Crookes Endowed School built in 1791, the Handsworth Church School built in 1800 and others in Parson Cross and Shiregreen (who only took in six pupils each), Ecclesall, Brightside and Stannington.

Sunday Schools were also introduced towards the end of this century, initially in private homes but later in adapted or purpose-built establishments, and although religious instruction was a major part of the teaching, reading and spelling was also taught. By 1791, 770 pupils were attending ten Sunday Schools located in the Park, Spring Croft, Broad Lane, Backfield, Hollis Hospital, Queen Street and Pond Lane. This figure would rise dramatically over the next 30 or 40 years.

A broad estimate of literacy amongst the population indicated that the number of men who could read and write rose from about ten per cent in 1500 to about 50 per cent by the mid-1700s. The percentage of women who were literate was about half that of the men.

It is not surprising that women in these times were less educated than the men. As housewives and mothers of fairly large families, their time was more than adequately used in cooking, cleaning and caring. Given the opportunity, their academic skills will usually equal and often exceed those of their male counterparts (as is now evident in late 20th-century school reports), but in the 18th century, opportunity was not often available. Domestic issues were far more important.

Although the market place and a few shops were available for provisions, local dairymen began to trade as the number of households owning a cow rapidly declined. Before horse-

drawn carts carrying churns of milk became the norm, milking a travelling cow on the customer's doorstep (with the occasional "gift" of free fertiliser) was the standard way of delivering milk!

Home-made butter and cheese was skilfully produced by most housewives in their kitchens, using a variety of utensils and mixing bowls available to them. Iron bars and grates were now used in the kitchen fireplace with wood still being the main fuel. Cooking was basic, and iron pots and utensils easily produced a tasty broth, a suet pudding or boiled fish. Clay and later brick ovens provided the essential daily bread or slowly roasted meat and built-in charcoal ranges gradually appeared in the homes of the better off.

Lighting was still only provided by Rushlights, made from rushes (a water plant), peeled and dipped in melted animal fat, or candles made from tallow (boiled and separated animal fat) and pure cotton wicks. The Rushlights were cheap to run, and four to five hours worth of light could usually be obtained for less than a farthing (about one tenth of 1p in today's money). Although the candles cost twice as much for only two hours light, they were more popular as rushes were not always easy to come by. Beeswax candles were, however, popular in the homes of the rich (as these gave a brighter flame, less smoke and generally smelt better), although by the end of the century oil lamps were in use.

With such primitive means of lighting combining with the comfort of fiercely burning logs in open fireplaces, the risk of fire was always significant and the year 1703 saw the introduction of Sheffield's first fire engine. This early fire-fighter was basically a hand cart with a pump operated by large handles which was kept at the Parish Church and was the first real advancement on the leather fire buckets which had previously hung there.

Hygiene in the home continued to be a constant problem and would remain so for the next 150 years or more. As water on tap was not available, it was used sparingly with personal washing usually involving the occasional use of cold water, and bathing (in metal tubs) probably only taking place in the homes of the better off. Going to the toilet, an essential activity for all classes of people, did, however, vary with affluence. Those who could afford them used hinged lid chamber pots kept under the bed or pots enclosed in a wooden stool, often with padded seats, which were emptied as and when required, probably in streams and rivers if these were nearby or on open land if this was more convenient.

In town, the poorer working classes still relied on pots and buckets inside the home and an earth closet outside. This probably consisted of a wooden seat with one or more holes cut out under which suitable buckets or containers were placed. A bucket full of dry earth was always available, some of which was thrown into the closet after each use. It is presumed that the whole affair was contained in a timber (or later brick) outhouse and emptying was carried out as and when required, sometimes into the open ditches which ran down the main streets of the town for many years up to the 18th century. During this hundred year period, pipes made of oak were being used to transport water from reservoirs and it is probable that the beginnings of a buried drainage system emerged at the same time.

Washing clothes presented a different problem and many housewives used to carry out this chore at the many wells which were scattered around the township. This, however, created health hazards as the hitherto pure water became contaminated and laws were passed banning such activities.

Did You Know that the expression "going batty" which is slang for "going crazy", derives from the old custom of beating clothes with a wooden bat to get rid of most of the thick or loose dirt before washing, often in cold water and lye? Lye was a soap substitute and was often made by adding urine to water, although pigeon or hen dung was equally as effective, and all were good cleansers. It is also of interest to note that the wooden tub into which the washing was placed was called a "buck", from which the name of a small tub, a bucket, developed.

Whilst paid washer women existed in town for use by the better off, most housewives elected to do their own, albeit probably only once a month. Hot water was rarely used, and hard soap was not generally available other than that imported from Europe by the rich. Most soiled clothes and linens were soaked in a solution called lye. This was produced by pouring water over fireplace ashes to separate out salts which then formed the alkaline cleansing solution. It was important to use the ash of burnt wood or vegetable matter to make this soap substitute, with apple tree wood being reputed to produce the wash which was "whiter than white".

Mangles were used in the households of the rich at the end of this century to iron sheets, table cloths and linen although they later developed into mechanical wringers used for squeezing water from wet clothes. Hot irons were already in use and were heated over fires on a three-legged metal stand called a trivet, which was attached to the base of the fire grate. The trivet was also used for the cooking pot, and later the kettle, to stand on.

(c) Travel and Communication

During the first half of this century, Sheffield's export trade to other parts of the country or even abroad was still carried via its network of packhorse routes over hills and down dales to their destinations. Bawtry was the centre of exportation in this area as not only were goods able to be transported via the Rivers Idle and Trent to inland locations, but more importantly they were able to progress via the River Humber to Hull and thus to the continent. Good quality continental iron and even groceries travelled the same route back for sale and use in Sheffield.

By 1732, however, the River Don was improved and made navigable as far as Tinsley. Incoming goods were then transferred from here to horse-pulled wagons for the last stage of their journey to Lady's Bridge at the edge of town.

The old packhorse routes were, nevertheless, totally unsuitable for wheeled traffic and, as the demand for more goods and their prompt delivery increased, such vehicles of transportation became essential. The lack of good transport routes prompted the town's important traders and merchants, together with the Cutlers' Company and the Town's Trustees and Burgesses, to pressurise the government into creating legislation which would enable existing roads to be improved, or new roads to be built by private endeavour. In return, permission would be granted for the private operator to erect gates or barriers (called turnpikes) at which tolls could be collected from the users of such roads. Thus, the idea of turnpike roads was introduced, their management and operation being undertaken by Turnpike Trusts which were comprised mainly of Sheffield's leading citizens and businessmen. In the hundred years covering the last half of this century and the first half of the next, about 18 toll bars were erected and anyone wishing to get into or out of the town had to pay for the privilege.

The standard of the turnpike roads, whilst being a great improvement on the old packhorse routes, was, nevertheless, fairly basic and a surface of broken stone on wider roads with reasonable drainage was the norm. Fencing, strengthening and widening of old wooden bridges and the provision of

The Turnpike (Toll Bar) at Collegiate Crescent, Ecclesall Road.

stone, timber and sometimes cast-iron "mile" posts were carried out and the improved transportation network resulted in increased trade. Later turnpike roads were better designed and constructed by professional civil engineers such as Thomas Telford and John Macadam, and it was the former who constructed the new road to Manchester via the Snake and Glossop in the first quarter of the 1800s.

Coach travel became possible with the advent of better roads, and the first horse-drawn stagecoach made the difficult journey between Sheffield and London in 1760. Twenty-five years later, the first Royal Mail coach service between London and Leeds via Sheffield & Barnsley was introduced, its stopping place in Sheffield being the Angel Inn in Angel Street. In 1788 the arrival and departure point became the Tontine Inn in Beast Market (previously Bull Stake and now Haymarket), where the coach left at 4am every morning for its eventual arrival at the Bull and Mouth in London.

Postal deliveries to other more local towns and villages were still made by Post Boys on horseback, some as young as 12 years old, and after an incident relating to a lost or stolen

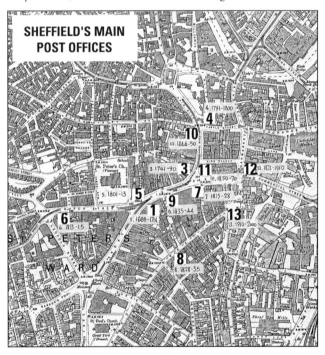

letter containing £100 on the Buxton to Sheffield run in 1797, a minimum age of 16 years was recommended for such a responsible post.

The post masters or mistresses during this century changed hands several times with Jonathan Turner taking over from George Carr in 1696, Martha Turner being post mistress between 1713 and 1740 and Samuel Simmons taking over the new post office in Market Place (at the top side of what was the "hole in the road", now Castle Square) for the next 43 years. The end of the century saw post master

Simmons, who was a stationer by trade, handing over to Miss Lester for about five years before the post office moved once again to a location at the corner of Snig Hill and Castle Green Head (now Castle Street) where it remained until 1800 under the supervision of Rice James. The new incumbent earned a generous £60 a year, this being an increase of £10 on his predecessor's salary, and he not only sold stationary in his new premises, but specialised in selling the "most genuine medicines" as well.

Perhaps one of the most significant aspects of communication to develop in the 18th century was the emergence of the daily newspaper which, in the absence of radio and television which dominate today's society, represented the biggest voice and influence of the people of the

Hartshead.

time. *The Sheffield Weekly Journal* was the first newspaper in the town and made its appearance in 1754. Within two years this newspaper was bought by *The Sheffield Weekly Register and Doncaster Flying Post*, which was printed in Doncaster. The *Sheffield Register* emerged in 1787 in its own right and continued under this name until 1794 when, under the new editorship of the famous poet James Montgomery, it appeared on the Sheffield streets as the well-known *Sheffield Iris*.

It is interesting to note that James Montgomery was an outspoken editor who was twice imprisoned for three months for publishing libelous comments in his paper before his retirement at the age of 54. He continued to live over his printing shop in Hartshead until his mid-60s before finally moving to a comfortable residence at The Mount in Broomhill, where he lived until his death at the age of 83.

Chapter Eight

1700 to 1800

"YOU know," said Mr S as he tried a few puffs on his long stemmed clay pipe, "I can't imagine what people see in this new leaf called tobacco. It's got a rather a strange flavour and it always seems to make me cough."

"Well, its very fashionable amongst those rich enough and daft enough to buy it," came the response, "so if I were you, I wouldn't bother."

Mrs S was usually to the point but she did, of course, appreciate how things were changing in their rapidly growing community. Unfortunately, many of the changes were not, for the vast majority of people, for the better.

"It's all right producing new steels, new silver plate, hundreds of different tools and tons of coal, but who's raking in all the money? You've got the iron industry controlled by a group of Gentlemen Ironmasters who live in great big houses in the suburbs, the cutlery trade controlled by rich "middlemen" who deal with London Merchants, and most of the mines owned and controlled by the Duke of Norfolk!"

"I take your point love, but we're not too badly off really. I'm running three hearths in my workshop at present and it's keeping our little family business going quite well."

But Mrs S wasn't just thinking about themselves. It was the conditions under which everyone was working. There was the smoke and the heat from the forges, the deadly dust from the grinders' "hulls" on the rivers and the long, hard hours worked by everyone.

Saw grinder.

resistance was accompanied by sparks of defiance as it spat out streams of steel and stone dust which gleefully infiltrated the ears, nose and throat of its aggressor.

The man in the next trough had been there eight years, but at the age of 27 he had the appearance of someone twice as old. His drawn lean face, permanent stoop and short rasping breaths were easily recognisable as the "tradesmarks" of a grinder, and it was a sobering moment when the gaffer announced next day that the poor soul was "done for".

"Grinders Asthma" was an occupational hazard in these difficult times, but little did Mrs S's nephew realise that it was to get worse before it got better!

Life had to go on, however, and it was cleaning day in the S household and both children and father knew to keep well away. The beaten-earth floor of the past had now given way to stone slabs and the old loose straw or reed covering had been replaced by one of Mrs S's specially woven mats. "Times are so much easier these days," she thought to herself.

She had two besom brooms in the corner of the kitchen, one which she referred to as "old faithful" made from birch twigs bound tightly round a wooden handle, and the other made from the softer foliage of heather. Whilst the birch was invaluable in removing the "muck and rubbish" brought in by her inconsiderate family, the heather was better for the corners and those areas where dust rather than mud was the offending matter.

For those extra gentle touches around the walls, windows and simple wooden furniture, Mrs S had persuaded her husband to make her a golden maidenhair besom from the delicate fern of the same name. Its fine hair-like stalks and

> **Did You Know that before the days of iron locks, the method of locking the door to the Cutler's Hull was to use a "hull boy"? This young boy slept in the Hull at night and locked the door from the inside by pushing a wooden block through a hoop into the door frame. As the cutler left his place of work at night he would call out a message to the boy left inside, so originating an old Sheffield expression: "Don't forget to put t'wood in t'ole!"**

It had only been last month when her nephew had gone down to occupy one of the troughs at the grinding wheel on the riverside. There was noise and vibration everywhere as the powerful water wheel turned the gears then the shafts of the huge grumbling grindstones which rotated incessantly in the watery troughs which kept them cool. When the rough steel blades attacked the hard, turning stone, its screech of delicate foliage, once skinned and combed, transform into a soft, pliable chestnut coloured "duster", ideal for use on fabrics, furniture and carpets. It was unlikely, of course, that many of her neighbours would require the use of such a fine cleaning aid as most homes in the town were far more basic and rundown than hers.

As she put the finishing touches to her brushing and dusting chores, she recalled the exacting demands placed on her eldest daughter, who was now in service as a Housemaid at Mrs Posh's large residence in the suburbs.

"Do you know, mum, I have to get up at 6 o'clock and have the fire grates cleaned and all the downstairs rooms swept, dusted and ready for use by the household before I have my break at eight o'clock. And that's not all, at half past eight, I have to go upstairs, turn down the beds and open all the windows to air them before they're able to be made as well as tidying up, emptying the chamber pots, sweeping and dusting. I'm totally shattered by lunchtime, I can tell you."

Mrs S had, of course, been totally sympathetic with her daughter's rigorous morning schedule, but recalled with just a little envy the wonderful new cleaning aids that she was able to use as part of her duties. There was the fancy shaped library duster for example, the round furniture brush, the new fangled brush and crumb tray, the wonderful long-handled cornice brush and the very handy picture dusting brush. Perhaps the most unusual brush that her daughter had described was that used for furniture shaped like a porcupine, whilst the one that was easiest on the back was the long-handled dustpan and broom.

But it was time to get back to reality and continue with her chores. "Day-dreaming never got any work done," she reminded herself, "and there's the work surface to clean next." This bare wooden table set against the wall was a regular harbourer of germs as raw foods and cooked foods shared its surface every day. Mrs S had already bought some soap from the "sope boiler" in town but had never liked the odd smelling, greasy

product with the consistency of putty and was grateful for the expensive, imported hard soap that Mrs Posh had sent her.

Half an hour of good scrubbing later, the task was complete, and she treated herself to a mug of weak tea which she'd heard tasted even better with a drop of cow's milk in it. The water had already boiled in her new iron kettle with its easy-to-pour spout, although she did think it was going a bit far to have one of those earthenware teapots which the well-off were buying when you could just as easily mash the tea in the mug.

"Some people will buy anything just to be fashionable," she muttered to herself as she munched the last oatcake which had been waiting patiently for her in the earthenware storage jar on the kitchen shelf.

It was the heavy iron frying pan which presented Mrs S with her greatest challenge as it sat there with its burnt-on greasy sides and base, staring up at her defiantly with its black deep-set eye. Grasping its long handle, she took it to the little stone sink which nestled in the corner of the kitchen on its two brick supports, and set it down on the firm, solid surface for action. An initial assault with a short wooden scraper managed to weaken its resistance and set the scene for the battle to come. After what seemed an age, and only armed with a thick cloth, "black soap" made from ashes, sand and linseed oil and lashings of "elbow grease", she finally rinsed the pan with boiling water to signal the triumphant end to her struggle.

"I'm glad that's only once a month," she gasped with

exhaustion, "I think I'd rather go to war than do that very often."

Mrs S's final task of the morning was more of a pleasure than a chore as she always enjoyed cleaning the knives which her husband had made for her. He didn't like to see the little blemishes and spots of rust appear on the sharp steel blades, and his understanding wife was more than pleased to oblige by regularly strapping them on the leather covered knife board with the aid of a little emery powder.

"By the "eck lass, I can almost see my face in them," was his usual appreciative remark on such occasions. "I couldn't have done much better myself."

* * * * * * * * *

Shopping in town was something Mrs S enjoyed now that more choice had arrived on the streets. Butchers and bakers intermingled with ale houses and Inns, whilst new little tea and coffee shops offered their wares to the rather better off. Shoemakers and tailors rubbed shoulders with button makers, glovers and sadlers, whilst the market place sold almost everything you needed. Bull Stake had earlier been renamed Beast Market and then again further changed to Haymarket, probably to eliminate the stigma associated with bull-baiting, although she couldn't for the life of her understand why High Street had changed its name to Prior Gate.

It wasn't just the shops that attracted her, it was the hustle and bustle of activity that she loved. Not that she cared for the new Barber's Shop which had recently opened. There was always plenty of activity in there, but the cutting of hair and shaving of beards were not the barber's only occupations. He proudly announced on his sign that he also undertook the

delicate operation of "bleeding" as well as the pulling out of teeth, and the occasional screaming and shouting which came from his open window was at least some indicator that his combined trade was doing well.

There were, of course, more doctors in town, but their charges were rather prohibitive to the poor classes who still preferred to depend on cures such as a pine-cone for averting "evil eye" or an Orris root necklace around baby's neck to prevent convulsions. Mrs S wasn't too sure about the cure for fever, however, as the recommended sealing of a spider in a goose quill which is then hung around a child's neck "as low as the stomach" didn't seem quite right to her.

Of course, for shopping she needed money, and the copper farthing and halfpenny in general circulation were the two most useful coins in her purse. "Mind you, its not like the olden days," she muttered, noticing the ridiculous tea and coffee prices at about 3s a pound and feeling even more grateful that Mrs Posh was able to let her have the tea "dust" from the bottom of her storage jar each month. Silver coins were also circulating widely for use on the larger household purchases, and whilst Mrs S used the silver penny, two pence, three pence and groat from time to time, it was the much better off who could afford to buy with the sixpence, shilling, half-crown and crown.

"I don't know why they make these golden guineas," Mr S would always remark to his wife when they discussed the cost of living from time to time. "We'll never use them, that's for sure." Of course, life was different for those who had acquired or inherited wealth, and the half guinea, one guinea, two guinea or five were commonly used in such circles. There had been times during the last century, Mrs S recalled, that thin brass halfpenny and penny tokens had been used due to the shortage of small change in silver. Tokens such as these would also be used again at the end of this century and the beginning of the next for a short time.

"I'm getting as bad as that husband of mine," Mrs S suddenly thought as she snapped out of her day-dreaming and hurried down Prior Gate to catch the post at Miss Lister's Post Office in Market Place. Mrs Posh had asked her if she could drop off an important letter to London and had already given her the seven penny charge.

"I think I'll go and have a look at this new Tontine Inn that's been built in Haymarket while I'm at this end of town," she decided. "I can nip straight down King Street but I do wish they hadn't moved the Bakehouse, and I still prefer its old name of Pudding Lane."

It was good timing on Mrs S's part, for as she turned the corner into Haymarket, the yard bell rang at the Inn and two pairs of beautiful chestnut horses were led out amid a clatter of hooves on cobbled stones and cheers from the ever-present crowds of people standing by.

The Angel Inn had been the main coaching house in town until the building of the Tontine and still carried out plenty of trade there. Coach travel was now big business and with the introduction of the mail coaches it had grown enormously. Mrs S recalled when the first coaches had left Angel Street for London about 25 years ago and took about

Did You Know that the Tontine Inn was so called because its cost of around £5,000 was raised by a financial agreement called a "tontine"? This arrangement enables subscribers who have invested in a project to receive equal shares of the annual rents and profits for a specified time. This inn, built in 1785 on the site of the old Woolco store in Haymarket, now occupied by Wilkinsons and others, was bought by the Duke of Norfolk in 1850 so that he could demolish it and erect the Norfolk Market Hall, which thrived on this site for over 100 years.

three days for the journey at a cost of £1 17s (£1.85). The journey now took just over a day on "The Express".

The Castle Barns had stood on the site of the Tontine for many years and Mrs S remembered these being used to accommodate the cattle and other animals on market days as well as corn and hay. "Now its all this heavy traffic," she mused as the Royal Mail coach for London pulled out and was immediately replaced by an incoming coach and several other departures. "Well, that's progress for you. At least it can't get any worse!"

* * * * * * * * *

Despite the progress made in their small cutlery workshop, the S family were still fairly poor, and success depended on "the whole family pulling together" as Mr S always put it.

"It's alright you wanting the kids to help out in the workshop, but what about their education?" Mrs S reminded her husband yet again.

"You never give up do you?"

"We had this discussion some time ago when you wanted our son to go to the Free Grammar School at Townhead. I didn't like the idea then and I don't feel any different now."

"Yes, but husband, times change don't they. It's our young daughter I'm concerned about. She needs a proper job which will keep her on the straight and narrow. If you walk round town at night these days, there's lasses hanging around on street corners with all sorts of fellows and they've all been drinking. And have you seen those filthy dark places they hide in? If the girls don't catch a disease from the lad they go with, then they catch one from the germ ridden gennels that they mess about in."

"Now come on, dear, its not all that bad you know. There are plenty of good lasses and lads in town although I do accept that conditions are getting worse with the population having grown so fast."

"Well, its not just that is it," continued the very determined mother. "Just think about poor Mrs Weaver's daughter. She had two babies out of wedlock, one when she was 16 years old and another when she was 18. She spent three years in gaol for that second one and she'd still be there now if Mrs Posh's friend hadn't bailed her out and stood surety for her."

"All right, all right, you win, but what have you got in mind? She's only seven you know."

"Well, there are two options as far as I'm concerned. Do you remember that meeting we went to at the "Sign of the Harrow" in Sheffield Park District a year or two back organised by Shrewsbury Hospital's Chaplain? It was a real success and because the Park's grown so much with mostly poor people living there, they managed to organise enough charitable money to build and run a school."

"Won't it be full by now?" Mr S quickly and hopefully responded.

"It may be but I favour the new Girl's Charity School at the junction of Virgin's Row and Campo Lane at the back of the churchyard. They're allowed to start at seven years old as long as their eyes are all right, they've got no diseases and they're not deformed."

"Well that is good of them I'm sure," came the sarcastic response. "I just hope the teaching staff are as perfect."

This particular school had been the "brain-child" of Edward Goodwin, the Curate of Attercliffe, who had liaised closely with James Wilkinson, the Vicar of Sheffield, who fortunately was fairly open minded about forms of worship and various religious beliefs. The principle upon which the school had been established was that of being able to rescue poor girls from vice and immorality and thus guide and educate them for a career in domestic service. In pursuance of this, emphasis was placed on moral excellence, uprightness, patience and chastity with an obligation to be dutiful and earnestly religious.

"By the sound of things, she'll probably be a Saint by the time she comes out of there, never mind being a domestic servant," continued the cynical father. "I just hope it works, that's all. Mind you, at a cost of fifteen hundred quid to build, it should be good!"

There was little point in further discussion, and Mrs S intended breaking the news to her husband later that this was in fact a boarding school which provided free education, training, clothes and lodgings until the children reached the age of 13 or 14, at which time they were placed out to service. The demand for domestic servants of good quality was in fact very high at this time as large fashionable properties grew up around Hartshead, Paradise Square and on the west side of

"To put it briefly Mrs S, the first lesson emphasises that each girl must be good and God will then love her, the second lesson asks them to love God and try and please him and he will then be their friend, and the third lesson emphasises the need to always speak the truth."

"What about the fourth lesson?" chimed in the attentive young girl. "I thought you said there were four?"

"Hush dear," said Mrs S, colouring up at her daughters forthrightness, "the headmistress hasn't finished yet."

"Well, Miss S, it's good to see that you have been listening, but patience is a virtue we encourage here. But to answer your question, the fourth lesson applies to more practical things and reminds you that you must keep your clothes clean, wash your hands and face, comb your hair and always tie up your shoe laces."

The puzzled little girl looked down at her grubby, bare little toes poking out of her rather well-worn "flip-flop" sandals, and casually pushed her equally grubby little fingers through her tousled mop of blond hair. Words were not really necessary as the looks on all their faces said what each was thinking.

Whilst parting was painful and full of tears, the joy of reunion on visits and holidays was desperately looked forward to. Daughter S delighted in telling her mum how the girls cleaned the rooms, washed their clothes, learnt to spin, sew and knit, learnt to bake and cook and even how to brew ale. She wasn't however, so keen on washing the pots and pans, scrubbing the floors and beating the carpets and she was "even told off just for talking too loud".

In their discussions at school on the principles of Church religion, many references were made to the different Churches and Chapels which had sprung up in Sheffield by this time.

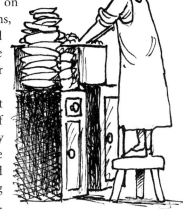

The Roman Catholics, for example, had built their first chapel attached to the "Lord's House" which had been built in 1707 for the Duke of Norfolk at the junction of Fargate and Pepper Alley, whilst the Quakers had established a meeting house in Meeting House Lane, although this was later to be replaced by a better building at Hartshead. The nonconformist Upper Chapel on Norfolk Street existed early in the century as the Presbyterian Meeting House at the bottom of Pepper Alley, whilst the new St Paul's Church of "Peace Gardens" fame found itself located in beautiful surroundings fronting the rural Pinson Lane.

"We talked about John Wesley as well, mummy," said her remarkably knowledgeable child on one of her later visits home. "I bet you remember when he came to Sheffield in 1741 don't you, and spoke to a huge crowd in Paradise Square

town towards Broomhall and it was the rich and influential owners of such properties who had contributed towards the school's development and operation.

It was a nervous little girl who arrived for the first day at her new school. Holding her mother's hand, she stood out amongst the older girls in their plaited straw hats, plain blue dresses and little checked aprons.

"Do I have to wear one of those mummy?" she whispered, pulling a face. "Everyone looks the same."

With a reassuring word and a quick little hug, Mrs S took her daughter into school, explaining that it was better to all look the same, then there would be no tendency to be jealous of what other girls might wear.

"We teach English, religious instruction and the principles of Church religion," the headmistress explained after sitting Mrs S down on a hard chair, whilst daughter S stood dutifully to one side. "We then train them in the arts of knitting, sewing and spinning as well as domestic management so that by the age of 13 they will be able to successfully serve their elders and betters."

Mrs S was pleased that the husband hadn't come with them that morning. He wouldn't have been the most tactful of persons to deal with the headmistress at this critical stage of school entrance.

"And this, Mrs S, is a copy of Reverend Goodwin's introductory exercises which we shall expect your daughter to learn and obey as soon as possible."

Luckily, Mrs S was able to read, although many of her friends were not so fortunate. The single sheet of paper was headed "The Poor Girls Primer" and set down a few basic lessons to be learned and remembered.

Did You Know that the first Preparatory School in Sheffield was opened by Miss Wragg in 1876 for the education of "children of Sheffield Gentlemen"? Its first premises were opposite the main entrance to the present Sheffield University, following which it moved to 383 Glossop Road in 1883, before finishing up in Westbourne Road in 1883. At this time it became the Westbourne Preparatory School.

behind the Parish Church? Well, his Methodists have built a Chapel at the corner of Chapel Walk and Norfolk Street now, just across from Nether Chapel."

"You've certainly learned some stuff, young 'un" said her father, not wishing to be kept out of such intellectual conversation. "I hope you'll make good use of it. As for me, I'm totally confused with all these different types of Church. I don't know why they just don't stick to one type for everybody and be done with it!"

Mother and daughter gave him a disapproving look before he continued.

"Having said that lass, I'm very proud of the way you've progressed. You're an example to us all and let's just hope some of it will rub off into the next century."

The Ninth Hundred Years (1800-1900 AD)

(a) Size and Growth

This crucial period in Sheffield's history was dominated by over 60 years of Victorian rule during which time the relatively small town merged with its neighbouring parish townships to form a huge industrialised city.

By the time Sheffield was incorporated as a Borough in 1843 (and became locally known as "the Corporation"), its population had increased from 45,000 to about 120,000, rising to a staggering 400,000 or more by the end of the century.

The new Borough of Sheffield incorporated six main townships, these being the Central township, Upper Hallam, Nether Hallam/Heeley and Ecclesall townships to the west, and Brightside and Attercliffe townships to the East.

By the mid century, at which time the population was 135,000, 62 per cent of the inhabitants were living in the Central township (83,000 people), about 18 per cent were living in Ecclesall township (24,000 people) and most of the remaining 20 per cent were spread around Nether Hallam, Heeley and Attercliffe. By far the largest township in area was Upper Hallam which occupied about 40 per cent of the Borough, although its population of 1,400 was without doubt the smallest.

Forty years later, in 1891, the picture had changed significantly for although the total population had increased to 324,000, that of the Central township had only increased by less than ten per cent. This was mainly due to the fact that not only was it already fairly densely packed with people, many dwelling houses gave way to shops and offices, and street widening schemes were carried out. Brightside's population, on the other hand, increased dramatically from 12,000 to 67,000 over this period, whilst that of Attercliffe increased from 5,000 to 36,000, both due to the explosive increase in the heavy steel industry.

The men in the heavy trades came to live near the steelworks in Brightside and Attercliffe (including Carbrook and Darnall), whilst those in the lighter trades made their way to Heeley, Crookes, Walkley and Hillsborough.

Although the Central township had little new space available by the mid-century, there was still a large demand by manufacturers wishing to be located near their supplies, sub-contractors, business agents and merchants. This resulted in many large dwelling houses being converted and adapted to industrial use, whilst at the same time rows of tightly packed houses were built to accommodate the workman who wanted to live near to his place of work.

Whilst much of the increase in the population was the result of natural growth, a significant proportion was due to immigration of people from outside Sheffield who were attracted by the prospect of work in the heavy industries. This was particularly true in the second half of the century when about 60,000 of the 190,000 population growth came from all the surrounding counties, as well as from Ireland, to find work.

Housing and industry at Heeley Bottom.

Typical housing layout.

> **Did You Know** that the first electric motor to be used to "blow" the Parish Church organ (now the Sheffield Cathedral) was introduced in 1894?

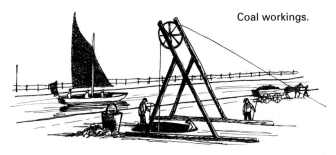

Coal workings.

The growth in industry and people during this time of remarkable change was accompanied by improved roads, the building of the canal, the coming of the Railway, the building of schools and the provision of hospitals. Unfortunately, it also saw deaths due to cholera, the massive destruction caused by the Great Sheffield Flood, and poverty, death and disease caused by appalling working conditions and lack of sanitation. As ever, change comes at a price as it marches relentlessly onwards.

(b) Local Rule and Government

The 19th century began as it finished, by the building of a new Town Hall. The one built 100 years earlier at the south-east corner of the parish churchyard with its three unhygienic, dark prison cells underneath, was considered by the community as a whole to be a disgrace by the time it was demolished in 1808. Accordingly, despite having problems with its cost, the Town Trustees funded a new, larger building at the corner of Waingate and Castle Street which is still standing today. Apart from being used for official meetings, it was also used as a prison and for court hearings. It was enlarged in 1833 and again in 1867 when the Borough Council took over the lease from the Town Trustees, an underground passage also being constructed to link with new police offices which had been built in Castle Green.

It was 1894 when construction of the new Town Hall began. New Church Street ran through the centre of the site and many a building was demolished to accommodate this magnificent seat of local government, not the least of which were three public houses, the Cutler's Arms, the Old Green Man and the Grapes. Such was the price of change!

In 1832, the Reform Bill (known as the "Great Charter") became an Act of Parliament and Sheffield was allowed its first two MPs. Regrettably only 3,500 male householders were allowed to vote, none of whom were the poor majority as voting restrictions related to wealth in these days. The poor people's candidate was not, therefore, successful and the election result caused much unrest and violence which resulted in the unnecessary and unjustified deaths of five protesting rioters. Later in the century the situation improved, and in 1878, the "working man's candidate", a liberal by the name of A. Mindella, was successfully appointed as an MP for Sheffield with the support of most of the unions.

It was, however, in 1835, that the chain of events began which changed the face of local government in Sheffield for ever. The "Municipal Corporations Act" had been passed by parliament specifying that a number of named towns

Sheffield Town Hall, which was completed in 1898.

(including Sheffield) could apply for a "Charter of Incorporation" as a Borough. This Charter would not only allow the formation of the Borough Council (Sheffield Corporation), but it would give the town permission to appoint salaried officials in the Town Hall, appoint a Commissioner of Peace and a Quarter Sessions Court. Unfortunately, the majority of the influential people in the town feared that higher rates would result and opposed any such application for the Charter. Most of the local people did, nevertheless, support the proposals and by 1838 a Chartist movement supporting the Charter, one man one vote and other radical parliamentary reforms began in Sheffield, which became the centre for a nationwide campaign.

The leader of the Sheffield movement was a young married man by the name of Samuel Holberry who lived in Eyre Lane. On 11 January 1840 he was arrested for plotting an armed rising to capture the Tontine Inn and the Town Hall and was sent to York Castle goal for four years. Eighteen months later, on 21 June 1842 at the tender age of 27, he died in captivity and received a martyr's funeral which saw 50,000 people line the route of its procession to the General Cemetery on Ecclesall Road.

Whilst this uprising had not succeeded, it had set the scene for the struggle ahead, and on 31 August 1843, Royal Assent to the Charter was given and Sheffield Borough Council was born. At its first elections in November of that year, 56 Councillors were elected to form its first Council, William Jeffcock becoming its first Mayor and Edward Bramley being appointed Town Clerk.

It was 50 years later, in 1893, that Queen Victoria bestowed the title of City on Sheffield, and the Duke of Norfolk was subsequently chosen and sworn in as the City's first Lord Mayor. During the intervening period, the Borough Council added many functions to its early responsibilities of lighting, police, sanitation, finance and local streets. These included the taking over of Highways from the 1819 Town's Improvement Commissioners and Parishes in 1864, taking over the Fire Service from the various insurance companies in 1869, electing a School Board in 1871 under the provisions of the 1870 Education Act, appointing a Medical Officer of Health in 1872, applying building bye-laws to new Housing in 1880, opening its first sewage works in 1886, and taking over the waterworks in 1888.

Following its achievement of City status, it took over the tramway system in 1896 and the Electricity Company in 1898. In 1899 it also bought for municipal control, the markets from the Duke of Norfolk who, as Lord of The Manor, had owned them for 500 years.

Whilst the Borough Council did not take over responsibility for the police until 1844, the first semi-organised Police Force was appointed in 1818 headed by Colonel Francis Fenton as Superintendent (later Surveyor) with a small band of men employed as constables. By 1836, under the control of its new 200 guineas a year Surveyor of Police, Thomas Raynor, the force consisted of five sergeants and 16 privates, who really looked the part in their blue coated uniforms.

Within another four years, an Act of Parliament authorised the appointment of a 72-strong force at a total weekly cost of £60 19s 0d a week, comprising of a Surveyor of Police, an inspector, four sergeants, 22 policemen and 44 nightwatchmen. With weekly wages of £1 for sergeants and 18s (90p) for the "copper on the beat", there were few luxuries for any but the "top man".

The Mayor and Corporation of Sheffield *c.*1887.

Did You Know that in the early 1700s several hundred crimes could be punished by hanging? The list was reduced by 100 in 1823, and by 1861 only murder, high treason, piracy and the destruction of military establishments were punishable by death. By 1969, the death penalty was abolished altogether.

From 1843, when Sheffield became a Borough, the post of Chief Constable was introduced and the size of the force rapidly increased to over 200 men by Thomas Raynor's retirement in 1858 at the age of 71. His successor, John Jackson, subsequently held the post for the next 39 years during which time the force continued to increase reaching 470 men by the time of his death in 1898.

Rules relating to the building and running of workhouses were introduced in 1834, and a Poor Law Commissioner for the country was appointed to administer them. Areas of the city were given powers to combine so that they could organise poor relief locally, and each area was then called a Union.

This "union" of areas resulted in the formation of a "Sheffield Union", comprising the townships of Sheffield, Handsworth, Brightside and Attercliffe, and an "Ecclesall Union", comprising Ecclesall, Hallam, Totley, Dore, Beauchief and Norton. Both Unions were run by Guardians of the Poor who provided workhouses. The Sheffield Guardians converted an old cotton mill at Kelham Island, whilst the Ecclesall Guardians provided one in Crookes and one in Psalter Lane. This latter workhouse was replaced in 1843 by a much larger building in Nether Edge, which eventually became the Nether Edge Hospital.

There were many rules in the workhouses, and one particularly harsh one was the introduction of more segregation of the inmates with separate apartments and places of work being provided for seven different classes. These classes were Aged and infirm men; Aged and infirm women; Able-bodied men and youths over 13; Able-bodied women and girls over 16; Boys between the ages of seven and 13; Girls between the ages of seven and 16 and children under seven years. The dreaded workhouse was a "last resort" for most people, despite its declared good intentions, and the separating of husbands from wives or parents from children only added to the distress already experienced. A later Act of 1847 did, however, show some compassion by allowing husbands and wives over the age of 60 to stay together.

Further important legislation was introduced later in the century, including the Artisan Dwelling Act of 1875, which allowed local authorities to demolish slums, and the Housing of the Working Classes Act of 1890 which allowed the Corporation to built new houses. Powers relating to the crucial aspect of improving public health were contained in the Public Health Act of 1866, which imposed a duty on the council to improve sanitation and appoint sanitary inspectors; a requirement which was long overdue. The subsequent Act in 1875, which laid down standards for sanitation, was a natural and important step along the road to reasonable living conditions, and with the notification of infectious diseases being made compulsory by the end of the century, at least progress was being made.

It can be seen, therefore, that in this century of massive population growth, the needs of the Sheffield people created new systems of organisation, policing and control, which, although far from ideal, paved the way for further progress in the future.

(c) Working Life

The transition from the 18th century to the 19th century was an important time in Sheffield's working history. Improved roads had created better access to markets and many small manufacturers had developed into wealthy merchants through travelling across the country selling cutlery, investing their growing capital into turnpike roads and reaping profits from the tolls. The enclosure of lands had also given them opportunities to build.

Sheaf Works.

Steam power was now beginning to revolutionise industry, and with one steam-powered engine being able to drive 100 grindstones, or steam bellows being able to pump air through ten or 12 hearths and forges, the hundred or so water wheels which lined Sheffield's rivers were on the verge of gradual redundancy.

William Greaves & Sons.

By 1819 Sheffield's canal was also complete, and high quality bar and pig iron from Sweden could now arrive quickly and in greater quantities directly into the town centre.

The earliest steam-powered works were built in the Kelham Island area in the 1790s, on what, at that time, were flat green fields on the outskirts of town. However, the huge Sheaf Works of William Greaves and Sons, built in 1823 alongside the new canal was the first factory in Sheffield to carry out all the manufacturing processes from raw materials to finished goods. Bars of raw iron were able to be off-loaded from barges close to the huge cementation furnaces from which the resulting blister steel was refined in nearby crucible furnaces. Steam engines then drove machines to make tools, cutlery and files which were then packed, ready for sale and export from its magnificent new office building (now the Sheaf Quays Public House).

Whilst water-powered works like the Abbeydale Hamlet continued to employ 20 people to produce their quality cutting edge tools, a steam powered cutlery works was built on a similar sized site on Cornish Place (off Green Lane) in 1828. These works of James Dixon and Sons used a single, large engine which turned 100 belt-driven machines in dozens of workshops, and enabled 500 people packed like sardines to work there at its peak.

Steam had certainly made its impact, and by the 1880s the number of riverside water wheels had reduced to about 30, whilst grinding workshops throughout the town were powered by between 400 and 500 steam engines. People employed as grinders found themselves working longer hours in more cramped conditions.

The development of the steam engine by James Watt in 1782, together with the rapid expansion of the whole steelworks industry, had also led to a large demand for coal. The main collieries established in the town were in the Park District where conditions for miners were poor, particularly for young children who worked underground from the age of seven.

Large numbers of men, women and children were working in a variety of trades in the town at this time. Apart from the cutlery and other steel industries, there were people quarrying stone, making bricks and building houses. Many built dams, dug drains and laid pipes.

Working conditions in factories and workshops were very poor with the lack of adequate lighting and ventilation combining with long working hours. The working week was up to 70 hours long over six days, although a Saturday half-day was introduced in the 1840s. Twelve hour shifts were not unusual in some steel trades and the few holidays which were allowed were precious to the workers. A day at Easter, another at Whitsuntide and half days for Shrove Tuesday and Bonfire day were the norm with many in the steel trades also having ten days off without pay after Christmas for stocktaking.

Although girls worked in factories in jobs such as file cutting, and later in making steel hoops to be worn under crinoline skirts, three quarters of those under 20 worked in domestic service, where the "upstairs and downstairs"

arrangement existed. Many a young servant sweated over her chores in a damp, filthy basement, swilled out bed chambers or scrubbed kitchen floors with only one or two days off a year.

The main "light trades" of this century were basically those making goods of iron and steel (eg cutlery), the silver and silver plate producers, and the ancillary trades such as handle and cabinet makers. By about 1850, forgers and smiths were able to earn between £1 ad £2 a week, whilst grinders were the highest paid group at between £1 and £2.50. Many others earned much less, with burnishers and finishers (usually women) only managing to take home about 50p.

Self employed craftsmen with specialist skills, working usually with one or two apprentices or helpers in workshops converted from houses, were called Little Mesters and were the backbone of Sheffield's cutlery and toolmaking industry. They were small "masters" in their own right, often carrying out two or three of the specialist activities before passing the product on for completion by another.

By 1838, the first railway was steaming across the open land of the Lower Don Valley and the first large steelworks were built alongside it. Charles Cammel's Cyclops Steel and Iron Works was the first to move close to the railway in 1845, and it settled on a green field site in Savile Street East. Within five years, this was followed by Thomas Firth and Sons' Norfolk Works, also on Savile Street East, where railway parts, cannons and steel for Colt Revolvers and Enfield rifles were produced. Spear and Jackson, saw makers, had also decided to "open shop" next door. The addition of John Brown's Atlas Works in 1854 thus created the world's first area for bulk steel production and was the beginning of what later became Sheffield's East End "black belt".

The Bessemer Converter.

Bulk steel was now being produced in greater quantities, and by the time that the revolutionary Bessemer Converter was introduced in 1860, production had increased from 3,000 tons to 100,000 tons a year in the space of 60 years. When Charles Cammell and John Brown decided to adopt the new Bessemer process, they found that a 100-fold increase in production could be achieved. It was a sight to remember for the new breed of steelworker as they watched the huge furnace being "charged" (filled) with molten iron whilst lying on its side and then returned to its vertical position and air blown through from beneath. This process, which allowed oxygen from the air to combine with the iron to remove its impurities, took about 20 minutes to convert 25 tons of iron into steel. During this time, the huge flames and great clouds of sparks which forced their way out of the hole in the top of the furnace flashed like an angry volcano.

It was now possible to make hundreds of railway lines and huge girders for bridges and in 1860 John Brown first rolled

Steel works.

armour plate at his Atlas works for *HMS Warrior*, Britain's first iron-clad battleship. During that year, Samuel Osborne's moved to their Clyde Works on the Wicker (now the Afro-Caribbean Centre) and by 1867 Vickers and Sons moved from its town works at Millsands to the River Don Works on Brightside Lane. Within a year Edgar Allen's Imperial Steel Works had opened in Tinsley producing rails and tramway equipment, and by 1871, Brown Bailey and Dixon Iron and Steel works opened in Attercliffe on the site of the present Don Valley Stadium.

Not to be out-done, Hadfield's Hecla Works (named after a volcano in Iceland) opened in Newhall Road, Attercliffe in 1872, before deciding to extend 25 years later to its giant East Hecla Works on the site of the present Meadowhall Shopping Complex. The two other firms of note at this time were

Thomas W. Ward, who moved his break-up and dismantling business to the Albion Works on Savile Street in 1887, and William Cooke, whose works on Attercliffe Common at Carbrook in 1889 were later changed to that of Tinsley Wire Works fame.

By 1872 John Brown's Firm had grown from 200 to 5,000 men, Thomas Firth's from 20 to 2,000 men and Charles Cammell's from a dozen or so to 4,000 men. But, by 1873 demand began to fall and the depression years of 1874 to 1879 saw wages falling by 75 per cent in some places. They were described at that time as being "at starvation level", and these were certainly hard times for many Sheffielders.

Twenty years after Henry Bessemer brought his "converter" to Sheffield, Open Hearth furnaces were introduced to the industry. These made even larger quantities of steel, but were also used elsewhere in the world with great success. This resulted in bulk steel beginning to move away from the city by the end of the century, and Sheffield now became a centre for "special steels".

Henry Osborne, for example, produced high-speed drills and saw teeth which hardened as they were used. Robert Hadfield invented manganese steel which was extremely hard and used for such things as excavator teeth, railway points, tank turrets and even soldiers helmets. He also invented silicon steel which was a good conductor of electricity and ideal for use in electric motors, transformers and generators.

Despite the huge progress made in the heavy steel industry, employment in the "Light" Cutlery, Silverware and ancillary trades continued to rise over this century, being 21,000 in 1851 and rising to 32,000 40 years later. Employment in the heavy steel trades was only about 5,000 in 1851, whilst the 1891 total had increased to 21,000. Although the number of cutlery and silverware workers remained fairly constant over the next 30 years or more, those in the heavy industries continued their rapid rise and had reached 65,000 by the end of the first quarter of the next century.

Wages for cutlery and silver workers during the last half of the century hardly varied at all with forgers earning about £1.25 to £2.00 per week, grinders about £1.50 to £3.00 per week and silver workers about £1.50 to £2.50 a week. These were similar to those of their heavy steel worker colleagues who could earn anything between £1.50 and £3.00 a week as "first hands", although the wages of "second hands", "third hands", assistants and labourers were significantly lower.

The production of Old Sheffield Plate, which had seen enormous success since Boulsover's discovery almost 100 years ago, was beginning to decline by the 1840s at which time the new cheaper process of electroplating known as EPNS was introduced. One major company which emerged about this time was Walker and Hall, who's silver and cutlery works existed in Howard Street for nearly 100 years. Mappin and Webb was another big name, whose large works in Norfolk Street eventually transferred to its current location in Queens Road.

So there we have it. Cutlers, toolworkers, silversmiths and heavy steelworkers dominated employment by the close of the century, often working in the same factory or works as diversification and change progressed. The heavy thumping of the 70 or more giant Nasmyth hammers in the huge forging works plus the immense heat of the magnificent glowing furnaces contrasted greatly with the dust ridden hulls of the grinders or the delicate work of the silversmiths; but all provided employment. It is sad to think that the average age at death of many of its workers was only somewhere between 37 and 44 years old.

Drop hammer on Brightside Lane.

The story of Sheffield's remarkable growth as an industrialised city would not, of course, be complete without reference to its ever growing number of trade unions. By the beginning of the century there were over 50 such organisations representing the "light trades", which culminated with the setting up of the "UK Alliance of Organised Trades" in 1866 with its headquarters in Sheffield. Although it broke up the following year, it was the forerunner to the later TUC, and Sheffield pursued more local involvement with the setting up of the Sheffield Federated Trades Council five years later.

Whilst the need for trade unions was indisputable in the face of appalling conditions and low wages, they did themselves no good at times, with outbreaks of violence against unpopular employers, workmen who refused to join the union, and members who fell behind with their subscriptions. Hundreds of cases of "rattening" took place, where grinders' work was stopped by the stealing of the wheel bands which turned the grinding wheels, and by the 1950s and 60s this had extended to incidents of shooting, gunpowder attacks, wrecking of houses and murder. At a commission of enquiry into these "Sheffield Outrages" held in 1867, William Broadhead, the Secretary of the Saw Grinders Union, admitted his guilt. Despite the lessons learnt

and the legalising of unions by the Trade Unions Act of 1871, "rattening" continued for another ten years!

Trade unions for the thousands of labourers in the large steelworks and engineering works were still in their infancy even in the 1890s, although organisations were established in the mid and late 1800s of which some employees were members. These included unions such as the Associated Iron & Steel Workers of Great Britain, the Sheffield United Steel Melters Union, the Amalgamated Society of Steel and Iron Workers and the National Amalgamated Union of Labour.

It was not until the 20th century that these unions really gained strength and influence.

(d) Domestic and Social Life

Life in the 1800s should have been one of progressive improvement, particularly for the last 60 years as the new Queen Victoria, guided by her beloved husband Albert, tried to rule by example. She revolutionised the image of the monarchy, which up to then had been viewed as immoral and extravagant, into one of high morality and hard work, giving the country a new set of ideals. Expectations do not always result in achievements however, and good intentions do not always succeed. Let us have a look at Sheffield to see how it fared.

The standard of working-class houses deteriorated in town during the 1840s and 1850s as the population increased.

Rows of back to back, grey slated brick buildings began to line the streets for the skilled working classes, who lived "cheek to cheek" with their neighbours. In the terraced accommodation of this type, three walls were shared with their neighbours, and the one and only outer door led directly on to the street or a back yard.

For those "lucky" enough to have their exit on to the

communal, unpaved yard, access to the primitive outside toilet (usually called a privy in those days) saved a walk on to the street to the nearby shared passage in order to get to the yard and do what was necessary. At busy times, however, many would have to queue as, depending on their location, each privy served between two and 12 households. Ashpits were also provided for rubbish, but as household "slops" were often thrown in them, they became almost impossible to empty. This unenviable task fell on the Corporations "night soil" gangs who were employed to empty both ashpits and privies as well as the "overflow" from them both. The foul smelling mixture was eventually put on to a tip, the largest of which was at Corker Bottom in the Manor. This tip took three quarters of the city's nightsoil by the end of the century, much of the rest being tipped on the Bole Hills at Crookes. You can imagine what the locals thought of this practise as they opened their windows on a warm sunny morning to take in the "fresh air"!

Water from private companies was available to about three-quarters of Sheffield's homes at this time, although it was usually cloudy and affected by rust from the iron pipes. It was supplied to standpipes and pumps in the yards for just two hours on three days a week and had to be stored in tubs and barrels where it often became stagnant and foul.

Many of these "residential" areas also accommodated workshops and factories as well as the noise, smoke, dust and smell which went with them, although they were convenient for those employees who lived there.

The houses themselves were simple and basic and often consisted of a cellar and three little rooms. The outside door opened into the ground floor living room which also acted as the kitchen, scullery, dining room, washroom and bathroom, as well as being a drying and airing area for the laundry. Standing on the cold flag-paved floor was the stone sink with its lead pipe leading out into an old stone sewer or

directly into the street or yard. The cosy little fireplace fitted with an oven for baking and a side boiler for hot water was always the focal point of the room with cooking often taking place on griddle-cokes at the front of the fire. At the back of the room a steep dark staircase led up to the wooden floored bedroom which did its best to provide sleeping facilities for mother, father and young children. Although rarely lit, a second small fireplace also provided warmth when desperation demanded it. The small, dark attic was the last port of call if you had sufficient breath left to reach it or hadn't tripped on the last flight of stairs. Its low small windows made it look rather quaint set against the steeply sloping ceiling, and the older children who slept there were usually happy with their special room. If times became hard, as was often the case, then the attic was let to a lodger whilst the rest of the family re-shuffled, and the living room acquired one more use.

Rents for these homes worked out at about 2s 6d (12p) a week with the landlord paying the poor rates and water rates and the tenant paying those to maintain the highway. For those who could afford to buy a house, which were few and far between, a sum of £60 to £70 including ashpit, yard and street paving was the price they would have to pay.

Whilst these cramped little homes were put up in their thousands for the mass of Sheffield's workers, many casual labourers lived in far worse surroundings. These poor workers were mostly those who had come over from Ireland in an attempt to find work in the growing town, and they usually occupied slums in the most insanitary districts. They shared their homes with pigs, dogs and cats, as well as with criminals and paupers who lodged with them.

When, in 1864, "back to backs" were prohibited by law, there were 38,000 such houses in the city and overcrowding was becoming a problem. Tens of thousands of better designed houses were subsequently built in the 1880s and '90s from London Road to Heeley and Woodseats, City Road to Intake, Langsett Road to Hillsborough, Burngreave Road to Pitsmoor and in Firth Park and the East End. Sheffield's suburbs had arrived, and this was just the beginning. Even picturesque Crookes, the bracing "holiday resort" of West Sheffield, was suburbanised in the 1870s and 1880s as rows of brick terraces mingled alongside old stone cottages which were most unwilling to leave.

Back in town however, all was not well. Whilst some working-class areas such as West Street and Division Street were fairly well built with clean paved streets, most others were in an appalling condition. The worst of these were the often flooded Ponds Area, the dense "warrens" of The Park district, the low-lying and often flooded streets along both sides of the River Don above Lady's Bridge, the marshy courts of The Wicker, the closely packed courts off Fargate and Snig Hill and the area behind the Parish Church.

Perhaps the most notorious of these slums was the latter, known as the Crofts adjacent to Paradise Square. Amongst its small courts and filthy yards many people died of hygiene related diseases. Seven two-roomed houses in Pea Croft were identified as accommodating 62 people at a rate of nine

Interior of late 19th-century slum house.

people per house with only one privy between the lot of them. With water available for only a few hours on three days a week, the whole combination was one of squalor, stench and disease and it was with relief that the City Council commenced its slum clearing programme here in 1898.

It was not only the houses which were the cause of concern at this time. A cholera epidemic had killed 400 people in 1832, stagnant sewer water accumulated in valleys in front of dams and affected low-lying properties, courts and alleys accumulated ashes, slops and excrement for weeks, and even the Churchyard became a mass of human decomposition and appalling stench as too many dead bodies were packed closely together. The three rivers flowing through town also carried filth, dirt, dust, dung and lifeless bodies of small animals and all in all, the quality of life for many of the townsfolk was appalling. By 1860, Sheffield was probably at its lowest ebb in terms of sanitation and health, a situation made worse by the stubborn unwillingness of the borough council to take appropriate action in the face of much public unrest.

The standard of living for the working-class family also left a lot to be desired as even by the mid-1800s there were no carpets in the houses; not even in those of the better paid, skilled workers. Home made furniture and clothes, all children sharing beds, and the pawning of "Sunday suits" was the norm, with tea, coffee and sugar being luxuries much of the time. Bread, potatoes and cabbage often formed the daily diet, with meat being eaten only in good weeks.

Things did, nevertheless, improve towards the end of the century for those with some skills although the numbers of very poor continued to rise. Linoleum and carpets were being used on the floors, the straw mattress was being superseded by feather and flock, cheap sofas and couches appeared in most homes, and sewing machines and pianos were being bought by instalments.

This was also the dawn of the well-known Co-operative Societies, with the Brightside and Carbrook and the good old "S & E" beginning their "love affairs" with the Sheffield shoppers.

But, of course, life was for living outside of the home as well as in it. Many schools had continued to emerge, although education was still largely in the hands of religious bodies. By 1843 only half the town's children of school age attended a day school of any kind, and this was usually only for about one year. They mainly learnt the three R's and the basics of religion. As a result, about two thirds of the working class grew up in ignorance, with only half of Sheffield's workmen being able to read or write during the 1850s. There appeared to be a fear that educated workmen might forget their proper station in life, and the town's authorities chose not to give "learning" any financial priority.

However, in this "educational wilderness" for many of the poorer working classes there was a ray of hope, with the creation of the Sheffield People's College. This college of "further" education for adults was opened in 1842 by

Reverend Bayley, the minister of Howard Street Congregational Chapel. Attendance was allowed before and after work, and apart from some time being spent on the three R's, subjects taught included mathematics, science, English, language and history. The college, which later ran day classes for children, not only provided learning for the ordinary working-class students for the next 25 years, it also gave them an invaluable spirit of independence.

Blame could not, of course, be simply put at the door of the administrators for lack of education, as in many local industries children were made to help in their father's workshops from the tender age of seven or eight. It was surprising, however, how many children were "packed off" to school during times of depression when dad no longer had any use for them!

> **Did You Know that the first school to be opened in Sheffield under the 1870 Education Act, which made schooling between the ages of five and 13 compulsory unless the child lived more than two miles from the nearest school, was Newhall School in Attercliffe? The school was adjacent to the Newhall Grounds race course, and in November 1882 it had to closed early due to the crowds of "rough men and cabs" expected at the race. The following year, a dispute at the "Newhall Grounds Handicap" necessitated 100 policemen in attendance to keep order.**

The introduction of the Education Act in 1870 was the obvious beginning of better things to come as it not only enabled School Boards to be set up, it made education compulsory for children between the ages of five and 13. By the end of the century school enrolments in the City had reached about 70,000, although school attendance often fell well short of this mark.

But what of the schools and colleges themselves? Whether for the poor or the rich, progress was certainly made and their pupils were as different as chalk and cheese.

Take the Ragged School in Baker's Yard, Pea Croft, for example. The 280 children who attended there were those that other schools would refuse to admit or whose parents could not afford even a penny a week. Most were barefooted, ragged and hungry and had hitherto depended on stealing their daily bread. They were often to be found scavenging in the markets, eating the sweepings which had been heaped into one corner and allowed to rot. Regular attendance at the school was more or less guaranteed, as bread was provided for them daily, for which the children were truly grateful. In the first six years of the school, over 760 destitute children were admitted of which 83 had no mother, 236 had no father and

54 had neither. Many of the others had been abandoned by their parents who were either in prison or had been transported for some felonious crime.

Charity Schools were also provided for those who were poor with the rebuilt Boys Charity School on the corner of East Parade providing basic education. It also provided sparse meals and cold water washing and bathing in outside troughs for 100 pupils in 1845. The blue cloth coat over green corduroy trousers combined with large white collars and blue muffin caps were always a "give-away" of the pupils charitable status.

Reformatory Schools made an appearance in the late 1850s for juvenile delinquents as an alternative to gaol or whippings. St Joseph's Reformatory at Howard Hill in Walkley was one such institution opened by the Roman Catholics in 1861. It provided domestic service training for wayward girls in an effort to deter them from crime.

Many fee-paying scholars attended private schools for their education, these including the Milk Street Academy run by Mr Abrahams of Holy Green House on Sheffield Moor. His successor and son-in-law, Richard "Dicky" Bowling, taught many famous Sheffield people and was a great believer in physical correction to ensure success. I don't think his harsh methods would be supported by most of today's society; or would they?

> **Did You Know that Sheffield's Central Library started in the ground floor of the Mechanics Institute at the corner of Surrey Street and Tudor Street in 1856? During that first year 104,887 books were issued. Sheffield now has 28 libraries to which two millions visits are made a year. At least one million items are now available to library users most days of the week.**

Hebblethwaite's Academy in Paradise Square was perhaps the most famous of all, beginning in 1829 when a 21-year-old school apprentice noticed some vacant premises there. It was to be 36 years later when Edward Hebblethwaite's school closed, having gained the reputation as being one of the best of its time, and having produced scholars who later occupied high positions in life.

Last but not least were the new "Corporation Schools" which were built under the direction of the new School Board set up in 1870. Schools of great architectural merit were built in the first four years of this century, such as Newhall School on Sanderson Street between Attercliffe and Brightside, Carbrook School on Attercliffe Common (now The Player's Café adjacent to the Sheffield Arena), Crookesmoor School on Oxford Street and Springfield School in Broomspring Lane. Many others were also built in Attercliffe, Broomhill, Netherthorpe, Lowfield and Walkley.

The old Carbrook School, now the Player's Café.

Did You Know that the College of Art and Crafts established in Arundel Street in 1843, eventually became the School of Art? It was taken over by the City Council in 1902, and the following year, its Education Committee put forward a fairly controversial proposal to allow nude models to be employed there for the first time. Despite the concern of the Lord Mayor, who opposed such a measure, the proposal was agreed, and a little bit of history was made.

This then, was the main basis of schooling and education in Sheffield in Victorian times. Today, however, higher education is open to increasing numbers of people, and it is worth noting the origins of some of the educational establishments we now have in the city. Collegiate School, for instance, built in open country on Ecclesall Road in 1835 for better off Church of England children, is now the Collegiate

Crescent site of Hallam University. Similarly, Wesley College opened in 1838 in Broomhill Village for children of wealthy Methodists and Non-conformists is now the King Edward VII Comprehensive School. In 1843 the School of Art was founded off Glossop Road before moving to Arundel Street 12 years later, and in 1880 the Central Secondary Schools were opened in Leopold Street. Firth College, later absorbed by the Sheffield University, also opened on this site, to be joined later by the Pupil Teacher's Centre in 1899. At the other end of the scale, the Nether Edge Workhouse School was opened in 1842 and gave education to many who would otherwise have received none.

But "all work and no play", so they say, "makes Jack a dull boy". So let's have a whistle-stop-tour of some of the pleasures of 19th-century life.

In 1820 it was common for "little mesters" to take some time off work to watch cricket on Wednesdays. The new team playing at Darnall usually provided a good match and a glance at the signboard clearly showed that someone had shown initiative in choosing the clubs name. The Wednesday Cricket Club had been born, and history was in the making. Later matches were played at Hyde Park and then at Bramall

Lane, but it was at a special meeting of the club held on 5 September 1867 in the Adelphi Hotel on Arundel Street, that an important decision was made. In order to keep the members together during the winter months, a football section was formed.

The Wednesday Football Club's first ground was at the "highfield", the site of the current Highfield Library, and its first match was against Dronfield on 31 December 1867 at Dronfield. The Wednesday won by one goal to four "rouges", a "rouge" being an "almost goal", scored when the ball goes through an "outer goal" area marked by two extra goal posts.

Did You Know that before the road bridge was built which carries Leppings Lane over the River Don just outside the entrance to Sheffield Wednesday's football ground, the route for pedestrians towards Wadsley Bridge was a row of stepping stones? Animals and carts were able to ford the river at this point, but those on foot had to leap from stone to stone, which, during the early 1700s, acquired the name of the "Lepping Stones".

Sheffield Wednesday football team pictured in 1878.

Meantime, in 1854, in the same Adelphi Hotel, a site was being chosen for a cricket ground which the Duke of Norfolk said he would support. This site, on open fields at the side of a pleasant rural lane well away from the smoke and grime of the town thus became the home of the Sheffield United Cricket Club, with its own new grounds at Bramall Lane. The first cricket match played on this ground was between the "First Eleven" and the "Twenty Two" on 30 April the following year, this being followed in August of 1886 by the first County match between Yorkshire and Sussex, which the home side lost.

It was not until March 1889 that this cricket club also decided to have a football section, and the Sheffield United Football Club was born. Unfortunately, the new club expected to be able to use players from amateur clubs such as the Sheffield Heeley or Owlerton Football Clubs. When such expectations did not materialise, United advertised for players, firstly in the local newspapers and later in provincial and Scottish papers. By May 1889, the new team was formed and within four years Sheffield United FC became one of the 16 leading clubs in the country.

It is interesting to note that the first two matches played between the rival Wednesday and United teams resulted in a win for each on their own ground. On 15 December 1890, Wednesday beat United 2-1 at their Olive Grove ground (which they occupied from 1887 to the end of the century before moving to Owlerton), whilst the return match a month later on 12 January 1891 at Bramall resulted in a 3-2 victory for United.

But this, of course, is not the whole story of Sheffield, the "home of Association Football". It's first game was played in 1793 at Bents Green between Sheffield and Norton. The six men of Norton were dressed in green, whilst the six men from Sheffield were dressed in red. The game continued for three consecutive days and, with the score uncertain or unknown, ended in fighting and bloodshed.

The club which is considered to be the world's first real football club and which is the oldest existing club in the world is Sheffield Club, whose records reputedly go back to 1855 but was officially founded in 1857. These Gentlemen of Sheffield initially played matches among themselves on the East Bank, but on 12 February 1861 faced the Gentlemen of Hallam on their own ground.

Hallam FC was itself founded in 1860 and not only does it have the distinction of being the second oldest football club in the world, its ground at Sandygate is the world's oldest. Sheffield FC won this first match 2-0, and it lasted two and a half hours. The return match, however, was a different story. Strengthened by players from the hamlet of Stumperlowe, Hallam FC fought like tigers, and after three hours of play, which completely exhausted the two 14-men sides, Hallam emerged victorious.

It was probably fitting that the first football match ever decided on the famous ground at Bramall Lane was between these two oldest teams. It was played on behalf of the Lancashire Distress Fund in December 1862 with the three-hour game ending in a goalless draw!

Not everyone wanted to watch or play football, however, and more leisurely pursuits were now available. Perhaps a night out at the Surrey Music Hall in West Bar was more suitable, with a choice of theatre or dancing in the huge ballroom where massive mirrors and beautiful pictures graced its walls. For a more "high-brow" evening of classical tastes, the Pavilion in Surrey Street was rather charming, especially as it gave away legs of mutton on Friday nights. If you fancied a stroll down Angel Street, you would have found the Fleur de Lys on the site later occupied by Cockaynes and Schofields, whilst the 2,000-seater Albert Hall which opened in 1873 on the site of today's Cole Brothers store was also a major attraction. Towards the end of the century the famous Empire on Charles Street was the City's favourite, but whatever your tastes, there were plenty of places of entertainment to choose from.

Did You Know that a 6ft-high, bronze statue of Peter Pan surrounded by woodland animals and birds can be found in the Rose Garden of Sheffield's Botanical Gardens? It was erected in 1953 and was donated by the late Sir Charles Clifford, who had expressed the view that he wished to encourage more children to use the beautiful gardens.

If daily recreation was preferred, you could take a stroll through the Botanical Gardens, opened in 1836 with its three large conservatories of plants with tinted glass corridors. This was a particular favourite with young ladies. Its bear pit was also a big attraction for the children who threw buns to the two brown bears which climbed its central pole for their treat. Weston Park, with its small museum adjacent to the Mappin Art Gallery, provided an interesting afternoon in the later 1800s, unless you lived more to the south of the city, in which case a visit to the Ruskin Museum in the former Meersbrook House would be more convenient. For the benefit of those

who lived more to the north of town, steel giant Mark Firth, a well liked and respected man who was elected Master Cutler three times before becoming Lord Mayor in 1874, presented to the city 35 acres of land which were part of the Page Hall Estate. This area of beautiful greenery, now known as Firth Park, provided a pleasant and peaceful parkland for public recreation.

Despite the unavoidable picture of "doom and gloom" which has emerged from our look at some of the aspects of living conditions this century, particularly as it relates to the average, working-class Sheffielder, there are many positive aspects which must be pointed out.

Did You Know that in 1833 the small dispensary in Westfield House on West Street, which was the forerunner to the Royal Hospital, used 3,500 leeches in one year as part of its medical treatment? Specialist "leech women" placed the blood sucking leeches on patients in order that "bad blood" could be sucked away and effect a cure. Medical opinion of today now appears to support the theory behind this long abandoned practice.

The rewards had been great for those people who had shown foresight, initiative and determination in building up the city. Their achievements included huge industries which gave work to thousands of people, factories and workshops for the cutlery and silverware trades, banks and financial institutions to manage the city's economy, and a host of professional, commercial, construction and trading opportunities and organisations in the city to the general benefit of its population. Fine stone houses, mansions and halls were built in the suburbs to accommodate these self-made entrepreneurs, and many of them are still standing today. One such example is Endcliffe Hall, built in 1860 at Ranmoor by John Brown.

Healthcare was also improving in the borough as the General Infirmary continued to expand and became the large Royal Sheffield Infirmary in 1897. Another famous hospital started as a small dispensary for the "sick-poor" on the site of the present Central Library in 1832, before moving to West Street a year later where it developed into the General Hospital in 1860 and the Sheffield Public Hospital in 1875, before being rebuilt as the Royal Hospital in 1895.

Botanical Gardens, Broomhill.

The Jessop Hospital for Women in 1978.

Nether Edge Hospital developed from the Ecclesall Union workhouse-cum-hospital in 1842, whilst today's massive Northern General Hospital complex developed from the Sheffield Union Hospital at Firvale in 1881. The Sheffield Hospital for Women was also opened in 1864 in Fig Tree Lane off Hartshead with six beds in a large Victorian house. Thomas Jessop, of the large east-end steelworks fame, then bought land at Leavygreave Road and built the Jessop Hospital for Women at a cost of over £26,000, which took over from its Fig Tree Lane beginnings.

The Children's Hospital in 1981.

Did You Know that in the early 1800s, Ward's "Extract of Rosemary Oil" was sold to "stay the falling off of hair" and "preventing it becoming grey"? Also at this time, "Lettuce Lozenges" were recommended for coughs, and breathing difficulties such as Asthma, whilst Caster Oil was "found to be beneficial in curing ring worm". Last but not least, "Croton Tiglium Oil" and "Croton Pills" "never failed to act on the bowels, however obstinate the constipation."

Specific provision for children began with the Sheffield Free Hospital for Sick Children, which was founded in Brightmore House at Brookhill in 1876. Within a year it was dealing with nearly 15,000 attendances and in 1880 it moved to 269 Western Bank as the Children's Hospital. Despite being extended between 1888 and 1896 it was still short of room and new premises were built for it at its present site at the corner of Western Bank and Clarkson Street, which officially opened in 1903. Many extensions and improvements took place over the next 70 years and by its centenary year in 1976, this now world-famous hospital had dealt with more than one and a half million patients.

Last but not least were the infectious diseases hospitals, and in 1881 the Borough Hospital for Infectious Diseases was built on Winter Street for victims of smallpox and other such infections. It was later changed to St George's Hospital for the treatment of tuberculosis. Lodge Moor Hospital was subsequently built in 1887 as a direct result of a serious smallpox epidemic, and began life as 12 wooden huts surrounded by a fence on the lonely and bleak Lodge Moor. Three hundred men were employed by the Town Council to work day and night to erect these simple wards which, when complete, formed the Borough Smallpox Hospital. With its £60-a-year matron, 18 nurses, 16 servants and two porters together with its temporary resident medical officer on a wage of three guineas (£3.15) a week, the hospital became operational and even acquired a horse-pulled ambulance at a cost of £88. It would be some years later when its name was changed and its functions extensively broadened.

Did You Know that a "cure" for rabies was available in 1832 which contained the extracted juice of a plant from the cactus family? The "mode of operation" recommended for administering the medicine was the same as that being used in South America, namely: "Put the patient up to his neck in sand, and then pour two ounces and a half of extract down the throat by force as soon as possible after the bite."

Our look at domestic and social life must, of course, take account of developments which have taken place which directly affect us, the most important of which relate to the essentials of water, gas and electricity. Space, unfortunately, allows us only to scratch the surface of these major topics.

Our famous Barker's Pool was removed at the end of the last century, and by 1830 the Sheffield Water Company was formed by an Act of Parliament with powers to build new reservoirs, the first of which were the Hadfield Dam at Crookes and the middle dam at Redmires. 1845 saw another Act of Parliament for two more reservoirs at Redmires and two small dams in Rivelin Valley, followed nine years later by authority to construct two reservoirs in Bradfield Dale and one in Loxley Valley. Following the tragic collapse of the Dale Dyke Dam in 1864, the Town Council took over the Water Company in 1888 to continue improvements to the town's water supply. At this time Sheffield had about 68,000 houses supplied with water, although most still used standpipes and pumps. One house in 30 had a fixed bath and one in 17 had a WC, although, needless to say, the working classes had neither.

Did You Know that the rich could buy a portable bath complete with apparatus for heating, in 1827, for seven guineas (£7.35)?

Gas had arrived quite early in the century and by 1818 the Sheffield Gaslight Company was formed. The following year, on the 6 October, Sheffield's first gas lamps were installed, and remarkable though it may seem, 130 years would pass before they were all replaced by electricity! By 1834, a second company had been formed, which ten years later amalgamated with its rival to form the United Gas Company. Not to be outdone, the Town Council also set up in business in 1850, and once again a merger of the two rivals resulted in a new "United Gas Company" being formed five years later. By 1874, the Gas Company offices opened in Commercial Street at about which time cooking by gas started in Sheffield for those who could afford it. It was not however, until 1893 that about three-quarters of all householders were consumers.

Sheffield's new gas lamp at Wicker Arches.

The number of gas lamps had risen from nearly 1,200 in the 1850s to over 6,000 by the 1890s. This must have created significant employment for the lamplighters, who had to travel the town each evening with their ladders, climb each lamp and light the gas with lucifer matches before returning the following morning to turn them all off again. These matches were the fore-runner of the modern match and had been invented in 1827 by a pharmacist by the name of John Walker. They were originally called friction lights and cost 1s

(5p) for a tin of 100. They were simply thin, flat sticks of wood, the head of which had been dipped in a specially mixed paste which, when nipped in a fold of sandpaper and pulled smartly out, would ignite. The sandpaper, incidentally, was included in the price.

It was not until 1886 that the town was first supplied with electricity by an enterprising man by the name of John Tasker who had a small concern called the Sheffield Telephone Exchange and Electric Light Company in Sheaf Street. Private supplies via overhead cable were common up to 1892, at which time Tasker's company was asked by the Town Council to provide underground electricity supplies to the Borough of Sheffield along its main streets. Within two years he had sold off his telephone interests, renamed his company The Sheffield Electric Light and Power Company, and opened a new larger generating station in Sheaf Street. By 1896 new offices were erected in Commercial Street opposite the Gas Company, and he was eventually taken over by the City Council in 1899 with still only 688 consumers on his books. This new exciting technology had yet to really "take-off".

Before we leave this section on what we might call essential services, it is worth noting that the Town's Fire Service progressed from a small "Insurance Fire Brigade" in 1804, which only turned out its hand-pulled engine for those fortunate house-holders who had taken out an insurance policy with the company, to one operated by the Town

Council in 1869 whose first fire station was in Norfolk Street. All fire engines were horse-drawn up to 1907, at which time the town bought its first motor driven one. The fire station itself had moved to Barkers Pool in 1870, Rockingham Street in 1883, and much improved premises at West Bar by 1900, where the horses were stabled immediately behind the vehicle for a "quick turnout". Further improvements were, of course, yet to come.

(e) Travel and Communication

By the time that the Borough Council was formed in 1843, the main road network was operated and controlled by the Turnpike Trusts. These collected tolls at its 18 or so toll bars across the Sheffield area, and it was not possible to get in or out of town without stopping at one. The Broadfield Bar, erected across the country lane leading to Beauchief, now called Abbeydale Road, lasted for 72 years before being removed in 1884, whilst the longest lasting bar was erected on what is now Pitsmoor Road as early as 1759. Its replacement in 1836 incorporated two large gates which swung across

Toll House and Gate at Hunter's Bar.

would finish their speeches so that it could begin its proud inaugural journey to Rotherham. It took 17 minutes that day for the new smokey trip, but within two years travellers from Sheffield could change there and hop on a train to London with the whole seven hour journey costing only £1.

The Manchester, Sheffield and Lincolnshire Railway was next to arrive and did so in style by reaching Sheffield at Bridgehouses Station in 1845 after crossing the Pennines through the Woodhead tunnel. Three years later saw the achievement of one of Victorian Britain's most impressive civil engineering works as the huge stone viaduct from Wicker Arches across the back of the Canal Basin was constructed. By 1849 the line east to Grimsby and Lincoln, and London via Retford, were complete, these being followed in 1851 by the opening of the Victoria Station and the building of its magnificent hotel ten years or so later.

Pitsmoor Road and Burngreave Road and by the time of its closure in 1876, tolls had been taken there for 117 years. It was also about this time that the bar at the junction of Attercliffe Road and Saville Street was removed. The last bar to go was that on Ecclesall Road at Hunters Bar. This bar took its name from Mr Hunter who lived in a small house nearby and its closure on 31 October 1884 was met with great cheers from the large crowd which had come to watch. The original stone gates were then used for the entrance to Endcliffe Park, where they remained until the present traffic roundabout was built in which they now stand, more or less on their original

It was not until 1870 that the Midland Railway huffed and puffed into Sheffield at the Midland Railway Station, but by the end of the century there were five stations within half a mile of the centre. The three passenger stations at that time were the Midland Station at Sheaf Street, Victoria Station adjacent to the Canal Basin and City Station at Broad Street. The Wicker Station now dealt only with goods, as did the Park Goods Station at the Canal Wharf.

Commuting to town by train was also available for those who could afford it from Millhouses and Heeley, and for those keen to get to work on time, services were available to Attercliffe, Brightside, Darnall, Neepsend and Wadsley. The magic of rail travel was here to stay… or so we thought until the "Beeching Tragedies" was published 60 or so years later and both history and progress was destroyed at the blow of an axe!

Did You Know that in its first year of operation, the Sheffield to Rotherham trains carried 455,375 passengers who paid £13,304 16s 3d for their fares?

---

position.

It was the last day of October 1838 when steam railways came to Sheffield. The "Fire King" hissed impatiently in the new Wicker Station in Saville Street wishing the dignitaries

Travel by road became easier, cheaper and more available during this exciting century of change, although use of the expensive horse-drawn Hanson Cabs was only made by the

The Wicker Arches in about 1900.

A horse-drawn carriage.

Horse tram in High Street about 1900.

very well-off at the prohibitive cost of 1s (5p) a mile. This taxi facility was available throughout the whole of this 100-year period for the upper classes, with the richest people also having their own horse-drawn carriages and stables at their West End houses.

For the growing middle-classes and the better off working craftsman, the introduction of the Horse Omnibuses in 1838 was a real treat as the first buses trotted along to the new Wicker Station from the toll bar on Glossop Road and also from Sheffield Moor. Within ten to 12 years, these private bus operators were a familiar sight on routes all over town as the powerful horses raced alongside their rivals to be first to pick up their threepenny fares.

For the thousands of people earning less than £1 a week, this threepenny "town to terminus" fare was still too much to pay, and their usual five mile "hike" to and from work each day using "shanks's pony" would continue for a few years yet. The new routes out to the south and west, including Heeley, Hillsborough and Broomhill, encouraged new housing in these suburbs, and by 1900 they had reached up to Commonside and Springvale, Abbeydale, Nether Edge and Ecclesall and even as far out as Woodseats, Dore and Totley Station and Lodge Moor Hospital. During bad weather and on steep uphill journeys, additional horses were provided, with a penny extra being charged on the journey up to the Springvale Hotel, where a change of horses at the stables just below was always welcomed by the tired animals.

When horse trams were introduced in 1872, with the Corporation laying the tracks and private companies running the trams, they were very basic with hard wooden slatted seats, straw on the floor to help to keep passengers' feet warm and two oil lamps for lighting. This new tram service overlapped with that of the Horse Omnibus, which continued until the early 1900s, but the fares on some of its routes were cheaper, particularly on the early workman's service at 6.30am. This encouraged a greater use by more people, and new terraced housing grew up around the tram terminuses as a result.

In Heeley and Hillsborough, many better off workers left their grimy town houses to rent refreshingly clean little dwellings in an environment far removed from that of the dust, noise and smoke they had left behind. For the first time, the availability of reliable and reasonably cheap transport could at least give some respite to some of Sheffield's working-class families. The numbers of office workers and professional people were also on the increase and they similarly took the opportunity of moving home, this time to larger, more attractive estates like Nether Edge.

It was 1896 when Sheffield Corporation took over the Tramways Company, at which time there were 44 tram cars and four omnibuses pulled by 310 horses on nine miles of

Did You Know that in 1878, the "Red Flag Act" limited steam road vehicles to 4mph, and required that a man waving a red flag had to walk or jog in front of it whilst it was moving? By 1896, the speed limit on the highway had risen to 14mph, and the red flag man was no longer required. The car speed limit was subsequently increased to 20mph in 1903 and again to 30mph in 1935.

track, all operated by 182 employees. Drivers and conductors worked 15 hour days with the driver's daily pay being 4s (20p) and that of the conductors, 2s 6d (12p). Within three years the first green electric tram ran between Nether Edge and Tinsley and by 1900, now in its posh new livery of blue and cream, the one penny fare and its half penny stages were introduced. The tram was here to stay, or so we thought, until a "30-year hiccup" took them off our streets for a while 60 or so years later!

Not everybody, however, wanted to use the tram or bus, even though they were pollution free at that time. Take Arthur Blyde of Crescent Road in Nether Edge for example. He was the owner of a scissors manufacturing business at the Clintock Works in Milton Street and he loved to cycle to Baslow at the weekends. He also owned a motor tricycle in 1895, but with his sights set on a "motor car", he bought a Quadracycle which had two seats, a single speed, and a two and half horse power engine. He enjoyed "roaring" past the "toffs" on their Penny Farthings, ringing his bell as he peered through his large goggles to make sure that the way ahead was clear. The pedestrians thought it was outrageous. Little did they know what was in store for them.

Last but not least in this age of transport innovation, was the building of the Sheffield and South Yorkshire Navigation Canal between Tinsley and the Canal Basin, in 1819. The five mile waterway, which cost £102,000, was constructed using

picks, shovels, horses and wheelbarrows by dozens of professional navvies and unemployed cutlery workers. The boats which carried the cargoes of iron, steel, coal, timber, sugar and grain were called "keeles", which were powered by two square sails on a large central mast. When it was not possible to use the sail, horses could be hired to tow the keel, although many a hard-up boat family ended up towing it themselves.

But what if you wanted to communicate with someone without having to travel? Well, the postal system continued to improve with about a thousand letters a week being received in Sheffield at the beginning of the century. Letters cost 5d (2p) to Leeds and eight pence (3p) to London at this time, with the only "postman" in town being Thomas Taylor of Lee Croft off Campo Lane. His daughter took over his duties of letter carrier, to give it its correct name, on his death in 1814, and was often seen scurrying round town carrying her letters in a small hand basket covered with a white napkin.

Delivering letters was free within the town limits at this time and with the post office being centrally located, it was within ten minutes walk of most places. Clerks of principle merchants in the borough brought in and collected letters themselves three times a day, whilst two letter carriers and an assistant already took post to some outlying districts. From 1817 onwards, the Postmaster, William Todd, decided to introduce a Sheffield Penny Post for deliveries beyond the regular town delivery, with areas such as Dronfield, Bradway, Norton, Meersbrook, Attercliffe and Ridgeway paying the additional penny for its local service.

Postage was still very expensive, and by 1820, when the mail to London took 22 hours, the cost of a letter it carried was 10d (4p). However, by 1840, when mail to London was taken by rail, the one penny uniform postage rate was established for all standard letters, regardless of distance, and the beginning of the modern postal system was born. Eight letter carriers now delivered twice daily in town, with people such as Joseph Winterbottom, Samuel Cooke and Thomas Burdon, always greeting the householders with a cheery smile. Of the four village postmen, John Waller and John Witheford made their daily trips to Wortley and Norton, whilst George Bower plodded his way to Attercliffe, and James Johnson struggled on to Handsworth and Woodhouse.

With the system still growing, the number of weekly letters delivered rose from 34,000 in 1843 to 636,000 in 1910, at which time the number of postmen in the city rose to a massive 350, and the new Head Post Office was established in Fitzalan Square. A new industry was thus born, and the cheery local postman not only took us into the 20th century, he is seeing us into the next one as well.

There are still, however, two more powerful communication systems to briefly consider, both of which play a vital role in our lives today.

The first is the telephone which, in 1879, was introduced in Sheffield by John Tasker, who had a store in Angel Street, and a repair and engineering shop in Sheaf Street. Having sent his solicitor to visit Graham Bell's new invention in America (where Bell was currently living), he ordered telephones from the Bell Telephone Company, and set up an exchange on the top floor of his Angel Street Store. From having only 12 subscribers initially and lines available from 8am to 11pm every day except Sunday for an annual rent of £7, Tasker Sons and Company soon built up a national reputation, and he even installed private exchanges at Balmoral and Windsor Castle for Queen Victoria.

By 1888, with 400 subscribers on his books, Tasker sold out to the National Telephone Company, and the new telephone exchange in Commercial Street was enlarged.

Within five years it was serving 2,400 subscribers, with the large new switchboard being worked by 50 female operators. By the time the Post Office took over in 1912, 8,800 lines were in existence, serving over 12,600 telephones. Society's most convenient and well used facility had well and truly made its mark.

Perhaps the most influential of all communicators is the daily newspaper. The *Sheffield Iris* led us into the 19th century and lasted until September 1848 when, after a life of 54 years, it became Sheffield's longest surviving newspaper.

The *Sheffield Mercury* was published in 1807, followed by the *Sheffield and Rotherham Independent* in 1819, both being weekly publications like the *Iris* due to the crippling financial burden of paper duty and newspaper stamp duty which lasted until 1855.

On 8 June 1855, *The Sheffield Daily Telegraph* appeared for the first time, being a daily paper published at 8.00am, and costing one penny (less than ½pence today). *The Iris* and *The Mercury* were in due course absorbed by the *Sheffield Times* which had been published in 1846 as another weekly rival to the *Independent* and continued to be published weekly until 1873. *The Independent*, however, changed to daily publication in 1861.

The *Sheffield Evening Telegraph* put in its first appearance on 7 June 1887, its only local rival being the *Evening Star*, produced by the owners of the *Independent*. Within one year, the *Evening Telegraph* took over the *Evening Star* and the *Sheffield Evening Telegraph and Star* was born, only to be changed to the *Yorkshire Telegraph and Star* in 1907.

The *Sheffield Weekly Telegraph* was launched as a paper in 1883 but became more of a national publication by 1887, when it became simply the *Weekly Telegraph*, which existed until 1951.

Sports papers also emerged at the beginning of the 20th century, commencing with the *Early Bird*

racing paper which developed over the four years 1905 to 1909 and ceased publication in 1950. The forerunner to the *Green 'Un* was a six-page *Sports Special* printed on green paper, which hit the streets on 14 September 1907.

The *Sheffield Mail* had also been launched a second time by 1920, this continuing as an evening paper until 1931, when it was incorporated into the *Yorkshire Telegraph and Star*. Seven years later, in 1938, the *Independent* was eventually merged into the *Sheffield Daily Telegraph* and these two papers were now the only ones in publication and simplified their names to the *Sheffield Telegraph* and *The Star*. In 1965, the former became the *Morning Telegraph* and continued in print until 8 February 1986. Three years later, on 6 October 1989, the paper was reborn as the weekly *Sheffield Telegraph* and the new look tabloid *Star* incorporated colour and won the coveted Provincial Newspaper of the Year award in 1990.

As you can see, I've "bent the rules" for this last look at the 1800s by taking you through almost to the present date. In the interests of continuity, I felt that this was right, and what better vehicle could there be to "bridge that gap" than one which records and reports on all history as it is made: the newspaper.

The *Sheffield Telegraph* and *Star* offices at the High Street-York Street junction, about 1930.

Chapter Nine
1800 to 1900

THIS was the beginning of a new century and Mr S had decided to have a change of jobs. He liked being a cutler and his workshop was doing quite well, but with factories springing up all over the place and working conditions getting worse, he thought a change would do him good.

"You must be mad," said Mrs S "What can you turn your hand to at your age? You'll be throwing away a lifetime's experience for nothing. We all get fed up you know."

"I know all about that," explained Mr S, trying to be patient, "but we've got a 30-year-old son who's quite capable of running things in the workshop. If I don't make a go of it, I can always come back into the trade."

"Yes, but what would you do?" persisted his irate wife. "You've got me and our little son to think about and we can't live on fresh air!"

"Well, I'll tell you what I've got in mind," said the despairing Mr S, who never had liked being questioned about his decisions. "There are a lot of big houses and mansions which have been built over this last 50 years or so and they've all got long, wide chimneys which need cleaning. From what I'm told, there's good money to be made, and all you need is a climbing boy."

It was the stunned silence that Mr S hated most, as he knew it was usually followed by an explosion.

"YOU, A CHIMNEY SWEEP!" she exclaimed almost hysterically. "I've never heard of anything so stupid in my life."

Poor Mrs S was lost for words, but as she stormed out of the room in disgust, she knew that once her stubborn husband had made up his mind, there was no changing him.

Six months passed by and Mr S was tired of getting up at five o'clock in the morning to sweep chimneys, but he didn't dare complain to his wife.

Things had been going well until the government had passed a law making it illegal to use boys as chimney sweeps. Little-un, as his father liked to call him, was nearly seven years old and was good as a climbing boy. His thin little frame and shortness of height enabled him to crawl along the chimney flues fairly easily, although his breathing was becoming rather laboured at times.

"But this is the 1800s," muttered Mr S as he crawled out of bed and threw on his old working clothes, "and a chap deserves a bit of a lay-in of a morning."

He knew, of course, that the only way to dodge this law, which

was particularly unpopular with those chimney sweeps who used their own children as climbing boys, was to go to work early before most people were awake. That way, there was less chance of getting caught.

"Come on Little-un," growled his father trying hard not to be too irritable with his innocent little helper. "Put a spurt on or we'll be late."

Scurrying through the dark, deserted streets like two criminals on the run, they eventually arrived at a large, stone-built house which looked almost menacing in the early morning gloom. They were let in at the servants entrance round the back by the equally early-rising chamber-maid, who had already started on her chores. She ushered them downstairs to the large fireplace in the kitchen which smelt heavily of smoke and told them to be as quick as possible.

Thrusting a brush into Little-un's hand and making sure that a cloth was tied over his mouth and nose to filter out some of the fine sooty particles floating around in the air, Mr S pushed his reluctant young son up into the blackness above.

As Little-un groped his way along the still hot brick flues, cutting his knees and burning his thighs, crying quietly to himself, he must have wondered what he had done to deserve such punishment from his father.

Coming to a bend in the blackness of the chimney, he encountered the obstruction which had been causing the smoke from the fire to billow back into the cook's face and cause soot to collect on the master's special broth that previous evening. In an attempt to clear the blockage, he

Did You Know that using boys as chimney sweeps was made illegal in 1788? Despite this, the practice continued for another 100 years and in 1862 there were still 40 chimney sweeps recorded in Sheffield employing 22 climbing boys between the ages of five and ten-years-old. Their average life expectancy in the 1800s was only 15 years.

Recent new occupants of a large old house wishing to use the fireplace which had been blocked for many years, claim to have discovered the skeletal remains of a child in one of the chimney flues. This came to light when a chimney sweep was called in to clear an obstruction and the grim reminder of 150 years or so ago came tumbling down with the soot.

squeezed his tiny frame further in but, with a sudden movement of the fallen debris, he became wedged.

A sudden shower of soot into the fireplace below followed by muffled cries of help alerted Mr S to the child's plight, but no amount of encouragement to his son would help. After half an hour of Little-un struggling in vain, the desperate father, fearing for his son's life, asked the chamber-maid to fetch help.

The local builder was summoned but it was nearly two hours after becoming stuck before a sufficient part of the chimney was able to be demolished to enable the weak and frightened boy to be rescued.

Little-un did recover slowly but, as the black, searching soot had penetrated his throat and lungs and all but suffocated him, it was a good four days before he was able to speak again.

Mr S, meantime, had learnt his lesson, and decided to give up chimney sweeping for good and go back to being a cutler.

"It's about time you came to your senses," retorted Mrs S as she cuddled her young son. "You could have got him killed. Don't ever let me hear of you suggesting any such hair-brained ideas again."

Although he wouldn't admit it, Mr S knew that his wife was right. He had, however, heard that there were some jobs to be had in the local mine and that youngsters of Little-un's age could be hired as "hurryers" or "trappers" in the dark tunnels linking the foot of the pit shaft to the coal face.

"After all," he mused, "pushing and pulling wagons full of coal or simply sitting in the dark for a few hours, opening and closing the little wooden trap gates that the wagons have to pass through, should be a snip for Little-un after all he's been through. I wonder if I ought to mention it? Perhaps a bit later!"

* * * * * * * * *

Time had passed, and Mr S had got himself "back into gear" with his cutlery work and was putting in very long hours.

"You're looking a bit "peaky" these days, my love," said a concerned Mrs S "Why don't you take a couple of weeks off and take a few walks in the country? A bit of fresh air would do you the world of good."

"But what about you? Who'll look after the workshop?"

"The workshop will carry on without you for a short time, have no fear. Our Joe's a good lad and he's learnt a lot over all these years he's worked alongside you. As for me, I've got plenty of friends round here, and I might even stay a few nights with Mrs Weaver."

Mr S had to admit that he had been overdoing things for quite some time, and he did need a break. His cousin, he recalled, had a nice little "two-up and two-down" terrace over at Hillsborough which was within spitting distance of the beautiful Loxley Valley and the hills beyond. He could spend a day or two walking the hamlets, looking at the water wheels and mills on the rivers, and even walk up to see how this new Dale Dyke Dam was progressing on the hill overlooking Low Bradfield.

"I think you're right love," he said at last. "Cousin S has

often invited me over to stay with him, but I've never had the time in the past."

It was a beautiful, sunny morning when Mr S kissed his wife goodbye and set off for his first ever two week break without her.

"Now you be careful," she said with tears in her eyes, "and make sure you get out into that fresh air."

He felt strange as he made his way over to Angel Street to

catch the horse omnibus to Hillsborough, as he wasn't used to going places alone. Even the ride on the new bus would be an adventure, as this would be only the second time he had felt "flush enough" to pay the three penny fare for the privilege.

The first occasion, he recalled fondly, was the anniversary of his 25th year of marriage to his dear wife, and he had put aside 2s (10p) for a special day out. They had taken an early morning bus from the Yellow Lion in Haymarket to its terminus at the Red Lion in Heeley. The fare was three pence each, but the exhilarating drive on the top, open deck of the bus which swayed to the movement of the two galloping horses, had been an experience never to be forgotten. Mrs S had thought that this trip to the Red Lion was the extent of her treat, so it had been to her complete amazement that the happy couple had boarded a second bus out to the Big Tree at Woodseats.

This second stage of the journey had been even better than the first, as the two powerful white horses had proudly taken the excited passengers up the long winding hill to the rapidly growing village. The views over the Sheaf valley past Smithy Wood and Norton Hammer had been breathtaking, and as the horse omnibus had pulled into the forecourt of the Inn and parked under the grateful shade of the large tree which grew there, Mr S recalled that this had been one of the happiest days of their lives.

Did You Know that in 1898, a three-horse double-decker horse omnibus seating 26 passengers was run by John Heath, founder of the John Heath & Sons Funeral Services, from the Courthouse in Castle Street to Petre Street? The first bus left Castle Street at 8.15am and its one-penny-all-the-way fare made it the cheapest in the city.

The sudden clatter of hooves and the rattling of wheels snapped him out of his daydreams and he boarded the Hillsborough-bound bus. Climbing the steep little steps up to the top deck was always a bit of a problem, particularly when the horses, impatient to get on their way, were jostling about; but the best view was from up there, and this was part of the holiday.

The route along West Bar Green, Gibraltar Street and into Moorfields was flanked with an ever growing number of workshops, houses and factories. Even the main Walkley Road, on which the new General Infirmary now proudly stood, was becoming built-up, and Mr S wondered where it would all end.

By the time the huge Hillsborough Barracks appeared to his right, Mr S knew that his interesting ride was over. Bidding goodbye to the cheerful driver and his snorting horses, he made his way to his cousin's house for the beginning of what he expected to be a relaxing, healthy fortnight.

The first two or three days, as you might expect, were spent mostly chatting and drinking in one or other of the many pubs which served this area. However, remembering his wife's good advice, he spent several days going for walks in the refreshing country air. By the end of the week, he had ventured up to the banks of the almost completed Dale Dyke Dam. He marvelled at the engineering feat which safely contained the hundreds of millions of gallons of water above the valley below, but felt grateful that such a responsibility would never fall on him.

It was only the middle of March, but the sun was still shining in a pale blue sky and the view looking over towards Sheffield was like nothing he had ever seen before. The town itself was covered by a dark haze of smoke and fumes, which looked more like an unfriendly rain-cloud in the distance.

Elsewhere, fields, woods, hills and valleys tumbled over each other as they reached for the horizon, and Mr S could just make out the trail of white smoke left by the afternoon train as it chugged its way to Manchester. A mile below the dam, but looking much closer than that, sat the picturesque hamlet of Low Bradfield, with its low stone walls, quaint little church and clusters of stone built cottages. Water mills and farmsteads were dotted along the river valley until they disappeared from view, and for Mr S, this was the peace and relaxation he'd been seeking.

As the second week progressed, the weather changed and March winds began to blow. Mr S now spent more time inside than out and on the last day before his departure, he had lunch at a nearby pub. The winds had become stronger, and although his cousin had to leave for an afternoon shift work at Mousehole Forge at Malin Bridge, Mr S decided to stay and "down a few more" until the winds abated. But the weather got worse and time marched on and at last he decided he must leave.

It was quite late when Mr S finally arrived "home", pleased to be able to shelter at last from the clutching fingers of the tormenting wind which shrieked with laughter as it hurled broken branches and loose tiles around for amusement.

He was breathless by the time he reached the small flight of steps leading up to the front of his cousin's little terrace. Lurching through the door, he gratefully slammed it behind

Devastation caused by the Great Flood.

The Great Flood wrecked the nearest of this pair of cottages and drowned all but one of the family living there.

The clock on the old oak sideboard in the corner of the room struck quarter to midnight as he reeled back in disbelief and prayed that the merciless waters would at least spare this little home tonight.

"It must be the end of the world," Mr S gasped to himself as he slumped to the floor, wishing he'd stayed in the pub for that last pint.

The 12 booming strikes of the clock brought him out of his temporary stupor as it heralded in Saturday morning. Mr S certainly didn't want to die, but what could he do. What of his neighbours? How were they? He ventured back to the window. The wind had eased a little, but the mighty torrent roared on.

In desperation he went to the door and opened it with cautious trepidation. The noise was deafening and water surged and swirled past his feet, inches below him, trying desperately to reach up and claim yet another victim.

The moon was shining brightly now, and other doors and windows opened to reveal the pale, terrified faces of

him and heaved a sigh of relief as the destructive stormy night gave way to the relative peace of the small but cosy living room. Even the constant rattling of the loosely fitting window frames was almost a pleasure to his cold, aching ears as he settled down to a welcome cup of tea and a slice of best beef dripping in the faded blue, horse-hair chair.

It wasn't until he was halfway through his favourite supper, that Mr S became aware of another, strangely menacing noise from outside. It sounded like the distant rumbling of thunder, but gradually became louder and louder until it swallowed up the higher pitch of the still raging wind. A tingling sensation crept over his body and a gradual feeling of fear filled his heavily pounding chest as the roar outside became a crescendo.

Hardly daring to look, he rose unsteadily to his feet and staggered across the linoleum clad floor to the slightly misted up windows.

It was dark outside, the only relief being the intermittent shafts of moonlight which burst their way through the moody black clouds which were racing, as if their life, across the vast expanse of sky above.

He rubbed his hand over the cold surface of the moist glass and peered into the blackness beyond. The flickering light of the lonely candle, which stood by the side of the half eaten supper on the little table behind him, reflected annoyingly in the blackness beyond, and at first he could see nothing. Slowly, his eyes began to focus on a vast, swirling mass, not unlike the stormy clouds which appeared to have fallen from the sky with a deafening roar of accompaniment.

Suddenly, as if in answer to the turmoil in his questioning mind, the moon lit up the scene in all its awful splendour, and Mr S gazed in disbelief at the sight of utter devastation.

The street along which he had hurried home not more than half an hour before, was now a raging, swirling torrent of water whose destructive force had uprooted trees, torn down buildings and fences and swept along the furniture and contents of once precious homes further up the valley where huge waves of foaming water had engulfed houses in their path.

Did You Know that on 11 March 1864, the almost completed Dale Dyke Dam, which was being built above the little hamlets of Low Bradfield, Dam Flask and Loxley, burst its banks half an hour before midnight and discharged most of its 700 million gallons of water down into the valley below at a rate of about 250,000 gallons a second? The onslaught devastated a large area of north-western, central and eastern Sheffield and resulted in 270 deaths, countless injuries, 800 houses destroyed and over 4,300 damaged. At least 15 bridges were swept away, along with riverside works, mills, farms and a local school. About 700 animals are also known to have perished.

Such was the power of the huge torrent of water that it created 50ft-high waves which crashed over rooftops and hurled enormous boulders into the air. It not only raced through Malin Bridge, Hillsborough and Owlerton on its way into town, but it also continued via West Bar, the Wicker and Savile Street on towards Brightside, Attercliffe and Tinsley and into Rotherham. The body of a boy from Malin Bridge was found there three weeks later.

The reservoir took 47 minutes to empty, and the "Great Sheffield Flood" was, at the time, referred to as England's greatest tragedy!

neighbours. Houses across the road were under several feet of water and lights flickered in the upstairs windows only.

"At least we've got each other," thought Mr S with some degree of relief.

It was nearly half past twelve before the raging waters began to subside. All manner of articles were floating and tumbling past, but Mr S's eye was suddenly drawn to a small white bundle swirling around in the foam, and caught up in the branches of a large tree which had reached out and entangled itself around the remains of his front garden fence. A whimpering cry reached his ears, and Mr S knew that the destiny of a baby's life was in his hands.

He hadn't got time to think as he found himself plunging into the deep, cold waters below him. Striking out with frantic urgency, he reached the semi-conscious child and somehow found the strength to battle his way against the dark, muddy flow to the safety of his home.

The embers of the dying fire which had been lit earlier that day were still glowing, and he placed the precious bundle in the warmth of its remaining heat whilst he went to find something in which to wrap the tiny miracle of life.

The next two hours were like a dream as Mr S, now in dry clothes himself, sat hunched up in the armchair, cradling his still whimpering charge hidden amongst the warmth of towels and an old blanket wrapped tightly round him.

A sudden banging on the door awoke the drowsy pair from their semi-slumber, and the welcoming sound of a neighbour's voice brought the realisation that the worst of his nightmare was over. Kindly hands gently took the baby from him, as words of praise tumbled over his numbed head from those who had witnessed his heroic deed.

He glanced up at the pale but friendly faces above him. Everyone was crying, mostly with relief, and they all thanked God they were still alive.

It was Sunday before Mr S eventually arrived home to the relief of his poor wife, who had been frantic with worry when she had read the tragic news in the Saturday edition of *Sheffield Daily Telegraph*. The report had been terrifying as it explained that the Dale Dyke Dam had burst its banks half an hour before midnight, and discharged most of its 700 million gallons of water down into the valley below. The paper had gone on to explain that the unstoppable watery onslaught had devastated much of the City, and hundreds of people were dead or homeless with many more injured, and thousands of houses damaged or destroyed.

"When I read that the water had poured through Malin Bridge and Hillsborough," Mrs S sobbed, "I thought I'd lost you. It even flooded down Attercliffe and Tinsley into Rotherham, you know."

Mr S was simply grateful to be alive as he put his strong arm around his wife's shaking shoulders. Never again, he vowed, would he leave her side, even for a relaxing break!

He never did find out who the baby belonged to or whether or not its parents were still alive. Perhaps they were amongst the 270 victims whose bodies were pulled from the mud, filth and rubble which identified the eight mile trail of devastation caused that fateful night. Mr and Mrs S knew that at least they had a lot to be thankful for.

* * * * * * * * *

This, as we know, was Victorian Sheffield, and Mr S had managed to get himself on to the Town Council at last. He was a caring man, and was concerned about the use of child labour in these difficult times. The committee on which he sat had asked him to do a bit of research into the problem, and what he had found had alarmed him considerably.

It was now usual for children to start work when they were about nine years old, at which time they could even earn quite good wages. The ironworks paid about 1s (5p) a day, whilst working down the pit could bring in about 8s (40p) a week for the youngsters.

Down in Attercliffe, several young children were employed in the coke yards separating out the shale, whilst some boys as young as six or seven operated the bellows for the spade and shovel workers. Girls under the age of 13 were even employed driving coal carts pulled by donkeys and ponies to earn extra money to make up the family wage.

> **Did You Know** that during the first half of the 1800s large numbers of Sheffield children were employed in poorly-constructed factories with poor ventilation and lighting, cramped conditions and unprotected machinery? They carryied out trades such as grinding knives and forks, handle making, file cutting, hair seat weaving, crucible steel manufacture, stone grave manufacture, saw making, silver plating, bone cutting, blade forging, nail and screw making. Due to the appalling working conditions, poor sanitation and the high rate of infant mortality, the average age at which people died in Sheffield was 24 years old.

There were, of course, some "cleaner" occupations, and half of George Basset's 150-strong workforce at his sweet factory was made up of children. The boys helped in the production of the sweets and the fetching and carrying of ingredients, whilst the girls worked in the warehouse doing sorting and packing. Inevitably, both sets of children helped in the eating of the famous "all sorts".

But it was his friends Mr and Mrs Weaver's sad situation which had shocked Mr S most. The hard times had hit them badly and they were struggling to survive. In desperation they had decided to put their six-year-old twins out to work to

Did you Know that Sheffield sweet makers, Trebor Bassett, celebrated 100 years of Liquorice Allsorts on 8 June 1999? The original products were sold separately with only modest success. However, when traveling salesman, Charlie Thompson, spilled his sample case on the floor in front of a customer in the late 1890s, the brightly coloured mix of "allsorts" looked attractively appealing, and history was accidentally made.

bring in some money. Their little girl had gone to a cutlery workshop, whilst her brother had started as a glazer at his father's grinding trough, sitting behind a spinning wooden wheel, putting a good finish to his blades.

"I know what you're thinking my old pal," Mr Weaver had said the day Mr S had chatted to him about it. "But what choice did we have? It was either putting the children out to work, or the workhouse for us all. We had an impossible choice to make!"

Mr S had agreed with his friend, but his colleagues on the Town Council had wanted to know more. In particular they wondered just what life in the workhouse was really like, and someone had to go and investigate.

It was no wonder, then, that Mr S now found himself heading the small group of investigators which set off on a cold, damp morning on their fact finding tour. Their destination was the Ecclesall Union Workhouse in Nether Edge, a magnificent stone building set in the country. It has already been described several years previously by a local manufacturer who championed the caused of the poor, as a "Horrible God-defying Place of Torment" and a "nursery for rearing prostitutes and vagabonds". With such an unsavoury pedigree, the investigators were prepared for anything, although the new laws had been passed which should have improved things.

Their knocks on the heavy wooden door with its cast-iron handle seemed to echo up into the misty vastness of the grey, almost intimidating front entrance as Mr S gave a little

shudder. Bolts crashed against metal stops in slow progression before the inevitable creak of the door announced that they could go in and be welcomed by their host. The silent, elderly servant who led the equally silent and apprehensive group into the large open entrance hall was predictably stooped and glum faced as he shuffled towards the next door barring their progression. For what seemed an age, the rattling of keys, the

turning of locks, and the banging of bolts and doors rang round their ears before they were met by the Workhouse Master.

"I'm afraid I'm rather busy this morning, gentlemen," he said with a fixed smile that made his bewhiskered face look even more sinister than it first appeared. "Mr Guardian will escort you around. I'm sure that you will find everything in order."

The next two sets of doors, which were securely locked behind them, led Mr S and his party to the cells of the "casual paupers" who arrived each evening seeking food and shelter.

"We strip 'em and bathe 'em as soon as they come in," said Mr Guardian in a blunt but fairly sincere sort of manner. "They get one of those dark woollen night dresses each and a couple of rugs and that's them sorted out for a few hours."

From what the group could make out, the workhouse accepted casual paupers of any sex, usually for two nights' shelter, with a superintendent and his wife being resident on the block to deal with them. Unlike some years previously, separate cells were now available for each sex, and "furniture" was provided for their personal use.

"Let's have a look then," requested Mr S in a slightly demanding voice. "I'm dying to see this wonderful new accommodation."

Mr Guardian turned yet another key in the heavy door which slowly opened to reveal a small cell with a large plank set on short wooden blocks tucked along one wall. At one end of the plank was another wooden block which acted as a pillow and, to the amazement of the observers, Mr G (as her preferred to be called) announced that the whole contraption was indeed the pauper's bed!

"But where's the chair and the table?" persisted Mr S.

"Well, the plank does for all three doesn't it? They can sit on it and eat off it! What more do they want?"

A sudden banging from the far end of the dingy little room, prevented any further discussion on the matter. In a tiny inner cell which led off from the room, was a small, white-faced man stooping over a pile of broken stone with a hammer far too big for him. He had paused for breath, but carried on hammering the stone as soon as Mr G came into view.

Stone-breaking was one of the tasks which the casual male paupers had to undertake in return for their night's lodging and board. Between 5cwt and 13cwt of stone (about 550 to 1500lbs) had to be broken up into tiny pieces and then thrown out of the inner cell in which they were working, through the two inch square holes in the iron grating window in its outer wall. This window, in effect, acted as a sieve, and ensured that the pile of crushed stone which ended up in the courtyard outside was the correct size for the Corporation to use for building roads and other construction purposes.

This work was tedious, tiring and "back-breaking" and was more reminiscent of that of convict-labour than that of working in return for a little charity and care. The previous occupier of this cell had, in fact, lost an eye when one of the sharp chippings had flown up into his face during his stint at stone breaking.

When the Corporation's demand for crushed stone declined, however, other tasks were specified. Nine hours work digging, pumping, sawing or grinding was one set of alternatives, whilst "picking" eight pounds of beaten oakum, or four pounds of unbeaten, was the most ridiculous of all.

Oakum is a loose fibre obtained by picking old rope to pieces and can be used in caulking, or sealing joints to make them waterproof. The rope provided was always hard and stiff and had sometimes been dipped in tar as a preservative. Beating with a hammer had the effect of softening it, this making "picking" slightly easier.

"It'll take a month of Sundays to pick four pounds of fibre from that!" exclaimed Mr S as they stood in the doorway of the next dingy cell watching its inmate at work.

The pathetic figure which sat there cross-legged on his plank-cum-chair, was huddled over a length of thick, black rope which his sore finger ends were desperately trying to untangle. He had a metal bowl at the side of him into which a few strands of fibre had been placed, but he knew he had to fill about six of these if he wished to eat later that day.

"It's bloody barmy this is," Mr S muttered to his council colleague. "I wonder what they make the women do?"

Mr Guardian had obviously overhead the comment and led the Town Hall delegation to yet another cell in which sat two women carrying out exactly the same work.

"I know what you're thinking, gents," said Mr G, "but we only expect the women to pick half the amount of oakum that the men are required to do. We do care for our inmates in here you know."

Trying hard to stifle his natural instinct to explode with indignation, Mr S listened as Mr G explained that the women were not always put on to oakum picking. They were often given nine hours of washing, scrubbing or needlework to do as an alternative, in order that they could be fed and receive lodgings for a second night.

It was, of course, necessary to feed the casual paupers in order to keep them strong enough to carry out their tasks, and Mr S read with interest the mealtime schedule and menu pinned on to the wall in the corridor. Breakfast was provided at 6am and consisted of a pint of gruel, made out of oatmeal, black treacle and water, together with six ounces of bread. The 12 o'clock dinner was not a lot better, although an ounce and a half of cheese accompanied half a pound of bread on this occasion, all being washed down with a tin mug of cold water. The management was not, however, keen for the paupers to get too used to such delicacies, so the 6pm supper reverted back to the morning menu of bread and gruel.

"We get about 100 casuals a week through here," said Mr G as they completed the first section of their tour. "That's 5,000 a year we have to deal with, and it's all free you know."

Mr S wondered to himself how much stone-breaking,

> **Did you know that the amount of food given to poor people in workhouses was controlled by a "Workhouse Regulations (Dietaries and Accounts) Order"? A "Haddon's Ingredient Calculator" was used for "at a glance" calculations of quantities for any given standard menu, which included such things as Gruel (oatmeal, treacle and water), Hotch Potch Stew (beef, flour, peas, barley, turnip cabbage, onion and water), and Broth (bones, vegetables and water). Puddings such as Batter Pudding (flour, milk and fat), Steamed Bread Pudding (bread, sugar, fat, currants and milk) and Seed Cake (bread dough, sugar, dripping and caraway seeds) were also popular at this time.**

scrubbing or oakum-picking the caring guardian would like to do himself for "free" board and lodgings! "Not a lot, I can tell you," he muttered to himself.

The 600 more permanent inmates of the workhouse had a different way of living to the casuals. This was made clear when the visiting group arrived at a number of wooden sheds in the yard which led off the doorway at the end of the corridor. Inside, groups of 12 to 20 men were supervised by a taskmaster whilst sawing and chopping up old railway sleepers for fire wood. They were paid for their work and thus earned their own living. A rate of 1s 10d (about 9p) a day was paid for the four "long" days of Tuesday to Friday, whilst Monday and Saturday only attracted a pay of 1s 6d (7p). Pauper women fared even better, as they were able to earn 2s (10p) a day in the laundry.

The next port of call was the huge dining room in which

rows and rows of long narrow tables stood smartly to attention a they faced the large, steamy kitchen at its far end. The long, hard benches were now filling up with hungry pauper men, women and children who were always grateful for their meal, as something was always better than nothing.

Today was meat dinner-day, and therefore the special weekly treat. In the kitchen, Mr S was amazed to see the huge legs of boiled beef which were being cut up into slices, briefly weighed and dished out on to the mountain of plates which stood nearby. These in turn were passed through to the serving counter at which fairly orderly queues of hungry diners had formed for their main meal of the day. A spoonful of boiled potatoes and a chunk of hard bread joined the meat and its watery gravy on the plate, and each person in turn was then hurried on, grasping the usual tin mug of water in his spare hand.

The sound of hundreds of spoons scraping on plates and tin cups clattering on bare wooden table tops blended remarkably well with the slurps and smacks of 1,200 lips, as dinner got well under way.

> **Did You Know that the Oxo cube's origins date back to 1847 when it was a nutritious liquid extract of beef known as "Lemco" after the Liebig Extract of Meat Company which produced it? The consignments of dried meat which were used to make this product, came from the town of Fray Bentos in Uruguay, and the crates in which they were packed were marked with the letters O.X.O. for easy recognition. OXO was registered as a British trade mark in 1900 and by 1910, the one-penny cube, each wrapped by hand, was for sale in the shops.**

"I wouldn't mind trying some of that beef," said the brave Mr S, who was determined to carry out his inspection to the full. "And I think I'll sample some of that bread as well."

To say that the meat was tough was the understatement of the year.

"There's more flavour in the missus's walking boots than in this 'ere meat," he spluttered after several minutes of unsuccessful chewing. "I just hope the bread's a bit better."

Needless to say, it wasn't. Mr S had heard about the many black beetles which found their way into the sacks of flour used for making the bread, but he was still shocked when he broke open his piece and found one lying there. As he hurriedly dropped the bread and its "sleeping" occupant on to the floor, it was instantly "seized upon" by several patiently waiting relatives of the deceased insect. Despite the cook's huge size ten feet crunching out their disapproval of the "little black monsters", Mr S and company decided that they had seen enough of the kitchen and beat a hasty retreat.

The Lunatic Wards were next on the tour, and Mr S was feeling rather apprehensive regarding these. Horror stories regarding the way they were run had often circulated the town, but the Council wanted to see "first hand" just how good or bad things really were.

In the past, things had been very grim. In the early 1800s, laws had been passed prohibiting physical beatings and chaining up of people of sane mind, although it is doubtful that much notice had been taken of such requirement for

many years. The chaining up of lunatics was, however, still legal. Mr S recalled the 1828 Act of Parliament which allowed paupers and criminally insane persons to be placed into lunatic asylums by a JP once they had been certified as such by a doctor. Once hidden from public view, treatment had been harsh and more like torture than medical care.

But this was the later 1800s, and things really had improved. The two lunatic wards accommodated 27 people of each sex, but so many were classed as insane in these times, when medical knowledge about mental illness was woefully lacking, that another 30 had to sleep in the main building with the rest of the inmates. The bare wooden beds in the wards were the same as those in the large, locked dormitories where the main body of the workhouse inmates slept. A few books and one or two bagatelle boards (a game where small balls are struck into numbered holes on a board,) were provided for the inmates recreation, but no one fancied a game when Mr S issued a challenge.

"They're all sat about doing nothing," said Mr S "What do they do for exercise?"

As if in answer to his own question, he glanced out of a side window where he saw several men and women slowly

 walking round and round a dreary, asphalt yard. This was the extent of their out-door pursuits and no work was provided to occupy any of them. Even music was forbidden, and only at Christmas, once a year, were they entertained.

"It's not as bad as I thought," said Mr S to himself. "Mind you, they'll obviously only show us the best bits, and heaven only knows what happens in the medical wards where some of them are treated!"

Mr S was gagging for a cup of tea as they all made their way to the hospital block where 180 patients were cared for by four nurses in bright white uniforms and faces to match. The hardworking young women were quite cheerful carrying out their tasks, but with patients spread out over four wards of 40 or 50 to each, one smiling nurse per ward was rather inadequate to say the least. To make matters worse, most of their time was taken up seeing to the patients clothes and bed linen, and very little time for nursing was available.

"Are these nurses trained?" asked Mr S "If so, it's not being put to much good use."

Trained nursing wasn't introduced, however, until 1897, so the patients depended on the daily "whistle-stop" tour of the workhouse doctor, one untrained nurse per ward, (although with only one nurse to every 90 patients at night-time) and a little help from "wardswomen", who were inmates carrying out extra duties in return for a meat dinner every day. The six chronic cases in the hospital did, nevertheless, receive a little more individual attention as these were placed under the care of an elderly pauper woman, who had no medical knowledge whatsoever!

The largest department in the workhouse was the Infirm Block, where people over the age of 60 spent their lives. Mr S was struggling by this time and was determined to ask for a cuppa" when he and his colleagues had looked around here. The day rooms and dormitories were overcrowded and dull and had been split into two classes of middle-age and old-age, as well as being separated by sex.

The middle-age accommodation was for those under 70 who mostly sat on hard forms, reading the odd book if they knew how, or chatting about old times to their mates. For those over 70, the comfort of a fireplace was allowed, together with a weekly allowance of an ounce of tobacco as a treat. Whilst most of these had outlived their spouses and children, in this century when the expectancy of life was nearer 30 than 70, one old chap of 103 still seemed to be enjoying himself as he pottered about the place, oblivious to any worries of the world!

"If you'd like a cup of tea, gents, I'm sure you'll be able to get one in these Old Married Couples apartments we've just built," said Mr Guardian as they made their way to the next small block. "We allow these old 'uns to brew their own tea, and they can fetch their meals from the kitchen when it's time."

The rooms for these couples were small and basic, but at least they enabled married couples over the age of 60 to be together.

As Mr S gratefully drank the weak but warm mug of tea that a rather charming but sad-faced old couple had willingly made for him, he pondered over the dilemma of the workhouse problem. Up to 1834, the town's poor had been able to receive help in their own homes from the Poor Rate which was paid by those with property. The new Poor Law which came into force in that year, meant that very low wages were no longer made up from the Poor Rates, and most paupers would only get help if they entered a workhouse. This meant that those with no jobs and those with poorly paid jobs had to go into the workhouse to survive.

This unhappy situation was compounded by the new workhouse rules which split up children from their parents and separated male and female of all age levels, except married couples over 60. The logic behind these rules was based on an attempt to prevent the serious problems of sexual promiscuity, bullying and other depraved activities that took place with the old system of intermixing.

"You can't win," thought Mr S "If you're poor and stay at home, you'll starve to death. Even though the breadwinner wants to come in on his own to earn money, he has to bring the family with him. If the whole family comes in, they're all split up. I think the old system was better myself. This new Law's only been brought in to save money being paid out in Poor Rates by people like me with a bit of property. It's just not right!"

So angry had Sheffielders been with this appalling situation, that 15,000 people had signed a petition to get rid of this law, which had been described as "the greatest curse that ever inflicted England". Sadly, it was to no avail.

"Come on Mr S It's time for the last part of our tour," said Mr Guardian, putting his head round the door. "We've just got the school to see, and that's your lot."

There were 32 boys and 32 girls in the two little classrooms when the tired visitors arrived. Under the watchful eyes of the schoolmaster and schoolmistress, each class sang in turn a pitiful little song which they had obviously learnt specially for the occasion.

As they stood their in their identical corduroy uniforms, Mr S was moved by the sadness in their eyes, the hopelessness

in their voices and the emptiness of the words which tumbled around his ears.

"What was the future for them?" he wondered. "Were they better off or worse off than Mr and Mrs Weaver's children?"

Perhaps the next century would give him the answer. Who knows?

The Last Hundred Years 1900-2000 AD

AT LAST, we have reached the last lap of our journey through time; we have arrived in the 20th century. It may be the beginning of the end of our interesting story, but it is also the beginning of incredible progress, "impossible" achievements and dramatic events.

Such are the happenings in this remarkable 100 years, that it is necessary to lay out the national back-cloth upon which Sheffield's history will be painted, in order that a better understanding of the 20th-century life of the Sheffielder can be seen.

Let us, therefore, have a brief look at the changes which have had such an important impact on our lives.

During this century medical knowledge and science improved beyond all recognition, from basic medicines and crude facilities, to life-saving drugs, powerful antiseptics and sophisticated surgery. Heart and liver transplants are now common, and even the cloning of "Dolly the sheep" is the first of more to come.

Travel speeded up, starting with the "little old banger" motor car, progressing through the old Ford Pop and the Mini, to the fast, luxurious models of today. Horse-drawn public transport gave way to electric trams, motor buses and taxi cabs, whilst those wishing to travel afar now hop on planes which can transport them halfway around the world in a few hours.

Satellites now circle the earth and man has even walked on the moon. Attempts to find life on Mars are still continuing, and space travel for us all doesn't seem too far away.

The advent of the computer has probably had the biggest impact on our lives, the micro-chip replacing the fried chip as the country's most important commodity. "Computeris-ation" arrived (as well as the unpopular decimalisation), and single machines began to do the work of hundreds of people, whilst thousands lost their jobs in pursuit of efficiency and progress.

The simple "wireless", meanwhile, progressed to the sophisticated radio, and the magic of the silver screen and talking movies moved over to make way for television and video. Communication was also revolutionised by a world wide telephone system, which was later added to by electronic mail and the magic of the Internet.

On a more domestic level, "mod cons" replaced "elbow grease" in the home as electricity brought in cleaners, washers and cookers to take some of the drudgery out of housework. Making a fire and smoking chimneys also became a thing of the past as gas fires, radiators and central heating brought instant warmth to our homes.

Dancing and music also dominated the social scene as the Black Bottom and the Charleston of the 1920s and 1930s developed into the Rock and Roll of the 1950s and 1960s. During this pop music explosion, teddy-boys were followed by hippies, mods and rockers, and punks as new generations tried to establish their identities.

People, of course, were the key to change and progress, and three of many spring to mind. Mrs Pankhurst and her daughters were leading suffragettes fighting for women's votes, Mrs Thatcher became the country's first woman Prime Minister, and the Royal Family suffered knocks, scandal and sadness as Edward VIII abdicated to be with Mrs Simpson, Princesses Margaret and Anne, together with Princes Charles and Andrew, were divorced, and the affectionately-called People's Princess, Diana, was tragically killed. This last, sad event shook the nation to its core, and millions of people worldwide felt that they had lost a personal friend.

Last but not least, on our back-cloth of time, we must remember the horrors of two world wars and the great depression of the late 1920s and early 1930s, when three million people were unemployed in Britain and families were starving everywhere. Add to this the more recent escalating abuse of drugs, the incurable illness of Aids and the destructive impact of modern day pollution on our environment, and we now have a broad picture of life on which to add some local detail.

Because the amount of change which has taken place this century is so considerable, the format for this last section of "potted" history has been expanded to cover more specific topics. Added to this, a large selection of old photographs have been included to bring the changes to life, and perhaps jog a few memories.

(a) Size and Growth

In 1911, the population of Sheffield was about 460,000, which included 30,000 or so which had been added by boundary changes in 1901 and 1911. By 1921, this figure reached 518,000, again including boundary extensions in 1913 and 1921, at which level it remained more or less constant for the next 30 years. The 1991 Census finally identified a total population of about 526,000, having brought in the districts of Mosborough (1967), Stocksbridge, Ecclesfield, Bradfield and Wortley (1974) in its boundary extensions, and represents the great City of Sheffield as we now know it.

The real expansion of the city in terms of new housing being built in the suburbs took place over the 20-year period covering the 1890s to 1910. The face of the city changed forever during that time, as new buildings practically engulfed areas such as Meersbrook, Millhouses, Sharrow, Fulwood, Ecclesall, Walkley and Crookes to the south and west, and continued with Firvale, Attercliffe, Brightside, Tinsley, Catcliffe, Darnall and Intake to the north and east. Hillsborough and Norton were also brought into the city during this time, following which their population increased considerably.

Terraced housing in Carbrook Street, Attercliffe in the 1960s. These young Sheffielders made the most of their surroundings.

By the 1990s, the city also had a thriving, integrated multicultural society, with about 26,000 or more of Sheffield's residents being Black, or from other Ethnic Minority Groups. The variety of nationalities in the city include Black Caribbean, Black African, Indian, Pakistani, Bangladeshi, and Chinese.

It is interesting to note that there are about the same number of males and females living in Sheffield at present, with pensioners forming one fifth of the city's population.

(b) Local Government

Up to 1903, there were only two political parties on the City Council, the Liberals and the Conservatives. By 1911, three trades union secretaries and a furnaceman had become councillors, and in 1926 the first Labour council ran the city. Labour successfully kept control of the city council for the next 44 years, until 1968, at which time the Conservative party took over for just one year. The next 30 years saw Labour back in power, but on the eve of the Millennium, after the May 1999 elections, the Liberals are now in control.

In 1927 the new Labour Council established a Direct Labour Department to build and repair houses, schools and other public buildings. At the same time it started a tram buildings department and an up to date municipal abattoir.

The City Council went from strength to strength and became the city's largest employer, peaking at about 34,000 full time and part time employees in the late 1980s, and costing in the order of £340 million during that year.

Up until 1974, at which time Local Government was reorganised, the Council had 20 major departments, including Public Works, City Engineers, Housing, Education, Social Services, Treasury, Planning and Architecture, Town Clerk's, Water, Transport, Recreation, Libraries, and many others.

In 1974, the South Yorkshire County Council was established and took over many of the city's functions, and it was not until 1986 that most of them were controlled by the City Council once again. This followed the Governments decision to abolish the large County Councils on the basis that they were too expensive to run and were unpopular with the grass roots electorate, who felt that the County Offices in Barnsley were too remote, and the question of "who does what" in Sheffield was too confusing.

Times, however, are changing rapidly, and over the last ten years, employee numbers in the City Council have reduced by half. In addition, many functions are put out to tender, and the Council departments such as Works, Recreation and Cleansing Services have to compete for work with the private sector. Some departments, such as those involved in civil engineering and architectural design, now act as consultants, and successfully bid for non-council work and make a profit for the ratepayers of Sheffield.

Money is, nevertheless, still very short, and in order to "make ends meet" and preserve important but "non-essential" services, the Council has handed over the management of its museums, theatres, leisure and sports facilities to Charitable Trusts. Whilst much of the money to support the buildings and services will still come from the Council, the Trusts will be able to raise extra money from the private sector and the Lottery to improve services and invest in their future. City Councillors sit on the boards of these Trusts, and so retain links with the public.

The Council is also putting out services to the private sector where specialist firms promise to do the work as efficiently but cheaper than the appropriate Council Department can achieve at present. One such example is the

Sheffield Town Hall with its 'egg box' extensions. The new water features and landscaping of the Peace Gardens complement the stone buildings.

contract to administer the Council's payroll and tax collection, which is expected to save several million pounds a year.

Last but not least, staffing has been reduced at all levels with a smaller, more compact management structure, combined departments and less people in all areas of work. Gone is the notion that the Corporation is the ideal employer, with a job secure for life. The "giant" protector of the public purse has now been reduced to a more modest size as it relies on private and public partnership for its service delivery. We can only wait and see how successful it will be.

Although I've probably said enough about local government, I really just ought to mention that it was during the 1970s that the controversial Town Hall Extensions were built. The "egg-box", as it is now referred to, was designed to complement the existing town hall with its matching stone finish, but bring out a contrastingly modern feel to suit the period in which it was built. Unfortunately, it failed to please most people, and now, 30 years on, the huge building is to be demolished to make way for an even more functional office block.

Now that the Peace Gardens have been significantly changed, its matching stone walls, steps, and garden features, together with its numerous fountains, have managed at last to gel the whole complex together. Indeed, the new creation blends in better with the "egg-box" than the town hall itself.

It is ironic indeed, that just when the area is looking its best, we have to destroy a landmark that does at last fit in well with its surroundings.

(c) Health and Poverty

"If you've got your health, that's all you need," is a statement made by many people these days. Whilst this is probably true, good health is often difficult to achieve unless you have a reasonable start in life to begin with.

This has proved to be the case over the centuries in Sheffield, as the very poor have carried out the worst jobs, for the longest hours, for the poorest pay. They also lived in the worst houses with appalling sanitary conditions where good health was never an option.

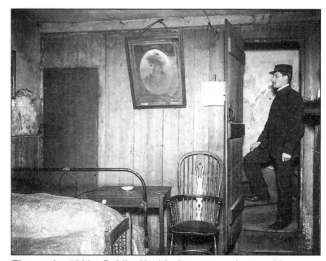

The early 1900s Public Health Inspector views with some concern the damp walls of terraced housing in Sheffield's East End.

If we take a brief look at the "best" and "worst" areas 100 years ago, we find that over a quarter of all babies (27 per cent) died before they reached the age of one in the industrialised districts of Attercliffe and the northern part of the central township. Compare that with one tenth of children under one year of age dying in the pleasant, rich suburb of Upper Hallam during the same period, and a relationship between poverty and health is identified.

Improvements in hygiene and medical care have, fortunately, drastically reduced these tragic figures, and the number of deaths of babies under one year old is now only about a fiftieth of all births (2 per cent), and is therefore ten times better than it was 100 years ago. Regrettably, however, recent surveys have established that the trend of the early 1900s still applies, as babies in the poorer areas, such as Burngreave, are six times more likely to die in their first year of life than those living in affluent areas such as Dore.

Evidence of the poor state of health of the nation as a whole in 1900 was illustrated during the Boer War in South Africa, when half the recruits to the army from the working-class areas were turned away because they were physically unfit to go and fight.

However, some good had developed from the tragedies of war abroad. The terrible conditions of the Crimean War of the 19th century, when England, France and Turkey were fighting Russia, resulted in the death of 20,000 British soldiers. 17,000 of these deaths were through disease, and it was only through the exceptional efforts of a British nurse by the name of Florence Nightingale, that many thousands more did not die. After this war, she introduced training for nurses and set up special schools, and by the beginning of this century, trained nurses were giving help to the sick. By 1902, a Midwives Act had also been passed requiring midwives to be trained and registered with a Central Midwives Board.

> **Did You Know** that in the late 1800s, poor children in Sheffield were wrapped in brown paper and lard to keep them warm in winter? They were also sewn into their clothes for up to six months as their parents couldn't afford to buy any warm ones.

But poverty was still a problem, and having babies they could not afford made mothers turn to drastic remedies. Although contraceptives in the form of condoms had been available at chemists from the late 1880s, their cost at about 15p a dozen was prohibitive, as a third of all families still lived on £1 a week or less. "Back-street" abortion was thus resorted to by many of the poor, with "old wives tales" remedies being tried in desperation. This resulted in terrible pain and suffering being endured by the poverty stricken, pregnant women.

However, by 1921 birth control clinics had been introduced with low priced contraceptives being made available. Abortion became legal in 1967, and by 1974 the Family Planning Act brought birth control clinics under National Health Service control, with free contraception and advice being made available.

> **Did You Know** that very large families in Sheffield were not uncommon in the late 19th and early 20th centuries? Fred and Joseph D, for example, had 19 children, 14 of whom survived. Child number three had a daughter who became a fan dancer at the Hippodrome Theatre, who subsequently became engaged to (but never married) John Walsh of the department store family. The 13th daughter was equally "struck" with fame. She married George Binns, the Sheffield barber who funded the first wooden seated Charabanc which subsequently evolved into the Booth & Fisher bus company. Joseph the father, had a more modest claim to fame as he ran the bar of the prestigious Grand Hotel in Barker's Pool, now the site of the "Fountain Precinct".

Although the National Insurance Act had been introduced in 1911, with provision being made for pensions, unemployment and sick pay, medical treatment was not free until the introduction of the National Health Service in 1948. Whilst the National Insurance Act had given sickness benefits for those in work of 50p a week for men and 37p a week for women, the decision to make health-care free to everyone in the country was the most important social event of this or any other century.

It was, of course, inevitable that demands on this vast and costly service would continue to grow as more sophisticated medical treatment was developed and people lived much longer. This has led to a steady rise in private medical provision, with Sheffield having several private hospitals and care centres, used mainly by the better off.

Coupled with these health-care provisions, other measures had been taken early in the century with free school meals being given to poorer children in 1906, school medical inspections beginning the year after, and old-age pensions being introduced in 1908. Earnings had to be less than £31.50 a year to qualify for a pension, which began at 25p a week for single people over 70, and 37p for married couples.

Of considerable importance to the health and quality of living, was the introduction of physical improvements to the way people lived. This commenced with the demolition of slums in 1900, and continued, with a break during the wars, into the 1960s. The substitution of removable metal bins for the fixed ashpits containing refuse also started at this time, as did the conversion of privy middens into water closets feeding into sewers. This process took about 30 years to complete, during which time many toilets still remained outside.

Did You Know that double-seated toilets still existed in Sheffield in the early 1900s, when privacy and modesty were less important than necessity?

Early 1900s 'dustbin man' with rubbish and paper collection.

Piped water was also a major improvement in achieving better health, and by 1914, all but a handful of the city's 107,000 houses were on "on tap". Bathing was, nevertheless, still a problem as only a sixth of the city's houses had baths by this time, and the "warm front – cold back" process of using the zinc bath tub in front of the open fire was still the most common method in use. The Corporation did, however, provide Public Baths, and the number of bathers using them rose from 267,000 a year in 1899 to 709,000 in 1914.

The building of a new sewage works at Blackburn Meadows in 1905 was also a sign of better things to come. This was a big improvement on the situation which existed for most of the 1800s, during which time the town's sewage was discharged untreated into rivers. The old rubble sewers of the town were also beginning to be replaced by solid pipes, and streets and yards were being paved. Tarmac was used for road surfacing for the first time in Sheffield in 1905, with Wincobank Avenue and Glossop Road being the two roads to benefit.

If we take a brief look at poverty in Sheffield as we approach the millennium, conditions have vastly improved over those which existed 100 or more years ago. The standard of living for everyone has increased beyond recognition, with many families now owning one or two cars, most having televisions and telephones, and many having holidays abroad. Pubs and clubs are packed with people of all ages most nights and fast-food outlets rarely seem to be short of customers.

However, surveys carried out in the 1980s and 1990s have shown that a fifth of all households in the city are dependent on Income Support, and that such payments are generally insufficient to take families out of poverty. When comparing such poverty in different areas of Sheffield, it was shown that 41 per cent of the total households in Burngreave were dependent on income support, whilst at the other end of the scale, only 4½ per cent of those in Ecclesall were dependent. Other areas such as Castle, Manor and Park had similarly high percentages, whilst wards such as Hallam, Beauchief and Dore fared much better.

Poverty in Sheffield, therefore, still exists to a considerable extent. It is often accompanied by unemployment and boredom, from which vandalism and crime can so easily develop. The poor of today's civilised Sheffield are most certainly better off than their ancestors, but the quality of life of many Sheffielders is still sadly lacking.

The Royal Hospital, Division Street, about 1978.

The 20th century saw the rise and fall of many famous hospitals in Sheffield. By the 1950s Lodge Moor had expanded and become a national centre for spinal injuries, as well as specialising in care for the elderly. Regrettably, this wonderful site was closed in the 1990s to make way for a more lucrative development.

Sheffield Royal Infirmary about 1959.

LIVING IN SHEFFIELD — 1,000 YEARS OF CHANGE

Middlewood Hospital about 1975.

Lodge Moor Hospital.

Northern General Hospital.

The Royal Hallamshire Hospital.

all facets of health care, and is probably the most advanced establishment of its kind in the country.

As part of the City's expansion programme for hospitals, which has established the Northern General, the Hallamshire and the Children's as the nucleus of its provision, the large Sheffield Royal Infirmary sadly closed its doors mid-way through the century. This was followed by the later demolition of the Royal Hospital on Division Street and the closure of the Winter Street TB Hospital, which had changed its name to St George's by that time.

An RAF helicopter brings a patient with a serious spinal injury to Lodge Moor Hospital.

Whilst many other hospitals and annexes have been built city-wide, special mention must be made of the cancer hospital which was built opposite Weston Park. Along with Aids, cancer is the scourge of modern society, and hospitals such as this do much to pioneer successful treatments and cures for the patients who go there.

(d) Education

Education improved by "leaps and bounds" over this century. Following the Education Act of 1902, local Education

Jessop Hospital for women also continued to improve, and extended to accommodate 240 beds by 1978. This hospital is also to close, although its "state of the art" replacement in Broomhill is already in the course of construction. Its new site is adjacent to the 18-storey tower block of the Royal Hallamshire, which was built between 1957 and 1978 as the City's premier hospital.

It is, however, likely that the title of "premier hospital" will now be given to the greatly extended Northern General Hospital at Firvale. In hospital grounds which are so vast that a 15-minute frequency "courtesy bus" now runs within it every day, the "village" of new and improved blocks caters for

Crosspool Primary School, 1938.

Lowfields Primary School at Heeley Bottom in 1907. The pupils are practising for the forthcoming Empire Day pageant.

Authorities became responsible for the maintenance of all elementary schools. By 1915, about 83,000 children were being taught in schools in Sheffield at a cost of about £285,000 a year. Schools such as Lowfield Primary in Heeley bottom in 1907, and Crosspool Primary in 1938 are typical examples of those attended.

Pupils at Manor Lane Council School School in 1926.

Pupils at Sheffield St John's School in 1923-24.

Of particular interest in the early days of schooling, are the pupils themselves, who by the expressions on their faces and the clothes they are wearing, tell a tale far better than I ever could.

Education for those who matured early was provided at Grammar Schools from the mid part of the century. The fortunate pupil who was able to pass the "scholarship", and later the "11 plus", was able to attend those schools and receive a better education, with access to Universities thereafter. Schools such as King Edward the VII ("King Ted's"), Firth Park Grammar (the "Red Caps") and High Storrs were three such schools at that time.

King Edward VII School about 1972.

In 1969, however, Comprehensive Education revolutionised the school system. Boys were taught with girls in the new comprehensive, co-educational schools which were introduced across the city. The old Grammar and Technical Schools provided for children of both sexes from 11 to 18, whilst the old Secondary Modern Schools accommodated those from 11 to 16 years old. At that time, there were 31 such schools with 13 having sixth forms. Eventually, most schools were able to provide post-16 education for those who wanted it.

Private schools continued to provide education for those who could afford it, with the Birkdale School for boys being the oldest surviving, and the Ashdell Preparatory School for girls being at least 40 years old.

Sheffield College's Stradbroke Centre which was closed in 1998.

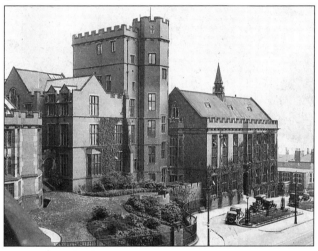

University of Sheffield about 1947.

University education was available in Sheffield from as early as 1905, when its buildings at Western Bank were opened with 100 full-time students. Nearly a century later, the University of Sheffield has become a vast business, with large land holdings and a student population of about 20,000 a year.

Hallam University also now exists in its own right, having developed from the Sheffield Polytechnic, which itself was formed by the merging of the Sheffield Colleges of Technology and Art in 1969.

Last but not least, Sheffield has about 50 centres offering adult education under the umbrella of the Sheffield College, with its four main centres at Castle, Loxley, Norton and Parson Cross. These centres provide learning for a host of

activities ranging from needlecraft to car maintenance, lip reading to photography, cookery to computers, horticulture to health and safety, and hundreds more.

There is little need for Sheffielders to be uneducated in today's modern society, as with a little time, effort and determination, virtually everyone can have access to this essential ingredient of life.

(e) Industry

The huge changes which took place in the 19th century, were equally matched by those which took place during the last hundred years, as the lighter trades of cutlery and silverware manufacture continued alongside the expanding heavy and special steels trades. Of particular importance was the

Sheffield Polytechnic viewed from Arundel Gate in about 1971.

Did You Know that Viner's Silverware Company of Sheffield did considerable business with Schindler & Co Limited of Bohemia through their London Office in the 1930s? Schindler's company manufactured all kinds of high-quality cut-glass goods for use by silversmiths and other manufactures. Oscar Schindler's list of uses, shown on the back of the company's business card, was far shorter than the one he produced in the 1940s during his unselfish help of persecuted Jews during World War Two.

invention of Stainless Steel in 1913 by a Sheffield born steelworker by the name of Harry Brearley. His invention revolutionised steel production, and influenced both heavy and light trades alike. A brief look at each would probably help to paint the picture.

If we begin with the lighter trades, we find that during the first 30 years of the century, about 10,000 to 14,000 people were employed in cutlery manufacture, between 5,000 and 10,000 in the manufacture of files, saws and other tools, and between 10,000 and 12,000 in silver and other small trades.

The men were involved in forging, grinding, hardening and hafting (handle making) in the steel trades, together with plating, engraving, chasing and handraising in the silver trades. Women more traditionally carried out buffing, burnishing, spoon and fork filing, file cutting and scissor furnishing, and represented about a third of the workforce in these trades.

Wages in those days still discriminated against women who earned on average about 11s 7d (58p) a week and girls a mere 6s 10d (34p). Adult men, on the other hand, earned on average about 31s 2d a week (£1.56) with lads and boys only averaging about 9s 8d (48p).

There were dozens of works, both large and small, employing these workers, whilst many others were basically self employed "little mesters" who either worked on their own or employed one or two helpers. During World War One in 1914 to 1918, most of the large cutlery producers were instructed by the Government to produce items for the war effort, such as bayonets, helmets, magazine cases and the like. During the depression of the 1920s and early '30s which

Typical scene in a cutlery grinders' workshop in the 1920s.

Workers at the Cricket Inn road works in the early 1900.

followed, competition was fierce, and the "little mesters" tried to survive by cutting prices to the bone, and became unpopular with their much larger rivals.

By 1924, about 500 firms were involved in the manufacture of cutlery and about £1 million worth of products were exported. Australia was Sheffield's best customer, taking about one third of all its exports.

With the expectancy of a second world war looming, industry again picked up from 1935, and in 1939, when Germany invaded Poland and Britain declared war on Germany, the industry once again concentrated on the war effort. It was the consequence of this war that brought about the eventual decline of the cutlery industry, and to put this in context, a brief résumé of events leading up to this would probably be useful.

Firth Brown's Steelworks in 1980.

Following Britain's declaration of war on Germany, Japan bombed Pearl Harbour and invaded Singapore in 1941, thus unofficially declaring war on America and Britain. By 1945, both Germany and Japan had been defeated and occupied by the Allies. Germany was divided into two, with the Russians occupying the East, and the Western powers of America, Britain and France occupying the Western half. Communist governments were then set up in those countries liberated by the Russians, whilst those liberated by Western powers had their governmental systems restored. Europe was thus divided into two camps, Eastern Communist governments and western democratic governments.

You may be forgiven at this stage for wondering what this has to do with Sheffield's cutlery industry! Well, the explanation will now follow. In order to stop Communism from spreading to those countries whose economies were poor, America poured money and mass production know-how into Japan, with Western Germany also receiving much financial aid to rebuild its industries. By the mid-1950s, both Japan, with its low labour costs and new industries, and Germany, with its new automatic manufacturing systems, produced high quality goods at low prices which came on to the Western markets. By the early 1960s, Sheffield was struggling to compete with this influx of cutlery, particularly from Japan, and within a few years many of its cutlery manufacturers had closed down.

Although this situation stabilised in the mid-1970s, with Japan's prices increasing as its workers demanded fairer wages, cheap stainless steel products flooded in from Hong Kong. This was followed by cheap, poorer quality silverware and the added problem of poor quality copies also now coming from Korea. This latest influx of cheaper goods all but destroyed the "home grown" quality market, and by the early 1980s, the work force had shrunk to about 4,000, with only a few dozen "little mester" still operating. But the tale of woe stops there!

The city now has 100 or so cutlery and silverware manufacturers and wholesalers producing or handling goods of the very highest quality and Sheffield cutlery continues to be the best in the world, still being based on craftsmanship which has been built up over 700 years.

The story of Sheffield, of course, is also about its huge steelworks which continued to grow. By the beginning of the century, Vickers had bought a Birmingham gun and ammunition company to form Vickers, Sons & Maxim, and in 1903 Cammell & Company amalgamated with a shipbuilding firm in Birkenhead to become Cammell, Laird and Co. In the meantime John Brown and Mark Firth were taking steps towards amalgamation, and by 1931 had become the huge complex of Firth Brown.

A more modern method of melting steel was also introduced at this time as electricity was used as a power source. The Electric Arc Furnace was now in use in which tons of scrap metal awaited contact with long, thick carbon electrode rods which were lowered through the roof of the furnace. The massive current passing down these rods created blinding sparks and vast amounts of heat as they touched the steel scrap, which was turned to a bath of molten metal in one or two hours.

The numbers working in these heavy steelmaking trades rose quickly at the beginning of the century, being about 38,000 in 1910 and 65,000 in 1920, although during the peak pre-war years of 1913-14, the figure probably reached nearer 70 to 80,000. During this time, Sheffield was the industrial powerhouse behind the country's war effort. Its mills rolled armour plate for the navy's Dreadnoughts, huge guns were cast for ships and tanks, and thousands of shells were manufactured.

In the depression years of 1920 onwards, unemployment

BSC Tinsley Park. The casting bay, electric arc melting shop.

HMS Sheffield, broken up in 1959

'Shiny Sheff 3', a Class Type 22 frigate.

'Shiny Sheff 2', lost in the Falklands, with 22 dead and many more injured after being sunk by an Exorcet missile.

lay like a huge dark shadow over the city, and at its peak more than half the adult men in the iron and steel trades were out of work. Of a total registered city-wide labour force of 171,000 in 1932, more than 60,000 were unemployed, and Sheffield experienced one of its darkest periods. During the desperate years between 1922 and 1939, over 50,000 left the city to try and find work elsewhere.

Greater efforts were now made for improved efficiency, and further amalgamations took place over these years as Vickers joined with Cammell-Laird to become the English Steel Corporation, which in turn combined its stainless steel interests with those of Firth-Brown. The large works of Steel, Peech & Tozer also combined with Samuel Fox of Stocksbridge, together with several other complementary firms in Sheffield, Frodingham and Workington, to create the United Steel Companies Limited.

The 47-hour week was also agreed in 1918 between employers and unions, although overtime brought the usual working week up to about 55 hours. Wages were quite high for the iron and steel workers in smelting and rolling, at about £3 a week, although general engineering workers earned about 10s (50p) less.

It was during the 1930s that the *HMS Sheffield* was built by Vickers Armstrong. This Southampton Class cruiser, bristling with guns and torpedoes, was the pride of the Navy, and was nick-named the "Shiny Sheff" because of her stainless steel fittings from Sheffield. Following her launch in 1936, and after many years active service, she was eventually broken up in 1959, to be replaced 12 years later by a guided missile destroyer, the first of the Royal Navy's Type 42. Sadly, it was the Falklands War in 1982 which saw the early demise of "Shiny Sheff 2," which sank on 10 May, having been hit by an Exorcet missile. Twenty people died and 24 more were injured in the disaster. Let us hope that the new "Shiny Sheff 3," a Broadsword, Class Type 22 frigate, will fare better.

During the war years of 1939 to 1945, Sheffield's huge steelworks geared up once again to supply the Forces. The English Steel Corporation (previously Vickers), for example, had a huge, steam-powered drop hammer that forged crankshafts for spitfires and other planes. As this was the only drop hammer in the country capable of producing such forgings during the first two years of the war, Sheffield's contribution to Britain's defence by this product alone was enormous.

However, many more vital components for Britain's fighting machines were made including parts for tanks and battleships by ESC, gun forgings, shells and torpedo vessels at Steel, Peach & Tozer, armour castings for tanks at Edgar Allen's, armour plate and armour-piercing shells by Firth Brown's, and gun barrels by Brown Bailey's.

A visit to Tinsley Park Steelworks by the City Council's Clean Air Committee in 1964.

The demolition of Hadfield's great steelworks in the 1980s, on the site of today's Meadowhall Shopping Centre.

Sheffield Foremasters, Brightside Lane.

In the years following the war, demand for steel remained high, and order books were full, despite other countries developing as major competitors. Hundreds of different types of special and high grade steels were being produced, and Sheffield was still the "steel capital" of the world. The city also gained the reputation of being the world's cleanest industrial city during the 1960s, as the City Council introduced its smoke-control policy with strictness and determination.

But as time moved on, worldwide demand for steel began to fall. Competition became fiercer, and the need for efficiencies led to cost cutting and job losses. More sophisticated processes meant that less people were needed on the shop floor, and by 1970, the number of people working in the steel manufacturing industry had reduced to 45,000. This was still about a sixth of the city's working population, but the decline was to continue. Within ten years, this figure had reduced to 25,000, and the 1980s saw the closure and demolition of many of the city's great steel producing works. By 1987, only 6,000 people were working in this once massive industry, which at its peak had employed almost half the working population of Sheffield.

But all is not what it seems. Sheffield is still a major producer of steel, and many people still work in the steel related industry. About 7,000 people are still employed in steel manufacture, whilst another 13,000 or so are employed in the making of tools, cutlery and other metal goods. In 1992, the companies of British Steel Stainless and Avesta AB from Sweden merged to form Avesta Sheffield, whose impressive works stand proudly on Shepcote Lane and also in Stocksbridge. Now, Avesta Sheffield ranks as one of the world's leading manufacturers and suppliers of stainless steel, with a product range and an international network second to none.

Another famous works which still dominates the Upwell Street to Weedon Street section of Brightside Lane in Sheffield's East End is Sheffield Forgemasters, which was formed in 1982 by the merger of British Steel's River Don Works and Firth Brown in one of the Thatcher Government's

Phoenix steel privatisation schemes. Following a £26 million management buy-out in 1988 and, latterly, ownership by an American company, Forgemaster is now renowned as a world leader, and the recent improvements to the old Vickers Works on Brightside Lane have created an image of optimism for the future, rather than sad reflections of the past. Its works on Carlisle Street are of particular importance, as they produce the special "steels of tomorrow" which supply the steady demand from the Eurospace industry.

Last but not least in Sheffield's "Big Three" is the vast complex of British Steel at Stocksbridge, which almost overshadows the "township". This company, which was previously the old United Steels, makes a multitude of steels, and is a physical reminder of the days of yesteryear.

There are many other steel producers, fabricators, and stockholders in Sheffield which make up the whole steel picture, including the long established Tinsley Wire Limited of Attercliffe Common fame. A more recent company which has made its mark, for example, is Aurora Forgings on Meadowhall Road, which won the forging industry's top award for innovation in 1997 by developing a way of producing hi-tech hollow forgings for power stations. And so I could go on.

But the message is clear and should be remembered. It was not the steel industry that all but disappeared in our city; it was the huge works and most of its workers. Sheffield still produces the same amount of steel now as it ever did in the past, but without the aid of most of its people. New technology, computer controlled systems, all electric power and vacuum melting, still allow a million tons or so of "normal" and "special" steel to be produced each year. So let us all remember; steel is still shining brightly in Sheffield!

So what do Sheffielder's do, if they no longer sweat over furnaces in huge steel works?

There are about 200,000 people working in Sheffield. About 150,000 of these work in the service industry. This all-embracing title includes: council services, emergency services, professional services, finance and administration, education, health, hospitals and social services, distribution and catering, recreation, culture, sport and leisure, and retail outlets such as shops.

Another 40,000 people work in manufacturing industries.

About 20,000 of these are involved in an assortment of businesses, including mechanical and electrical products, household and office products, and the delights of food and drink. The other 20,000 work with steel, with about 13,000 involved in the production of tools, cutlery and all other metal goods, and 7,000 remaining in steel production itself.

That leaves about 10,000 people who work in the construction industry. Houses, roads, bridges, sewers and all other buildings come into this category, including the city council's own construction and maintenance workforce.

So there we have it. A city of variety and change. 40,000 of us make something, 20,000 of us sell something, 10,000 of us build and repair something, and the remaining 130,000 workers do their best to make sure we all have a happy and meaningful life. What more could we ask for?

(f) Roads and Transport

The Electric Tram had just arrived by 1900, and for the first four years they were all double-deckers with open tops. By 1903, the first covered top-deck tram had arrived, although it would be another four years before one would be fitted with glass to protect the driver. It was luxury indeed, however, in 1911, when the first totally enclosed tramcar hit the road.

Early 1900s electric tram in Walkley.

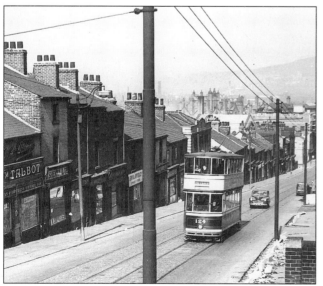

Mid-1950s tram on Duke Street.

Fares had remained at a penny a ride up until World War One, at which time they were doubled, and it wasn't until 1930 that they were reduced again to "three ha'pence". With all this extra money coming in, leather seats replaced the old wooden slats in 1926, and journeys now became a pleasure.

Apart from the time during the blitz of 1940, the trams ran continuously and with great demand. They could cope with nearly all weathers and, to coin a well-known phrase, they were the best thing since sliced bread!

However, the 1950s saw a rapid increase in the use of motor cars, and a decision was made, wrongly in my mind, that the tramcar routes should be closed. It was with enormous sadness and nostalgia that the last tram, No. 510, ran on 8 October 1960.

It was about the same time as the introduction of the electric tram that motor buses took to the streets, the first public vehicle being a "country bus" which ran along Manchester Road and out to Lodge Moor in 1913. Buses were also under the umbrella of the Sheffield Corporation Tramways, and in this year, the Tramway Department stock was 279 trams and ten buses.

> **Did You Know that in the 1930s, cyclists and ramblers often called at Wymingbrook Farm out at Redmires for a salmon tea costing about 11d (4p)? The Corporation bus ran as far as Lodge Moor Hospital on Bank Holiday Mondays, and passengers had to alight there and walk the rest of the way. Queues of up to 100 hungry people were not unusual at that time, and as well as selling teas, chocolate and crisps were also available.**

Bus body-building began at Queens Road Depot in 1915 for a 27-seat single decker, and by the following year, 21 buses were sharing the depots with 339 trams. During the war, about 1,100 men and 1,000 women were employed on the buses and trams, but when the men came home from the war, the position changed, with 1,500 men and 800 women driving and punching tickets. By this time, in 1920, 37 buses and 373 trams were carrying about 150 million passengers a year.

As with the trams, it took some time to provide cover to the top of the double-decker buses, but it eventually arrived in 1927. Bus types were also changing, and the 1930s saw the introduction of the Titanics. Demand was still rising, however, and a temporary bus loading station was built at Pond Street in 1936 to cope with the 247 buses which now shared the road space with 426 trams.

World War Two once again saw the depletion of manpower, and 1,600 women were called upon to help, mostly as conductresses. By 1946, the number of trams on the roads had not changed, yet bus numbers increased to 461. With the writing on the wall for trams, bus numbers escalated, and by that fateful year of 1960, when not a tram was to be seen after 8 October, 861 buses were polluting the streets with the ever-increasing number of cars.

Atlantean buses made their appearance at this time. They were 78-seaters with the engine at the rear. The entrance was also forward of its front wheels and the door was controlled by the driver. Gone were the days that you could sprint alongside as the bus pulled off and "just make it" via the door at the rear.

Now they're here to stay, but instead of being operated by the Corporations Transport Department, or from 1974 the South Yorkshire Passenger Transport Executive (which does much the same thing but sounds much more "posh"), private operators roam the streets preying on passengers and swallowing them up before their rivals can arrive. Mainline has been the biggest operator in the city, although this has now been taken over by "First Mainline".

I wonder how long they will last?

Did You Know that William Morris made his first Morris car in August of 1911.

Although we've started with public transport, it is the car that has created most of the congestion and pollution on the roads. Cars arrived in 1900, with the Hallamshire and the Churchill, and by 1905, the Sheffield Motor Company on Broomhall Street was making the Cavendish. For the sporty types, the Richardson Light Car, an 8 to 10hp, two or three-seater model was built in 1919 costing £250. Petrol consumption was guaranteed at 50 to 60 miles per gallon, and its friction wheel drive avoided the need for a gearbox! To say that it was simple was the understatement of the year, as it had no instruments, no front wheel brakes and simply operated by a chain drive to the rear axle. Compare that with today's Porsche at probably 150 times the cost, and we get some idea of a century's progress!

From these simple beginnings, over 50 million cars now travel the country's roads. Nearly half of all households have a car and over a fifth of them have two. The roads continue to

become more congested, yet people will not leave their cars at home. This is clearly shown by looking at travel habits over the last 45 years or so. In 1955, 46 per cent of people travelling used car, van or motorcycle, with 38 per cent using bus or coach, and the remaining 16 per cent going by train. By 1997 the numbers of travellers using car, van or motorcycle had risen to 88 per cent with only six per cent using bus/coach and train.

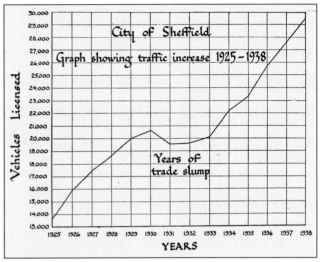

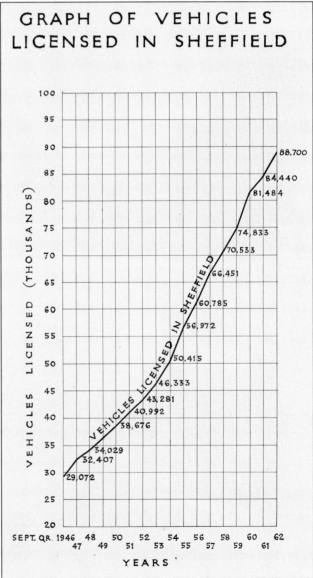

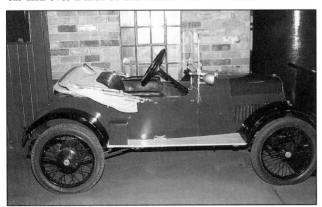

Richardson's Light Car, 1919.

But let us have a brief look at how Sheffield has dealt with this situation.

After World War Two, the City Council produced a major policy document entitled *Sheffield Replanned*. This document identified the then significant problems caused on the city roads by trams and buses, and the photograph showing Haymarket at that time is evidence of this. In addition, it identified the need for an Outer Ring Road, which more or less existed on the present road layout, an Inner Ring Road to facilitate the movement of traffic round the central area, particularly at peak hours, and a Civic Circle within which a civic and central shopping precinct would be located. The Civic Circle would thus provide for ease of movement of the large volume of traffic in the centre of the city brought about by the normal shopping and business activities of the city.

Traffic volumes had already risen by 100 per cent between 1925 and 1939, and the council considered it prudent to plan for a similar doubling of traffic in the future.

Despite road improvements being carried over the next 15 years or so, it was not until the 1960s that construction on the Inner Ring Road and the Civic Circle began. In its policy document *A Plan for Traffic*, issued in 1963, traffic surveys illustrated that the number of vehicles in the city had increased three-fold over the last 23 years, and designs had to be adjusted to suit. Indeed, with Department of Transport predictions indicating a further doubling by 1970, the Council decided to adopt these figures for the purpose of their road design. Thus, the 1939 figure of 29,000 vehicles was predicted to increase more than five fold to an estimated 167,000 by 1970.

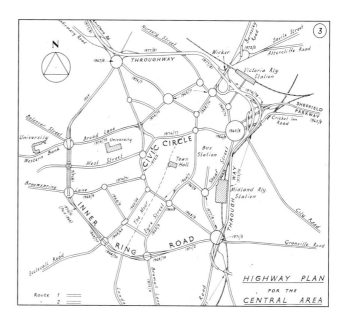

The first and only section of the Civic Circle was built in 1960s along with the famous Hole in the Road, and was known as Arundel Gate. Ambitious plans for the Inner Ring Road were also proposed, and the huge Tinsley Viaduct now brought the M1 motorway into the city. But, as traffic volumes soared, Government finance reduced. During the 1970s the Sheffield Parkway link to the M1 motorway was constructed, but the Government's policy regarding the provision of large, high capacity ring roads was also changing, and an emphasis on managing traffic rather than building urban motorways was its clear message.

Within another ten years, the number of vehicles coming in and out of the central area of the city had reached about a quarter of a million, with 200,000 of them being cars. The southern part of the Inner Ring Road between Bramall Lane and Shalesmoor was by now built or in the course of construction, although not to the scale originally envisaged. And the traffic still continued to increase.

The overall picture had now changed. People were also being given priority over traffic. No longer was it considered desirable for the public to go under subways or over bridges to penetrate the centre of town whilst the traffic retained all priority. The Civic Circle was no longer realistic, as it created a busy barrier to safe and convenient access by pedestrians to the centre. And the city could no longer cope with the demands on its roads, with traffic movement on a "knife-edge", ready to grind to a halt if an accident blocked a main carriageway, or we had more than two inches of snow.

This was life in the 1990s, and something had to be done. Traffic management now directs most through traffic on to a gradually improving Inner Ring Road. The Hole in the Road has gone, and Furnival Gate has been downgraded. An ultra modern, environmentally friendly and very regular tramway

system has been built to try and provide motorists with an attractive alternative to the car. The

Sheffield's unique, but no longer, Hole-in-the-Road.

Congestion in the Haymarket, just after World War One.

major bus companies are striving to improve the reliability and quality of their services and integrate with the Supertram System. But still the traffic continues to increase.

What is the answer? It's difficult to know. Some say that the motorists love their cars as much as their partners, and they're not given up easily! Only time will tell. There is no doubt that the completion of a good Inner Ring Road will go a long way to help. The continued improvement of good, reliable and attractively priced public transport is also essential. There is even talk of charging those who wish to drive into town, although this would probably only be as a last resort.

But the key to it all is YOU! Only the public can make it work. Attitudes are difficult to change, and force is always resisted. Discussion, co-operation and trust will lead to the answer, but when, I don't really know.

Finally, in this section on transport, a brief mention of four different modes of travel, often used for pleasure as well as necessity, need to be mentioned.

The much used motor coach began with the Charabanc in 1907. The first of these to be used in Sheffield was called The Roscoe, and with its solid rubber tyres and open-to-the-

The first SYR passenger train to Barnsley in 1854.

An express steam train flying through Darnall Station.

Early 1900s charabanc, all ready to take passengers of a pub outing.

weather seating, it gave an exciting ride to its 30 passengers. Unfortunately, this coach had an accident on its return trip from Hathersage to the George Hotel in Boston Street in August of that year whilst it was overtaking a carriage and two horses. Whilst only travelling at its maximum speed of 7mph, two men and a seven-year-old boy were killed as the coach hit a telegraph pole and crashed into a wall. Editorial comment at that time was critical of such huge machines travelling at terrific speeds, and posed the question "can there be any future in Sheffield for these motor vehicles?"

The "Sharrabang", as Sheffielders commonly called them

for the next 50 years, became the usual means of travel to the coast at holiday times. Many a child proudly told a friend, "We're goin' on a "Sharra" to the seaside today!"

The railways, of course, were already here, but during this century, the town centre services were consolidated and moved to the Midland Station. A reminder of what used to be still exists in the form of the majestic Victoria Station Hotel, which still stands proudly at the top of the Station Approach overlooking the City.

Gone, however, are the wonderful days of shrieking whistles, the sudden hiss of steam and the mighty belch of white and grey smoke as the magnificent trains of old lumbered out of the station. Gone also are the days when excited school children stood on fences, waving their arms and shouting with glee as the 6.15 Express thundered past. Nearly every child wanted to be an engine-driver in the good old days of steam. Now, the sophistication of diesel and electricity have increased speeds and shortened times of travel. But they have also got rid of the magic!

For the thousands of Sheffielders who now go abroad for their holidays, flying is the usual means of travel. Despite

Sheffield City Airport, opened in June 1997.

The opening of Sheffield's Victoria Quays in 1997.

being the fourth largest city in the country, Sheffield never had an airport. Many discussions were held at political level, both locally and nationally from the 1950s onwards, but it was not until June 1997 that Sheffield City Airport was opened. Built on the site of old Sheffield steelworks, which was subsequently worked as a 100-metre deep open-cast coal mine, Sheffield's long-awaited airport is thriving following its inaugural scheduled service to Amsterdam in February 1998. It is owned by Tinsley Park Limited, and also provides the base for the South Yorkshire Police Air Support Unit, who's helicopter regularly tours the city's skies on the look-out for trouble. Executive Aviation, who provide the "eye in the sky" light aircraft for local radio traffic reports, are also based here.

Lastly, I must mention the canal. This stretch of water from the city centre to Meadowhall has been greatly improved and is now used for pleasure trips in brightly coloured barges. The canal basin has been completely renovated, and was opened as Victoria Quays in 1997. The magnificent walk along the canal towpath has to be experienced to be believed, and for those who are fit enough, the return journey along 5 Weirs Walk on the banks of the River Don is equally as good. Sheffield has come a long way since the pollution and rats of yesteryear, and hundreds of fishermen now line the banks of both waters, catching fish once more.

So, now Sheffield has it all. Road, rail, air and water are at our disposal. We can go anywhere in the world by any means we wish. But I'm sure there's more to come.

(g) Recreation and Entertainment – Sport

This aspect of Sheffield's history has developed into one of the most influential and significant of any change that has taken place over this last 100 years, in particular sport.

Throughout the century, Sheffield's two major football clubs have developed into £multi-million enterprises, with Sheffield Wednesday still "lording" it in the premier division and Sheffield United hard on their heels. The 70,000 mostly-standing grounds of the good old days have become the 35,000 all-seaters stadiums of today. And what about the costs? In 1900, for example, Sheffield Wednesday paid out £360 in transfer fees and by 1925, the figure had risen to a massive £7,733. Today, the managers talk in £millions for anyone who might be classed as good! Gone also are the days of the maximum £20 wage for a star, as the player's agent (can you believe it) won't even start talking below "ten grand" a week!

Sheffield Wednesday team in 1950.

But there's one thing that is a little disappointing. It is the poorer support that the teams sometimes attract. With present day crowds of between 10,000 and 20,000 on a good day, they lag behind those of their predecessors. When The Wednesday played Manchester United in 1907, for example, a crowd of 43,143 came out to watch, and paid £1,100 for the privilege. A local derby fared even better, as in 1923 the game

Sheffield United team in 1953.

They're off! Greyhound racing in Sheffield.

against Barnsley brought in 66,250 fans and record receipts of £4,911.

I could, of course, write a book simply on these two teams, but I think we'll settle for an interesting set of statistics regarding the early period of their lives: Sheffield United and Sheffield Wednesday played each other 106 times during the period between their first match in 1890 and the end of 1925. Wednesday won 42 of these encounters and United won 36, with 28 being drawn. The goal tally was pretty evenly matched with United scoring 131 goals and Wednesday scoring 141. Most of the games were very tight, with the only real "thrashings" being 4-0 and 5-0 to Wednesday in 1918, and 5-0 and 5-0 to United in 1891 and 1896. All in all, the two teams were very evenly matched for the first 35 years of their existence, and have more or less kept that way ever since.

Huge crowds were often the order of the day at football matches. This pictures shows spectators at Hillsborough

Many other sports were played in Sheffield in the early years of the century. The Sheffield Hockey Club had its first pitch in the grounds of Woodthorpe Hall by 1900, and in 1902, the Sheffield Rugby Union Football Club was founded, playing at first on the ground at Sandygate before later moving to Abbeydale Park. Sheffield Tigers also had a ground at Dore.

Golf was very popular all over the city as it is now, and crown green bowling, tennis and fishing were not far behind.

Greyhound racing was introduced to the city in 1927 at the new track in Darnall, although confusion reigned on its first night of opening as the hare went backwards around the track! This sport is still going strong at the Owlerton Sports Stadium, where speedway and stock car racing have also enjoyed popularity for decades.

A particular favourite in Sheffield in the 1940s and 1950s was roller skating, and both children and adults alike could be seen in the parks, on the streets and in the many indoor rinks in the city. Many an enjoyable hour was spent in the large rink on West Street, the Empire in Aizlewood Road, or the American at the corner of John Street and Shoreham Street in the grounds of Sheffield United FC.

Ice skating became popular at the Queens Road ice rink in the 1970s, and this has developed into a major professional sport by the renowned Sheffield Steelers. Basketball has

Ice hockey with the Sheffield Steelers.

likewise progressed from a school day activity to one of international status, with the Sheffield Sharks and their "sisters" the Hatters beating all before them at present.

Swimming, of course, has always been popular and an activity which most children could enjoy. The Corporation's swimming baths have been attended by hundreds of thousands of people of all ages, and the magnificent new facilities built in the city during the early 1990s has also led

Basketball with the Sheffield Sharks.

Women's basketball with the Sheffield Hatters.

Sheffield's world champion Seb Coe in action.

to Sheffield hosting international competition in this sport.

The 1950s saw the building of the large, modern Athletics track in Hillsborough Park to satisfy a demand for facilities for this ever popular sport. The amazing world beater, Seb Coe, was a product of tracks such as these, but eventually Sheffield would do even better.

Snooker had always been popular during this century, but with the advent of television, it reached the national stage. Sheffield now hosts the World Championships every year at "The Crucible", and for two weeks in May, is on show to the world.

The hosting of the World Student Games in Sheffield in 1991 was the catalyst for its progression to becoming the country's primary City of Sport. State of the art sporting facilities were built at a cost of £147 million to accommodate the world's elite. The Olympic standard Don Valley Athletics Stadium, with its innovative award winning roof structure, was built in 1990 at a cost of £28 million, along with the Ponds Forge International Swimming, Sports and Leisure Centre costing about £52 million. The Don Valley Arena was

Snooker stars Steve Davies, Willie Thorne and Dennis Taylor get ready for the 1979 World Championships at the Crucible.

Prince Naseem in action against Freddy Cruz in October 1994, at Ponds Forge.

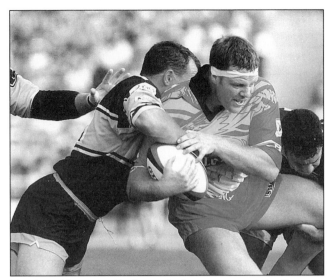

Tough tackling at an Eagles rugby league game at the Don Valley Athletics Stadium.

expensive, but bold initiatives taken by the City Council in promoting the city in this sporting way. One thing is for certain; sport is now a £multi-billion industry, and Sheffield at least "got in" on the ground floor.

Last but not least, I must mention the creative foresight of an enthusiastic skier which resulted in the building of the Sheffield Ski Village at Parkwood Springs. Now as Europe's largest artificial ski resort, it provides thrills and excitement to enthusiasts of all ages on its nine dry ski runs, which range from nursery slopes to those for the very experienced.

It can be clearly seen that Sheffield has much to be proud of as a city of sport. Let us at least enjoy it.

The Don Valley Athletics Stadium.

(h) Recreation and Entertainment – Parks and Gardens

Recreation, of course, is not simply sport, and for those less inclined to be so active, Parks and Gardens are provided in abundance.

Graves Park, which is Sheffield's largest, was formerly the garden estate of Norton Hall and was presented to the city in 1925 by J. G. Graves. It provides open land for walking, and lakes for boating and fishing, together with greens, pitches

the third of these "giants", and was built on the site of the demolished Brown Bayley's Steel Works in 1991 to accommodate ice skating and gymnastics, as well as being used for major music concerts and similar events. The main sporting provisions at this time also included an Olympic standard water polo pool and major sports hall at the Beulah Road Leisure Centre in Hillsborough, as well as the Waltheof Sports Centre for volleyball and basketball on Prince of Wales Road.

History will be the judge of the long-term success of these

Whirlow Brook Park.

and courts for several sporting activities. The park extends from Norton to Woodseats and includes a fine wood through which the public may walk.

Meersbrook Park, which was acquired by Sheffield Corporation in 1886, was originally the grounds of Meersbrook House, the home of a successful banker. Additions to the park were acquired in 1928 and 1964, and the large, attractive grounds have wonderful views over the city.

Hillsborough Hall was built on Middlewood Road in 1779 and was bought 100 years or more later by the Corporation and turned into a branch library. The estate and grounds of the hall are now known as Hillsborough Park, which for many years hosted the city's annual Sheffield Show, which has since moved its home to Graves Park.

At the other end of town, Corcord Park was presented to the city by J. G. Graves in 1929. This park, which is bounded by Wincobank and Shiregreen, is poplar with those who like sport as well as those who simply wish to gaze and wander, and includes tennis courts, football pitches, cricket pitches, bowling greens and a golf course, as well as a playground for children to play in.

There are, of course, many more parks, and worthy of mention are High Hazels Park at Tinsley, Crookes Valley Park on the western side of town, and Millhouses Park in the Sheaf Valley, which was given to the city in 1909 by Earl Fitzwilliam. Its swimming pool was converted to a wonderful Lido in 1969, but was closed some years later as the Corporation could not afford to maintain it.

The valley of the River Porter also has the beautiful open space of Endcliffe Park and Bingham Park alongside it, and a stroll through the adjacent Whiteley Woods leads to the relaxing Wire Mill and Forge Dams, where fishing is very popular.

Last but not least, are the colourful gardens and lawns of Whirlow Brook Park, which were opened to the public in 1946 following their presentation to the city, again by J. G. Graves. Whirlow Brook House was originally the home of Sir Walter Benton Jones but is now popularly used as a café.

So, if it's a relaxing walk which is required by the population of our great city, there are 4,000 or so acres of public open space to choose from!

(i) Recreation and Entertainment – Cinemas

Sheffield has always been a city where a night at the "flicks" was a regular weekly or even twice-weekly treat, and this century was the beginning of that pleasure for millions.

In the beginning, when the Lumiere Brothers invented the Cinematograph in 1895 and toured Sheffield the year after, cinemas were known as Picture Palaces. The first display of animated pictures in the city was during the 1896 Lumiere tour, and took place at the newly-built Empire Theatre. Early shows, which were without music or sound, were short and presented topics of interest in between the usual variety acts. Thus, in 1899 and then again in 1901, the film shows of great interest were the FA Cup Finals of those years in which Sheffield United starred in both.

The News Theatre, Fitzalan Square, as it was in the 1950s.

Elvis Presley's first film *Love Me Tender* was shown about 50 years later. The queues at that time went right round the block, and the screams and tears from his adoring fans inside set the scene for many years to come.

The Gaumont Cinema in Barker's Pool in August 1964.

The first purpose-built cinema in Sheffield was the Sheffield Picture Palace, which opened on 1 October 1910 with a showing of *A Little Heroine of the Civil War* and *Buffalo Hunting in Indo China*. It was at this 1,000-seater cinema that

Amongst the early cinemas in Sheffield was the Albert Hall in Barkers Pool, which opened originally as a theatre in 1873, before changing over to films in 1918. The Electra Palace also opened in Fitzalan Square in 1911, before later becoming the well-known Sheffield News Theatre in 1945. With yet another name change, it became the Classic Cinema in 1962, and remained as such until its demolition 20 years later.

Barkers' Pool was also famous for several other cinemas, with the Cinema House occupying the site of today's new Oxford House from 1913 to 1961. Opposite stood the Regent, which was opened in 1927 before going through a succession of name changes as Gaumont 1, 2 and 3, before finally closing

The Cinema House in Barker's Pool next to Wilson Peck's famous music store in the 1950s.

in 1985. Its replacement by the new Odeon two years later was, however, short-lived, as this only survived until 1994.

Other city centre cinemas of note include the ABC on Angel Street, built in 1961, which, when newly-named The Cannon in 1987, lasted only 18 months before closure. The Hippodrome in Cambridge Street was always very popular, having first been built as a variety theatre in 1907 before its conversion to films in 1931. Its closure in 1963 was a time to remember as it showed *Gone with the Wind* as its final film. Scarlet O'Hara summed up the feeling of the public at its last sad showing, as she finished the film with her famous words: "Tomorrow is another day."

Last but not least in the centre of town was the magnificent new Odeon in Flat Street, adjacent to Fitzalan Square. It was built during the emerging pop scene of the 1950s, but its longest-running film was the Julie Andrews special, *The Sound of Music*, which kept running for over a year.

We could, of course, go on, as many suburban cinemas spring to mind. Many will remember the Adelphi in Attercliffe, the Abbeydale on Abbeydale Road, the Essoldo at Sheffield Lane Top, the Picture Palaces at Crookes and Darnall, the Forum-cum-Essoldo in Southey Green, the Chantry at Woodseats, the Coliseum and the Palace at Heeley, the Kinema at Hillsborough, the Lyric and the Regal in Darnall, the Rex on Mansfield Road, the Roscoe on Infirmary Road, the Scala at Brookhill, the Palaces at Stocksbridge and Tinsley, the Palladium at Walkley and the Palaces at Woodhouse and Woodseats.

The new Odeon Cinema on Furnival Gate.

A total of 78 cinemas have graced our fair city over the years, with a peak of 58 existing between 1945 and 1950. Today we only have a few "mega" cinemas, with Warner Brothers at Meadowhall, the UCI at Crystal Peaks, the Odeon on Arundel Gate, and the giant new Virgin Megaplex at the Valley Centertainment Complex just off Broughton Lane.

We must not forget, however, that what goes around, comes around, and the new Showroom Cinema on Paternoster Row is now screening films of old which you might have missed or would love to see again.

Last, but not least, a special mention must be made of the film *The Full Monty*, which tells the story of Sheffield in the difficult years of the 1980s. The film broke box-office records, and really put Sheffield on the map internationally as the film was a big hit in the USA.

(j) Recreation and Entertainment – Theatres

Whilst not as abundant as cinemas during this century, a visit to the theatre was always a treat to remember. As already mention, the 2,200-seater Albert Hall in Barkers Pool started its life as a theatre, as did the Hippodrome in Cambridge Street.

The Lyceum Theatre in the 1960s.

Sheffield Playhouse in Townhead Street in 1979.

The old Empire Theatre, Charles Street.

The Empire in Charles Street was perhaps the most popular theatre in the city, with its magical presentations of laughter and song being given to thousands of Sheffielders for over half a century. When it opened in 1895, it had cost £65,000 to build, which was an enormous amount of money in those days. Its artists over the years have included many famous names, including Jimmy Jewel and Ben Warris, both Sheffield born and bred. Perhaps one or two will just be able to remember the stars of 1912, when Sara Bernhardt and Lily Langtry performed there at the same time that Anna Pavlova starred at the Lyceum and Annette Kellerman at the Hippodrome.

Alex 'Hurricane' Higgins and David 'The Silver Fox' Taylor at the Crucible in 1979.

The Lyceum, of course, is now the pride of our city, as it was restored to its former glory in 1991, having been closed down and used as a bingo hall about 20 years earlier. In the early 1900s it stood opposite the Theatre Royal on Tudor Street, a site now joined by the revolutionary thrust-stage

The BBC TV link-up to the Crucible Theatre for the World Snooker Championships.

Crucible Theatre, built in 1971. This theatre not only puts on top-class shows, but as already mentioned, it hosts the world-renowned Embassy World Snooker Championships in May of each year and is probably one of the best-known theatres in the country today.

(k) Recreation and Entertainment – Music

Whilst classical music has always been popular at the City Hall with its regular concerts given by the famous Halle Orchestra, it was the Pop and Rock of the 1950s and '60s which really stirred things up in Sheffield.

The Big Band sounds of Joe Loss or Syd Lawrence always filled the auditorium or the ballroom below, but nothing compared to the Rock Spectaculars which took over the stage in those days.

But let us quickly look back at some of those early Sheffield names which set the band-wagon rolling.

One local celebrity who did more than his bit to put Sheffield on the pop-music map was Peter Stringfellow. This ambitious young Sheffielder, who would never take no for an answer, fancied himself as a singer, but with a self-admitted rather poor voice, he decided to concentrate on promotions.

He originally worked as a second projectionist at the Regal Cinema in Attercliffe, but after seven months he moved on to better things. As a more senior projectionist at the Capital Cinema at Sheffield Lane Top, he thought he would make his mark. However, after making a complete hash of the first matinée showing of *Rock Around the Clock*, this job only lasted a few hours. His next venture as a curtain boy at the Lyceum Theatre, where Ronnie Carroll was singing, was no better and this also only lasted for a few hours.

His main rise to fame really began in 1962 when he opened a small "club" in St Aidan's Church Hall on City Road, which he rented from the vicar for £2 10s (£2.50) on Sunday

Dave Berry opening the new Birdcage Boutique at Cockayne's store in 1967.

evenings. Three up and coming groups played there for about £12 each, with the Pursuers being booked for the first gig. The following weeks saw Johnny Tempest and the Cadillacs and the latest local sensation at that time, Dave Berry and the Cruisers. The teenage audiences paid 3s each (15p) to get in, and the clubland scene had been set.

Peter Stringfellow now decided to call his converted church hall the Black Cat club, and paid Screaming Lord Sutch and the Savages £50 to perform there. This flamboyant pop star eventually turned his sights to politics and became the Leader of the Monster Raving Loony Party, with which he stood 41 times for Parliament without success before his sad death in June 1999. At the same time, Stringfellow booked a little known band from Liverpool to appear there in February 1963, although by the time that date arrived, demand for tickets was so high that he had to change the venue to the rather posh new dance hall called the Azena, on White Lane in Gleadless. At a cost of £40 for the hall, and £85 for the group and their manager, he presented The Beatles' first concert in Sheffield to a jam-packed, hysterical audience.

Two other venues were added to Peter Stringfellow's "empire"; another church hall which he called the Blue Moon just off Nursery Street, and a bombed building on Burngreave Road on the top side of Pitsmoor called Day's Dance Hall. The Blue Moon was opened Sunday nights and first hosted Freddy Starr and the Midnighters, whilst the Black Cat booked Long John Baldry and the Hoochy Coochy Men with a second singer called Rod Stuart.

Day's Dance Hall was renamed the Mojo Club (after Long John Baldry's song *Got My Mojo Working*), and for a £30 a week rental, opened as a pop music club with Jimi Hendrix and Ike and Tina Turner starring there in its early years. Rod Stuart appeared there as a singer in his own right in 1964, as did the Yardbirds with their lead guitarist Eric Clapton.

Last but not least in this era of pop, sex and booze, into which drugs had now made their impact, was Vance Arnold and the Avengers. This determined young plumber from Crookes made his main public debut on the Stringfellow promotion at the City Hall on 16 September 1963. Although he didn't do particularly well on this occasion, his persistence and grit, combined with a simple change of name, resulted in his eventual success. This was the beginning of the now international superstar, Joe Cocker of Sheffield.

It wasn't just our friend Mr Stringfellow who promoted the

Joe Cocker enjoys a cup of tea with his mum Marjorie at their Tasker Road home in Crookes.

pop-music scene however. Mr Harry Murray, the manager of the Gaumont Cinema in Barkers Pool introduced Saturday morning Pop Shows in 1959. These shows opened the doors for unknown talents to show off their skills, and the teenagers flocked in by the hundreds.

It should be acknowledged, however, that many groups who played in those days never made it to the top, nor even aspired to do so. With Noon and Night gigs at working men's clubs, they simply enjoyed playing, particularly at the Sunday noon spot when they were often asked to be the backing for the lunchtime stripper!

The Cadillacs in 1959.

Still going strong – The Cadillacs in 1999.

One such group, for example, was the Cadillacs, which also backed Johny Tempest for a while. It was started by base guitarist John Wilson and lead guitarist Barry Brompton, with rhythm and lead guitarist Malcolm Towndrow joining about one year later. Whilst four of the original group of five are no longer playing (although John Wilson admits to humming to himself on the way to the fruit and vegetable market at 5.30 every morning), electrician Barry and safety adviser Malcolm, still play the pubs and clubs two or three times a week to the delight of followers and fans. This duo, with the help of some electronic backing, still perform as the Cadillacs, and continue to be one of the most popular groups on the circuit, 40 years on!

As the years passed, Sheffield produced more home-grown stars. Tony Christie, the super-crooner of the 1970s is now 55, but has teamed up with the modern electronic beatsters All Seeing I. His comeback song *Walk Like a Panther* has hit the Top Ten, 23 years after his last chart entry.

The 1980s saw the rise of two mega-groups in Def Leppard and The Human League, whose record sales were phenomenal, both at home and abroad, with success in the USA being one of their major achievements. The Human League's *Don't You Want Me?* made No.1 both here and in the USA in the early 1980s! And who can forget Pulp and Jarvis Cocker, who rose in the 1980s and are still going strong today? Their latest song, *Disco 2000* is appropriately titled as we reach the Millennium.

Clubs and Pubs

The music scene in Sheffield today has continued to grow, with many new venues providing entertainment and pleasure.

Sheffield's new National Centre for Popular Music.

Crowds of 10,000 or so pack into Sheffield's Arena for regular live shows of international stars, whilst the Don Valley Stadium can hold three or four times that amount for the occasional pop extravaganza.

The clubs and pubs, however, are the nucleus of the exciting Sheffield of today. With clubland vibrating into the early hours of every morning, life doesn't just stop at the bewitching hour of midnight any longer.

Examples of today's city centre clubland scene include The Roxy on Arundel Gate, Uropa on Eyre Street, The Roundhouse in Ponds Forge and The Rhythm Room on Charter Square. The long established Leadmill is well-known across the country for its live music and alternative atmosphere, and the more recent Republic on Matilda Street has also gained national recognition. This club is the venue for Gatecrasher which is held weekly on Saturdays, and now attracts some of the country's top DJ's on a regular basis.

Out of town clubs have also become popular, with Pulse and Vogue drawing in the crowds next to the Arena. The Valley Centertainment complex nearby is the most recent of Sheffield's attractions, with Club Wow and Brannigans bursting at the seams to the pounding of popular music. Eating, drinking and amusements are also on-hand in this all singing, all dancing mini Las Vegas, with Quincey's, Fatty Ar-

Club Wow, Attercliffe.

buckles, Frankie & Benny's and The Hollywood Bowl providing what the customers want.

Last but not least, the city boasts pubs by the score which satisfy the needs of Sheffield's public. Although there are many traditional style pubs around, many "bars" and "café-bars" are now opening.

Division Street is now very popular, with The Forum, Halcyon, Bar Coast and Lloyds setting the scene. The Frog and Parrot is also in this area and boasts that it sells the "World's Strongest Lager", if you dare to drink it!

Other city centre pubs now include the Centro & Breeze, The Old Monk and the Bankers Draft, whilst the older pubs like the Sportsman, the Yorkshireman, the Brown Bear and The Surrey still pull in the customers.

West Street has always been a favourite with the University students, as well as city centre revellers in general. The "normal" pubs there of recent times have now changed to a mixture of theme pubs, Irish pubs and bars as they move with the times and the demands of a changing public.

There are, of course, hundreds more pubs across the city which provide drink, music and food. Family clubs and Working Men's Clubs also provide music and dancing to compliment the city's thriving social scene. Music and entertainment is now "big business"; but it also provides the essential ingredients of relaxation and pleasure, as we all try to "get away" for a few hours from the pressures and stress of our fast moving, modern society.

To underline the importance of music in our lives, Sheffield now hosts the National Centre for Popular Music, a complex of four huge, stainless steel "drums" which house everything and anything to do with music production, music history or the sheer pleasure of just listening. It was conceived nine years ago when the City Council established its Cultural Industries Quarter in the Paternoster Row area. With the support of an £11 million Lottery award and £4 million from European and British Funds, the centre opened in March 1999. Major sponsors such as Philips, Virgin, Vaux Breweries and many others have supported the project to which thousands of Sheffielders, young and old alike, are expected to visit for many years to come.

(l) Sheffield at War: 1914-18

Sheffield suffered from the two major world wars during this century. Whilst they brought inevitable death and destruction, we must remember that they also created hope, comradeship, a deep sense of caring and considerable pride.

Many lives were lost in World War One, as Sheffielders

went abroad to fight. Whilst training and preparation took place in the city, all the action took place on foreign soil in countries as diverse as France and Egypt. The only "invasion" of our shores was the "day of the Zeppelin" on 25 March 1916, when lives were lost in the city.

The Zeppelin was a huge airship designed and built in 1900, which was named after the German Count Zeppelin. It had guns on top of its hull as defence against planes, and a spy basket below which could be lowered beneath cloud level for navigating and directing bombing.

The raid over Sheffield lasted only 15 minutes during which time 36 bombs were dropped and 28 people (almost all women and children) were killed. The batteries of guns and search lights on the Manor, Wincobank Hill and Ecclesall were strangely quiet that night, and it was probably no coincidence that all the officers in charge were attending a ball at the Grand Hotel in Barkers Pool at the time.

But life was precious, and for those whose loved ones had waved a fond farewell, the torture of waiting and hoping was almost beyond understanding.

Let us have a brief look, therefore, at the impact of war through the lives of those everyday people of Sheffield who volunteered their services to Britain's Army at this time of need.

Private Richard Starling, Sheffield Battalion volunteer.

Private Starling was one such man, and be became a member of the 12th (Service) Battalion of the York and Lancashire Regiment, known better as the Sheffield Battalion. He was one of a thousand or more men who had "answered the call" and given up their homes, their professions and their businesses to form an entirely new regiment in a few days in September 1914. Their ages ranged from 19 to 35, and they were ready to die for their country.

The first home of the Battalion was Norfolk Barracks on Edmund Road, previously a popular place for boxing contests, in the ownership of the West Riding Territorial Force Association. Training and squad drill first took place on the Sheffield United Cricket and Football Club's famous ground at Bramall Lane. Extended order drill and attack practise took place amongst the trees of Norfolk Park, and for the first three months the men of the Battalion lived in their own homes. They were a proud lot in their dark blue-grey cloth uniforms, with a matching cap smartened by a thin red stripe.

Colonel C. V. Mainwaring had been appointed as commander, and the Battalion then moved to hutments on the new campsite on Redmires Road, which the Battalion

The Sheffield Battalion at their Lodge Moor Camp.

rented for £100 a year. The site had previously been an old racecourse built in the late 19th century, one of two in the city at the time, the other being on Crookes Moor near to Broomhill. It was one of the highest camping grounds in the country, and training up there in the wild winter storms was certainly good grounding for hardships to come.

The move to the site on 5 December 1914 was preceded by a march through the city, and was accompanied by driving rain and snow. Following five months stay at this camp, the Battalion moved out of Sheffield to Cannock Chase near the small market town of Rugeley near Stafford, before moving again to Ripon and finally on to Hurdcott Camp on Salisbury Plain. This latter part of the men's training was given to rapid preparation for active service, and it was now September 1915, just one year after their voluntary enlistment.

Within three months, the Battalion received orders to prepare for Egypt, and on 21 December 1915, they left England's shores on *HMS Nestor* on their fighting quest for peace. Their stay in Egypt, however, was only short, and by March 1916, they arrived in France where the full force of the

The Sheffield Battalion in Egypt.

German "fighting machine" met them. This was now real WAR!

But of course, this is a history of Sheffield, so there we must stop. 578 men from Sheffield's 12th Battalion died in action during the course of this war, and the lives of those who waited in vain would never be the same again. Yet one memory of these volunteers will continue for ever, as their favourite marching song *On Ilkley Moor Bar't* at will never disappear from Sheffield.

Sheffield at War: 1939-45

For Sheffield, the real impact of war was the "Blitz" of 12-13 December 1940.

Before that time, however, Sheffield was preparing itself, and in 1939 the Sheffield Branch of the Women's Voluntary Service was formed. Gas Masks had been distributed to everyone by this time, and a "Wear your gas mask everywhere" campaign had commenced.

In early 1940, the rationing of butter, sugar and bacon had been introduced, and before long most foods were rationed. The family Ration Book was one of their most important possessions at this time.

The Minister of War, Lord Beaverbrook, had also had the idea of showing that everyone in the country was "pulling together" for the war effort. He decided that all iron railings in parks and private gardens were to be cut down and used for steel production. Many will remember the little stubs and sockets on walls where the railings used to be. Unfortunately, from what we now learn, the Minister was badly advised, as there was no shortage of scrap iron at this time and most of the railings were dumped at sea!

Perhaps the best method of "setting the scene" for that fateful blitz night in December, is to quote you the thoughts of a Luftwaffe Pilot as he recorded the raid in his personal diary:

"We are to hit Sheffield tonight. Someone in the ground crew says he has been there, all steelworks.

We take off from Brussels and soon the navigator reports Zeebrugge and the North Sea below.

The flight is uneventful, cruising speed 3,000 K's an hour. Altitude 4,000 metres says the flight engineer.

Over land – no flak comes up and someone nervously says they know we are coming. There are rumours that Luftwaffe personnel who have crashed have been lynched by mobs.

This is the time we think of our family, wives and sweethearts.

A bright light in the dark sky ahead shows the work of the first wave.

About 50 K's from the target and the automatic bomb aimer comes operational.

30 K's … 10 K's … the bomb doors open.

We are over the target.

Below us looks like a sorcerers cauldron, luminous blobs flashing, bright glowing smoke.

The sky is lit by search lights criss-crossing the sky, dazzling as they find the plane.

The flak bursts ineffectively below.

Our 1,000 K mixed load of high explosives and incendiaries automatically drops one after the other.

Someone says it will soon be Christmas!"

Sheffielders salvage their belongings after a night of the Blitz.

Devastation in High Street during the Blitz, December 13th, 1940.

This airman, like many thousands of others, never did get home to see his loved ones. He died "doing his duty". This was war. This was a terrible waste of life.

The impact on Sheffield on that crisp, frosty night with a full moon shining was devastating, although it could have been worse. A protective blanket of fog had spread out over the huge steelworks in Attercliffe, and the main target of the Luftwaffe had been miraculously saved.

Nearly 800 Sheffield people perished, 2,000 more were seriously injured or wounded, and 40,000 were made homeless. Thousands of houses were damaged or destroyed, and the centre of Sheffield was a mass of burning, crumbling buildings.

Practically the whole city was without gas as 10,000 services were cut off. In addition, 300,000 people were without piped water supplies, street lamps were destroyed and 90 sewers were broken. Jessops Hospital had to be evacuated and Nether Edge Hospital received three direct hits, the staff carrying on there for two days before they too evacuated the building.

Schools were also badly affected, with eight being demolished and another 98 suffering varying degrees of damage. Public transport also received its share of German wrath as 31 trams and 22 buses were either destroyed or seriously damaged.

The winds that night fanned the flames of fury, and many well-known buildings were burnt out. C & A, Modes and John

Sheffield city centre at the height of the Blitz.

Wash's huge stores looked at each other in desperation as fire gutted their insides and huge twisted girders collapsed on to the street between them. Just around the corner in Angel Street, Cockaynes billowed out clouds of black smoke in defiance as it unsuccessfully tried to dampen the ravaging fire which consumed everything within it.

A stroll down the Moor was a similar scene as Robert Brothers crumbled under the onslaught, and Atkinson's proud corner store twisted and buckled to defeat in the intense heat of the blackest of nights. Silhouetted against the

The Women's Voluntary Service in action after the devastation of the first night of bombing.

bright orange flames were the burnt out shells of Sheffield's new trams, which only added to the desperate picture.

The single biggest loss of life during this tragic night was in the Marples Hotel in Fitzalan Square. A 1,000lb bomb crashed through the top of the seven-story high building full of men and women and blew the place apart. Seventy people were killed in one chilling blow, yet the city still carried on.

Despite a further attack by the Luftwaffe bombers two days later, during which further destruction and loss of life occurred, Sheffield began its harrowing but determined journey to recovery. Rest centres were opened for the homeless, and the Women's Voluntary Service worked day and night to help and comfort the shocked and bereaved families. Squads of volunteers were also organised by the City Engineers to rescue hundreds of people trapped amongst the debris of demolished buildings, and the water, gas and electricity workers toiled endlessly to repair their damaged services.

Out of the chaos and despair, rose a spirit of comradeship and self belief as people everywhere helped each other to survive. Their forefathers had seen it all before, and they had always come through. The challenge of the Blitz would be no different, as Sheffielders would never settle for anything less than success.

(m) Essential and Emergency Services.

A brief look at these services shows rapid growth in all areas. WATER: Piped water eventually made its way to most properties in the city during the first quarter of the century at which time the Derwent Valley reservoirs were built. In 1974, the Yorkshire Water Authority took over the old Water Boards and local Authority undertakings, and by 1978 the average amount of water used by each Sheffield household a day had risen to 50 gallons. For domestic and industrial use in the City as a whole, this figure was a staggering 57 million gallons a day.

We now take the provision of endless, clear, pure water for granted as we reach the millennium, and even complain if the supply is shut off for a short time in order to deal with an emergency. If we try and recall the misery and hardship that existed at the beginning of the century when stand pipes and taps in yards and streets were the norm, perhaps we will appreciate just how fortunate we really are.

GAS: By 1911, the old flat flame of the City's 11,000 or so gas lamps had been converted to incandescent "mantles", which were fragile, lace-like tubes fixed around the gas jet to give a glowing (incandescent) light. The lamplighter no longer needed to carry his ladder, and used a pole instead with a flame on the top. It was a sad day for the many gangs of children who followed the lamplighter on his rounds when electricity came in!

Cooking by gas had already started in Sheffield by the time this new century dawned, and was extended to industrial use by about 1914. By the time the gas companies had been nationalised in 1949, with Sheffield being served by the East Midlands Gas Authority, gas fires had made their appearance in peoples homes. These labour saving devices had originated using asbestos and firebricks which kept very hot, but had been replace by the honeycombed fire front in about 1925. Now, gas fires are set in attractive wooden surrounds and are an integral part of many modern homes.

By 1970, "Natural Gas" had been found under the North Sea and was able to be pumped "direct" into people's homes. All gas appliances in the city had to be "changed-over" to accommodate this new supply. This took three years to complete.

ELECTRICITY: The beginning of this century saw the introduction of electric street lamps in the city, with The Moor and Pinstone Street being the first two streets in which they were erected in 1907. The National Grid network had been set up in the 1920s, which enabled most homes to eventually have access to electricity for heat, light and power. In Sheffield, the City Council provided coin meters in 1923, to encourage the working class to have electric lighting installed. The meters accepted pennies and the customer obtained 187 minutes of light from one bulb for this amount. Once the installation cost had been paid for, the number of minutes per penny was increased to 249 for a single bulb. The number of people using this facility rapidly grew, and by 1926 8,000 applications a year were being processed.

By 1948, the electricity undertakings had been national-ised, and control passed from the Town Hall to the new

British Electricity Authority. Now, as with gas, this huge industry is back in private control and the Sheffield householder can use Yorkshire Electricity for his gas supply, and British Gas for electricity. It's a funny world, isn't it!

FIRE SERVICE: The 1900s saw rapid developments in this service in Sheffield. The first motor driven fire engine made its appearance in 1907, and within four years the service had four such fire engines and a fire brigade of 40 men.

Sheffield's new fire engine which pumped 1,000 gallons of water per minute, pictured in December, 1934.

Division Street became the new premises in 1929, where it remained until the 1980s before moving to its present large purpose-built fire station at the junction of Wellington Street and Carver Street.

Fire Services were also opened in the suburbs in the 1950s and 1960s, with stations being provided on Darnall Road, Mansfield Road, Low Edges and Rivelin Valley.

By the time the South Yorkshire County Fire Service had been created in 1974, it controlled 27 operational fire stations County wide. The number of fire appliances in use had risen to 70 and were manned by 1,250 uniformed personnel.

Changes are still being considered for further efficiencies to the system, and Sheffield can be proud of the service if now receives.

AMBULANCE SERVICE: Sheffield is also served by the modern and highly efficient South Yorkshire Metropolitan Ambulance Service, which employs about 600 people. The service has in excess of 235 vehicles, with 13 ambulance stations county-wide. About 700,000 patients are carried in vehicles every year, many such occasions being emergencies. The Sheffield public is fortunate to be able to have the services of trained paramedics with every Accident and Emergency ambulance which attends the 999 or doctor's call.

POLICE: Whilst not always being everyone's favourite people, the policemen of today carry out a most difficult and necessary job. The conditions under which they work and the traumatic events and circumstances which they have to deal with, make this job unlike any other that is carried out.

It is my experience of the police, through working with them for many years, that they are both dedicated and

sincere, although like most organisations, they will have their "bad apples" which can affect those around them.

But let us have a brief look at the police and criminal scene as it developed over the years.

The previous century had seen an upsurge in prostitution, mostly due to girls being put out of work during recessions in the manufacturing industries, and records in 1869 show that there were 94 brothels in the city.

It was, however, the antics of one Charlie Peace who hit the headlines during the 1800s. He was a ruthless killer, a skilful burglar and a master of disguise, who's favourite "hobbies" appeared to be music and womanising. He lived a fairly short and, for him, exciting life and died at the age of 46, having spent almost a third of it behind bars. At his trial in 1847, he was found guilty of committing a murder out of rage at being spurned by a woman. His hanging took place on 25 February of that year, and with his last words he sent his deepest respects to his wife and children.

In the early 1900s, illegal betting or gambling had become rife, particularly in the large East End works where, in 1913, it was estimated that about 80 per cent of the workforce were hooked on the habit. Apart from horse racing, other simple betting activities were common, one being "pitch and toss", whereby bets were made as to whether three coins tossed would come down heads or tails.

Sheffield 'beat bobbies' get their marching orders.

The main centre for this activity was the tossing ring at Sky Edge which is reported to have attracted hundreds of punters every day. In 1919 it was under the control of 29-year-old George Mooney and his gang, along with a small group of men led by 39-year-old Sam Garvin from the Park district of Sheffield.

After four years of working this pitch together, George Mooney grew greedy and pushed Sam Garvin out. This led to the creation of Garvin's notorious "Park Brigade" gang and the beginning of vicious fights between the two rival gangs for the next few years.

Following much bloodshed and terrorising of the public over this period, an elite squad of initially four hand-picked police officers was formed to suppress the gangs. With a free hand to use whatever methods they chose, the Flying Squad successfully fought gun, razor and cosh with fist, boot and truncheon, firstly under Chief Constable Hall-Dalewood and later under the better known Chief Constable Percy Sillitoe. He later became Director General of MI5.

Police cars take over from pounding the beat.

By 1928 the gangs had been beaten, although problems of bribery and corruption within the police force had left a sour taste in the public's mouth and resulted in 15 police officers being dismissed.

Following the war in 1945, the Police Force operated under-strength and by 1961, only 703 out of an establishment of 815 were in post. It was about this time that the notorious "Rhino Whip Affair" took place in Sheffield.

A Special Crime Squad had been formed in 1963 to deal with serious offences in order to increase the detection rate. Acting on information received, the squad arrested three known criminals and took them back to the CID headquarters in Water Lane for questioning. There, they were brutally and systematically assaulted with a police truncheon and a "Rhino tail", a type of whip made out of gut material.

Following complaints and an initial magistrate's court hearing, an independent enquiry was set up which found that the officers concerned were guilty of the vicious activities of which they were accused, but had in fact been encouraged by their senior officers. The City's Watch Committee suspended the Chief Constable, who subsequently resigned two weeks later.

It had been the press who had dubbed this serious incident the "Rhino Whip Affair", an action which had undoubtedly put it into the "public arena". Forty years earlier, similar action by Chief Constable Percy Sillitoe had been hailed by the press as justice. But times change, and the public now expected fairness in the pursuit of justice. The power of the press had achieved this, and the beginning of an age of better understanding and community co-operation had begun.

Crime in the city was, nevertheless, still high.

The good old 1950s Police Box.

The new, fast links of the railway and the M1 motorway "opened the gates" to new crimes involving drugs, vice and pornography which boomed in the permissive 1960s. Football hooliganism increased during the 1970s and the police were still kept at full stretch.

January 1981 saw the dramatic capture of the Yorkshire Ripper in Broomhill after five and a half years on the run. During that time he had murdered 13 women and attempted to do the same to another seven. The Sheffield police were praised for their action on this occasion!

The Miners' Strike of 1984 and the incredibly tragic loss of life at the Hillsborough football ground disaster in 1989 brought the police on to the national stage once more. The rights and wrongs of events which took place on those occasions are better left to the opinion of others who were most closely involved. Perhaps we should just ask ourselves how we would have coped in similar situations and what decisions we might have made.

As we move into the new millennium, however, we can be sure of one thing; the city will always need its Police Force which, like everyone else, is having to adjust to the demands and aspirations of an ever-changing society.

(n) Communication

It is probably appropriate here to scratch the surface of communication change over the last hundred years.

The magic of the TELEPHONE continued to increase as the Post Office took over from the National Telephone Company in 1912. New telephone buildings at Steel City House had automatic equipment installed on its top floor as a new dialling system for local calls was introduced in 1926. Telephone exchanges were also built at Woodseats, Broomhill, Firth Park and many more local suburbs, and in 1966 the Eldon House Exchange was built. Subscriber Trunk Dialling (STD) was introduced at this time, and within eight years International Direct Dialling had also been introduced. The system has continued to grow, and Sheffield people are now able to communicate by telephone to almost anywhere in the world at any time of day.

> **Did You Know that on the 23 September 1966, during the city's change over to Subscriber Trunk Dialing (STD), Sheffield was for one minute without a single telephone link to the outside world, the first time since 1879?**

In 1922, the BBC was founded and opened a local relay station in Corporation Street the following year. On 16 November 1923, RADIO (or Wireless Telegraphy as it was known) came to Sheffield. More than 1,000 wireless sets were sold in the first year, with the Northern Home Service being the only programme available.

Further improvements were carried out over the years, and on 15 November 1967, Radio Sheffield was established. Set in a large house in Westbourne Road in Broomhill, it had a staff of 16 and an output of four hours a day.

In 1972, Radio Hallam was instigated as a potential commercial station, incorporating advertisements in its daily broadcasts, and by October 1974, it was officially broadcasting from its studio in Hartshead.

Sheffield can now obtain a large variety of programmes on many different stations which give pleasure to thousands of local listeners.

TELEVISION made its appearance in the 1950s with small black and white screens and zig-zag flashing lines which brought gasps of amazement from its first ever viewers. Now pictures are in colour with size being no limit, and five channels to choose from for those without "SKY". If you are able to subscribe to the satellite channels or even those that are piped underground, you could watch the screen forever without seeing anything twice.

Times have certainly changed, both for the better, and perhaps also for the worse. Knowledge of the world can now be obtained at the press of a button, and education in most things is available on our screens. News as it happens can be shown in graphic detail, and drama and comedy can provide relaxation for us whenever we wish.

But violence and sex can sometimes go too far, and the pornography of old is probably the saucy titillation of today. However, society has changed, and we must be careful not to judge, as progress is inevitable.

Last, but not least is the COMPUTER REVOLUTION upon which society now depends, and about 38 per cent of households now own a computer. In particular, we've got the World Wide Web, the largest information system ever devised. The Internet delivers the web around the world for those who wish to use it. Thousands of web sites allow users to "surf the web" using a browser, looking for any information which might be interesting. Over 160 million people are "on-line" at present, each having an e-mail (electronic mail) address. This figure is expected to reach between 300 and 500 million worldwide by the year 2000.

This is without doubt the communication system of the future, and its progress is unstoppable.

(o) Domestic Issues

This all embracing title has been included here to pick up all those things we have not yet mentioned but are just as important to our daily lives.

In the light of all the changes that have taken place under this heading, information is given more in schedule form to make it easier to follow. Well, let's take a breath and begin.

Cooking
Solid fuel kitchen ranges for cooking were introduced early in the century.

The Aga cooker was introduced in this country in 1929.

Gas cookers were being used from about 1910-20.

Electric cookers were being used from about the same time.

Electric toasters arrived about 1920.

Microwave ovens were introduced about 1960.

Cleaning
The first carpet sweeper was invented in 1876 by Melville R. Bissell of Michigan, USA, because he was allergic to dust.

The Ewebank sweeper appeared about 1911 and cost 10s 6d (52p).

The first successful, practical, powered suction carpet cleaner was invented in 1901 by an English civil engineer called Hubert Booth. He formed the Vacuum Cleaner Company Ltd (now called Goblin) to build his machines.

A light and easy to use similar suction cleaner was invented by an American called Spangler in 1907. William Hoover bought the manufacturing rights and produced the first Hoover vacuum cleaner in 1908. In 1919 he adopted the slogan "It beats as it sweeps as it cleans."

Cylinder vacuum cleaners arrived about 1930.

Washing
Most washing in the first 40 years of the century was done in tubs using wooden dollys, a copper "poncher" and a wooden washboard with a zinc corrugated rubbing surface.

Hand operated washing machines made from wood were used in the early 1900s.

Electrically powered washing machines appeared in this country in the 1920s.

Electrically powered wringers and immersion heaters were added in the 1950s.

Automatic washing machines incorporating spin dryers were popular in the 1960s.

Dishwashers appeared in the 1970s.

Drying and Ironing
Early mangles were intended for smoothing and pressing.

Smaller mangles were developed as wringers.

Spinning in electric washing machines superseded wringers.

Dryers in automatic drying and washing machines completed the process from the 1970s.

Cast-iron flat irons heated over or in front of the fire were used in the early 1900s.

Electric irons came into their own in the 1930s when electricity was wired to homes.

They were very heavy and had no thermostat. They had to be switched on and off to control the temperature. Thermostats were fitted in the 1940s.

Steam irons first appeared in the 1950s.

Fridges and FReezers
Refrigerators, both electric and gas, were available from the 1920s.

Separate freezers developed in the 1960s.

Tea and Coffee Making
Kettles were in general use in the 1900s.

Electric kettles appeared in the 1920s.

The Goblin "teasmade" arrived in the 1930s.

The polished aluminium whistling kettle appeared in the late 1940s.

Plastic electric kettles came into general use in the 1980s.

Coffee was able to be percolated in the early 1900s.

Instant coffee mashed directly in cups was introduced by Nestle (Nescafé) in 1938.

Children at play

Early

Hopscotch	Yo-Yo's
Whip and Top	Skipping Ropes
Marbles	5 Stones (snobs)
Football	Roller Skates

> **Did You Know** that 1959-60, a good Yo-Yo cost about 2s 6d (12p)? In 1999, there are about 150 different types of Yo-Yo costing between £1 and £15, with sales in England being in the order of £40 million a year.

Later

Hoola Hoops	Space Hoppers
Pogo-Sticks	

Later Still

Skate boards	Cyber Pets
Roller Blades	Yo-Yo's (revival)

Some Early Children"s Comics

Dandy	Beano
Eagle (Dan Dare)	Bunty
Hotspur	Wizard
Sun	Comet

> **Did You Know** that the famous Sheffield Fletcher's Bakers, which began as a humble shop in 1923, progressed to be Britain's biggest independent baker by 1999 when it was sold to Northern Foods for £40 million? Its well-known jingle "Betta Fetcha Fletcher Loaf" was thought up by a bus passenger who had seen a similar slogan "Drinka pinta milka day" from the top deck of a bus going to work.
>
> His idea was gratefully snapped up by the company who paid the quick thinking bus passenger about a "tenner or so" for his contribution.

> **Did You Know** that it was about 120 years ago that a Mr Henderson invented his famous Relish, which is a mixture of malt vinegar, water, sugar, tamarind, salt, treacle, caramel, cayenne, cloves and garlic? Its recipe is still a closely-guarded secret. The one and only factory is in Leavygreave Road in Sheffield, at which half a million or more bottles of his special sauce are produced every year.

Some Typical Cost Changes: Food and Drink

	1900	1920	1940	1960	1980	2000
1lb Cheese	5p	7p	5p	15p	65p	£2.00
12 Eggs	6p	15p	9p	30p	51p	£1.50
1lb Sugar	1p	4p	1p	2p	30p	40p
1lb Tea	8p	13p	18p	36p	96p	£2.50
1lb Coffee	6p	25p	36p	65p	£4.00	£7.00
1lb Butter	6p	11p	5p	15p	70p	£1.80
1lb Bacon	3p	10p	6p	18p	90p	£3.00
1lb Margarine	–	4p	3p	7p	36p	£1.00
5lb Potatoes	1p	4p	4p	8p	35p	50p
Loaf of Bread	1p	2p	2p	12p	30p	50p
1pt Beer	1p	2p	4p	6p	30p	£1.75
20 Cigarettes	2p	5p	9p	25p	70p	£3.80
1lb Beef	5p	7p	5p	11p	£1.00	£3.00
1lb Pork	3p	4p	5p	13p	85p	£2.50

> **Did You Know** that Heinz Beans first came to Britain in 1901 as an expensive treat?

> **Did You Know** that Britons eat more flakes, muesli, porridge and sugar cereals than anyone else in the world? An average of 17lbs of such cereals is eaten every year by everyone in the country.

Some Typical Costs

About 1900:

Ladies' Knickers	13p a pair
Men's Shirts	6p each
Men's Trousers	37p a pair
Pair of Shoes	75p a pair

> **Did You Know** that "Dr. William's Pink Pills for Pale People" were available from chemists in 1901 as a cure for anaemia?

Blankets	30p a pair
Carpets (27" wide)	25p a yard
Gas Fire	£1.25
Carpet Sweeper	50p
Iron Kettle	13p
Hand sewing machine	£2.50
Servant's bed and mattress	£1.75
3 tablets of soap	5p
Labourer's wage	£1.00 a week
2-bedroom house	£200
Tooth extraction	5p each
Family car	£200

> **Did You Know that "Pears Transparent Soap" was available in 1827 at 1s (5p), 1s 6d (7p) and 2s 6d (12p) a block?**

About 1930:

Ladies' silk stockings	35p a pair
Ladies' moleskin coat	£150
Maternity corsets	75p
Men's shoes	£2
Gent's Wardrobe	£30
Oak draw-leaf table	£18
Armchair	£4.50
Wind-up gramophone	£8
Piano	£50
Wireless (radio)	£20
Enamel bath and fittings	£5
Aluminium Kettle	60p
Good Kodak camera	£5
Shorthand Typist's wage	£4 a week
Medium size car	£250
Bicycle	£6
3 bedroom semi-detached	£650

About 1960:

Men's Suit	£13
Men's Shirt	£2
Woman's Coat	£12
Woman's Shoes	£3.50
Brassiere	40p
Bed with mattress	£37
Good carpet	£1.80 per sq yd
Cooker	£35
Fridge	£55
Vacuum Cleaner	£37
12" Television	£70
Radio	£50
Record Player	£14
Unskilled man's wage	£10
3 bedroom semi-detached	£3,500
Road Tax	£12.10
Medium size car	£900

About 1980:

Shoes	£18
Coats	£40
Shirts	£7
Electric Cooker	£190
Gas Cooker	£140
Fridge	£105
Washing Machine	£145
Sewing Machine	£95
Electric Fire	£75
Blanket	£16
Skilled Male Worker's Wage	£48
3 bedroom semi-detached	£1,500
Medium size car	£2,500
Bicycle	£65

About 2000:

Ladies' and Men's Shoes	£30 – £60
Men's Suits	£150 – £300
Men's Trousers	£25 – £50
Ladies' Suits	£80 – £200
Ladies' Dresses	£30 – £150
Gas and Electric Cookers	£200 – £500
Fridges	£200 – £400
Washing Machines	£200 – £500
Automatic Kettles	£15 – £40
Music Systems	£60 – £600
Radios	£20 – £100
Vacuum Cleaners	£100 – £200
Televisions	£150 – £1,000
Clerical Worker's Wage	£120 a week
Manager's Wage	£300 a week
Executive's Wage	£700 a week
Top Footballer's Wage	£15,000 a week
Semi-detached house	£70,000
Medium size car	£9,000

(p) City Changes

This last section is included to give you, the reader, some visual examples of some of the changes which have taken place in the city over the last hundred years. Old photographs being back memories of how Sheffield looked, whilst a few newer photographs are included to highlight the differences. I hope you enjoy the trip down memory lane.

Let's start by taking a look at one of Sheffield's best-known stores – Marks and Spencer (or Marks and Sparks as Sheffielders like to call it). Here are the original Mr Marks and Mr Spencer.

Marks and Spencer's first shop was on South Street (now The Moor). Everything in the shop cost one penny, hence the name 'Penny Bazaar' on this 1911 photograph.

The Norfolk Market Hotel was another old landmark in Sheffield. It was built at the corner of Haymarket and Dixon Lane in the 1850s and remained there for about 100 years. The previous building on this site was the equally famous Tontine Inn, built in 1785, which was Sheffield's main coaching house. From here, stage coaches and Royal Mail coaches left daily for all parts of the country.

After World War Two, Marks and Spencer built their large new store on The Moor which remained open until the early 1990s. At this time, they built a new larger store at the Meadowhall Shopping Centre which became the 'flagship' store for the complex.

The remaining store in the city centre is on Fargate, and this is being increased in size to cater for local demand since the M & S store on The Moor was closed.

Did You Know that the site of the old Sheffield Grand Hotel in Barker's Pool is now occupied by the eight-storey office block known as the Fountain Precinct development, which was completed in 1978? The stainless steel Horse and Rider statue by David Wynne, which stands on its frontage adjacent to the garden and seating area, was presented to the people of Sheffield by the family of the late Hyman Stone, in his memory. Mr Stone was a well-known solicitor who later headed a large London firm, but nevertheless retained strong connections with the city of his birth.

This pre-war view of Castle Square shows the large Burton's store occupying the site now taken up by C & A. The good old 'bone-shaker' trams have now been replaced by the sleek new trams of today.

These two photographs of Fitzalan Square were taken before World War One and after World War Two and it is interesting to note how the taxis have changed from the horse-drawn hansom cabs and carriages to the 'black cab' still in use today.

Did You Know that there are 17 Sheffields around the world? These are in Illinois, Iowa, Jamaica, Massachussetts, Missouri, Montana, New Brunswick, New Zealand, Ohio, Ontario, Pennsylvania, South Dakota, Tasmania, Tennessee, Texas, Vermont and, of course, England.

Davy's food store and cafe were favourite calling places for shoppers in the 1950s and 1960s. In those days a tasty tea of bacon and eggs, plus a 'cuppa', could be had at the Mikado Cafe for 1s 6d (7½p).

Cole's Corner was probably one of the best-known meeting places in the city centre until the popular store moved to Barker's Pool in the 1960s. These two photographs, taken in early 1900 and 1964, show how the shop changed over the period it existed at the Fargate-Church Street site.

Cockayne's store on Angel Street began in a fairly modest way in the early 1900s. It was a popular family shop which was take over by Schofield's in the 1970s before becoming an Argos store in the 1990s.

The huge Walsh's store in High Street was opened in 1875 by an Irishman called John Walsh. By 1895 it had 36 departments from feathers to furniture, and became the city's 'premier shop' by 1920. Following its destruction in the Blitz of 1940, it was re-opened in 1953. In 1976 it became Rackham's and by 1987 was taken over by the House of Fraser. It was sold to the Liverpool firm, T. J. Hughes, in 1998.

This is an interesting photograph of how Snig Hill looked, with its narrow cobbled street, at the beginning of the 20th century.

In the first quarter of the 20th century, Pinstone Street was a busy place. In the background can be seen St Paul's Church which was demolished in 1938.

We now visit a few suburban locations, beginning with South Road at Walkeley. The absence of cars from this shopping street gives it a more rural setting.

If you wanted a drink in the early 1900s, the Cross-pool Tavern on Manchester Road could always be trusted to pull a good pint.

For those in the south of the city, drinking has been available for over 100 years at the Big Tree, as this late 1890s photograph shows. The public transport used to get to this village was the horse omnibus which, on a fine day, was a pleasant three-penny ride from the Red Lion at Heeley.

For those Sheffielders who liked tram rides in the early 1900s, an open-top trip out to the Darnall terminus formed an interesting afternoon.

Norton Lees was simply a rural village in 1900, and the horse-drawn cart was the only vehicle to 'pollute' the environment in those days.

Even Banner Cross was a leafy rural setting at the beginning of the 20th century. This early 1900s view looking down Eccleshall Road is a complete contrast to today's traffic-choked street.

Well, as you can see, Sheffield has changed considerably over this century. Life, of course, goes on and progress and change are inevitable. Let's make sure that we rise to this challenging change and create a better life for everyone.

Chapter Ten

1900 to 2000

I T WAS knocking-off time at Dixon's Cutlery Manufacturers and Silversmiths, and Mrs S trudged thankfully towards the door clutching the 14s she'd earned that week for 48 very busy and dirty hours. As one of 300 women and girl buffers employed at Dixon's, she was more than pleased to be on full-time at present as her husband was out of work more often than he was in.

Mr S, had started in the light steel business like his father and, as a saw hardener, used to be able to earn £2 a week. Times were hard in 1909, however, and even in full employment, which was rare, the most he could give to his wife for housekeeping and clothes these days was £1.

"And that's another thing," thought Mrs S as she looked round for her daughter. "The blokes here are on piece-work and can earn as much as 35 bob a week. It's just not fair!"

At that moment, 16-year-old Emily appeared, grinning broadly, with her big brown eyes shining clearly through the layers of grime and dust on her face.

"Here you are Mum. I've got 6s this week and you can have it all."

Her mother took the money gratefully and thought with interest that Emily's use of the word shilling was probably the result of her seeing rather a lot lately of that lad from the posh end of town out Nether Edge way.

"Well it's better than the half a crown you used to get when you first started here luv, isn't it?"

Holding the money tightly in her hand, she linked arms with her daughter and set off walking to their three-roomed home in Ball Street at Neepsend, her mind reflecting on the fact that she was the main breadwinner in the family at the moment. She didn't so much mind the responsibility for herself, but at the age of 36 with four children to support (one other had died at the age of three following a bout of measles), she worried about their future.

The children, who were five, ten and 12 years old, were at school, but were always missing lessons due to some illness or other. Take Emily for instance. She'd spent more time at home than at school and could hardly read at all when she left.

"Will Dad be home, Mum?" danced the cheerful voice in Mrs S's ears, jolting her out of her thoughts as they approached the long row of back to back houses where they lived.

"He'll be down at the pub if I know anything," she responded trying not to show her agitation. "He'll be spending our hard earned money."

We've done well this week though, haven't we Mum?" persisted Emily trying to make light of her father's shortcomings.

Mrs S turned to her daughter and felt a glow of pride and humility as she gazed at the ever-cheerful face which was able to brighten up even the most difficult of days. Yes, times were very hard. Most weeks the whole family had to manage on anything from 6s to 18s, and with four and sixpence a week going on rent, there was little left for even one good daily meal for them all.

Mind you, it was even worse for Mrs S's sister who rented two rooms on Woodside Lane for 3s 10d a week. Although her silversmith husband could earn 50s a week when in work, there was little available at present. With three young children to look after (three others having died), she was obliged to work intermittently at home for excessively long hours for about 8s a week, burnishing tea and coffee sets for the new Viner's Company on West Street.

Still she was grateful that such work was available to fit in with her domestic arrangements. Viner's was a new company, having been formed only three years earlier by Willie Viner, one of five brothers who came over to the city from Austria. Their Tiger Works on West Street only employed a few people, and some of their work was let out on a part time basis for "finishing".

Did You Know that Buffer Girls, the hard-working, fun-loving characters of the late 1800s and early 1900s, were very important in the silverware and cutlery trades? Stood at their buffing wheels for hours on end, they put the finishing shine to the steel and silver products in their care. The job was excessively dirty and, as well as wearing full-length aprons, they were usually protected from head to foot with brown paper or a copy of yesterday's Telegraph. With sleeves rolled up and hair pushed into a head scarf, these hard-talking, no-nonsense bastions of women's working class were, along with the "Little Mesters", the back-bone of this vastly growing Sheffield industry.

In the good old days, before she was married, she had been able to carry on her trade as a hollow-ware silver burnisher on a full-time basis and had managed to earn four pence an hour on piece-work. This had brought in about 15s a week, double that which she was able to earn now.

Reflecting on her sister's difficult situation, Mrs S felt that perhaps things were not so bad for herself after all, and that they would all feel better after a nice bacon buttie dipped in tomato juice for tea.

* * * * * * * * *

It wasn't only the buffer girls who managed to put on a brave face at work in these difficult times.

Take Mr and Mrs S's son Arthur, for example, who went to work at workshops in Fitzwilliam Lane as a forger at the tender age of 14 in the early 1920s. He loved his job, and his little square room with its thick stone walls and a single window was almost better than home, particularly in winter when the heat from the glowing coke fire which burned merrily in its hearth welcomed him on his nine o'clock arrival.

"Come in, Arthur lad!" growled Tom, his tough but kindly boss. "I know its "Saint Monday", but I want you to have a go at these blanks this morning."

Arthur was no stranger to Tom's forging shop, having been its unofficial errand boy and part-time assistant on his equally unofficial days off school over the last two years. During these times he'd often perched himself on top of the pile of coke to the right of the hearth to keep warm, breathing in deeply the odd smelling fumes which always made him feel rather dizzy.

"Them fumes will do you a world of good lad," was Tom's advice at the time, and who was Arthur to contradict the "expert"?

From his vantage point, he'd watched with interest as the strips of steel bar which had been collected from the Snow Lane warehouse had been carefully chopped down to length, heated up, and then hammered with great skill into knife blades of varying shape and size. Tom had let him practise on spare lengths of steel on many occasions, and if the truth were

known, he was proud of the way Arthur had picked up the technique.

This particular morning, Tom had arrived at the forge earlier to make a fire in the left-hand side of the hearth using old newspaper wrapped around broken sticks. Once alight, the flames searched hungrily for fresh pieces of coke to consume, their endeavours being helped by regular blasts of air from the hand operated bellows which fanned their flickering fingers into the black mass of coke.

It would be an hour before the fire was hot enough for forging, so Tom used his time to tidy up the place, clean up the hammers and tongues, and ensure that a bucket of cooling oil was positioned next to the anvil. He was an old hand at this type of work and, over the years, he'd built up his little cutlery business to include grinding, buffing and finishing shops as well as his forge. You might say he was a typical "Little Mester", one of hundreds who now operated in this busy but rather grimy town.

"Are you sure I'm good enough?" queried Arthur as he looked apprehensively at the large steel anvil which sat proudly on the timber stock which was embedded in the stone floor of the workshop. The yellow-white glare of the eagerly awaiting fire seemed to transfix him for a few moments and took him back to the time when he first saw the stock and wondered what on earth that old, solid section of gnarled tree trunk was doing half buried in the workshop floor. It was only when Tom and his mate had threaded a stout, steel bar through a hole in the shaft of the nearby anvil, and lifted it with difficulty on to the recessed top of the "tree trunk" that he realised its purpose.

"Come on dreamboat. We haven't got all day. You've practised plenty of times before. Now it's for real, that's all."

"Sorry Tom," came the mumbled response as he quickly tied his leatherette apron over his rather scruffy looking shirt and trousers whilst looking around for his mate. "Who's going to strike then?"

Now from the conversation so far, you would be forgiven for thinking that this knife making process was rather complicated. Well, you would be right. It wasn't simply a case of the forger beating hot metal into shape on the anvil. A striker stood opposite who also hammered the blade, with alternate blows to those of the forger. He used a long handled, heavier hammer which spread the metal as required and flattened it when asked to do so. It was up to the forger to control the thickness, shape and edge formation of the product, hopefully with the dual pounding of the hammers being accurately controlled.

"I'll strike today lad. You know what Joe's like on "Saint Monday". He'll probably not stagger in until after ten o'clock."

You might be wondering, like Arthur did when he first started, what this reference to "Saint Monday" was all about.

"It's like this ere lad," Tom had explained to the naïve boy. "We all work long and hard in this trade, particularly the grinders, who swaller more much and dust in a day at the grinding wheel than you'll manage in a lifetime. With Monday to Saturday working and 12 hour days, we all need a bit of lubrication down at the pub on Sundays."

A knowing look crept over Arthur's face as Tom continued.

"There's not many that can get fully tanked up on a Sunday and be fit enough for proper work on a Monday, so they all drift in and do a bit of tidying up in the morning."

Arthur still hadn't quite grasped the point. "But why call it "Saint Monday"?" he persisted.

"Use it lad, use it," came the exasperated response. "They're all sent home at lunchtime aren't they, although I must admit that most end up back in the pub. Do you get it lad? They're all "sent" home on a Monday!"

This rather embarrassing introduction to the Cutlery Trade's special day had certainly left its impression on our raw recruit, and he realised that today's task had to be completed by mid-day if traditions were to be upheld.

Without any more ado, Arthur grasped a strip of steel bar firmly between the jaws of his long handled tongues and plunged it into the now white hot "furnace" of burning coke. It wasn't long before the tortured glowing steel was ready to come out and submit itself to the skilful hammering of its assailants. The process continued as re-heating and hammering, followed by more re-heating and hammering, produced the long awaited blade.

Even now it wasn't complete. The blade needed to be hardened, and to achieve this Arthur once again heated up the steel, then plunged it for a second or two into the bucket of oil at the side of the hearth.

The sizzling protest of the burning oil indicated that hardness had been achieved, although Arthur ruefully reflected on the time when he had asked why water couldn't be used to quench the delicate blades rather than oil.

"Try it lad and you'll find out," had come the reply. Experience was always the best way to learn and this was no exception, as the boy's experimental plunge into water had proved. The cold water "shock treatment" was too much for the slender blade which quivered and distorted before it was able to be withdrawn. The oil, on the other hand, had absorbed the heat more gradually as it burned on initial contact with the hot blade, thus reducing the likelihood of the steel distorting.

Was that the end of the process? Not on your life. Arthur knew that he'd produced a good, hard blade, but it was too brittle and had no spring to it. So how did he sort this problem out? He decided to "temper" the blade by gently reheating it over the flame of the fire until his experienced eye told him it was the correct colour. He was sweating profusely by this time and desperately wanted a drink. He knew, however, as he carefully placed the hardened blade thick edge down in the slotted metal grid attached to the hearth wall, that this tempering process completed his task; or so he thought. "Only another five to go lad, then you can knock off for a bit."

At ten bob a week and too young to go to the pub, Arthur wondered whether this job was worth it after all, particularly as he sat down to his mug of tea and cheese sandwiches at lunchtime, feeling as though he'd done six days work in three hours.

"You've done a good job there lad. I couldn't have done much better myself".

This was praise indeed from the gaffer who continued, "I'll tell you what. I'll give the pub a miss this afternoon and treat you to this new, talking movie which is showing at the Central on The Moor. It'll never catch on mind you. All this talking will put people off watching, you take my word!"

As Arthur sat in the front stalls of the posh new 1,600-seater cinema, chewing his penny bag of tiger nuts and raisins and watching Al Jolson making "talking movie" history with his rendition of "Mammy", he recalled with some amusement his first few visits to Tom's forge and the well-meaning advice of coke-fume sniffing for better health.

Little did he realise that he would develop in the years ahead into one of Sheffield's finest edge tool makers, his work including among many other things the hand-forging of fine dress swords for British Army Officers on duty in India. As for the health advice, Arthur would finally retire from the cutlery and edge tool trade at the ripe old age of 81, even then feeling obliged to apologise to his employer for leaving them at a busy time! But that was in a dim and distant future.

* * * * * * * * * *

It was a sultry afternoon that found Arthur's Dad, Mr S, entering the barber's shop of George Binns and Sons in Pond Street. After having had his usual lunchtime pint at the Queen's Head just round the corner, he'd decided that his monthly "short back and sides" was just about due and would do wonders to cool him down.

George Binns' barber's shop in Pond Street, adjacent to Pond Hill.

"Afternoon George," said Mr S as he settled down into the vacant chair nearest the door and picked up the early edition of the *Telegraph*, noting that the new 1920's Morris Cowley 2-seater motor car was being advertised at only £175 "all-in".

The barber nodded and returned the greetings as he strapped the long shiny blade of his cut-throat razor before applying it to the well-bristled face of the customer he was already shaving.

> **Did You Know** that a secret tunnel existed in the time of Mary Queen of Scots, which linked Sheffield Castle to the Manor House (often referred to as Manor Castle), high on the hill at the top of Manor Lane? This tunnel is reputed to have been used as an escape route in the 1580s by Queen Mary during her 14 years of captivity in Sheffield, and several links to it have been identified over the years. George Binns barber's shop, for example, which was situated in Pond Street in the early 1900s, just round the corner from the Old Queen's Head pub, had a spiral stone staircase leading down to a well which was famous for its mineral waters. Old George always claimed that an entrance to a secret tunnel leading to the Manor House was also to be found at the bottom of these stone steps.

"Two or three minutes Mr S, and then it's your turn," continued Mr Binns, a man of modest stature with clear eyes and a face that suggested he knew a bit about life.

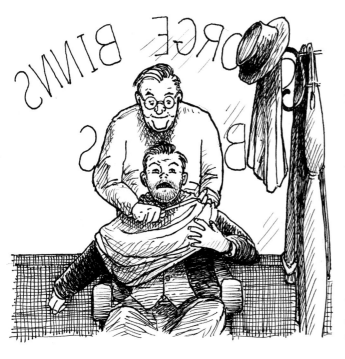

Returning his eyes to the newspaper, Mr S read with dismay about the continuing reign of terror created by the gangster George Mooney who seemed hell-belt on taking what he wanted out of life regardless of the suffering caused.

Pondering for a few minutes as to what makes such a person take up a life of crime, he reflected back to his own childhood and pictured the heavy, brown leather belt which his father had always kept hanging at the side of the fireplace at home. Misbehaviour in those days had always resulted in instant and fairly effective punishment, and Mr S winced as he recalled the pain.

It was, however, as a deterrent that he best remembered the belt. Its very presence had always had a calming effect on him, and many a proposed foul deed had dissolved in his mind at the thought of it hanging there.

"These gangsters could have done with a good dose of leather," he mused. "That would have sorted them out at an early age and avoided all this trouble."

Suddenly, as though from out of nowhere, the room was filled with people and Mr S snapped out of his daydreams. A dark-coated figure brushed past him and dropped heavily into the chair which, until a few seconds earlier, had been occupied by the freshly shaven and somewhat pale-faced individual now scurrying out of the front door.

Beads of sweat broke out on Mr S's forehead as the barber's next and totally unexpected words seemed to fill the room like a menacing cloud … "Sorry Mr Mooney, Mr S is next."

Now bravery had never been on the top of Mr S's list of personal qualities, and it wasn't likely to change now. With a wave of the hand and an utterance more like he was choking rather than speaking, he relinquished his turn in the chair to its present occupant.

"As you like" said Mr Binns, now turning his attention to his somewhat special customer. "Shave or haircut Mr Mooney."

"Shave, and I never pay!" came the curt reply.

It wasn't until the infamous face was covered in rich soapy lather and the razor sharp blade was hovering over the owner's pulsing neck that the barber chose to reply.

"All my customers pay Mr Mooney."

With the exception of Mr S's pounding heart trying desperately to burst out of his chest, not a sound was to be heard. The gangster looked at the hovering blade, then at the determined face above him, then back at the blade.

"George Binns, you're a brave man" roared Mooney, his face breaking into a broad grin. "I'll pay you and I'll be pleased to do so."

From that day, George Mooney was a regular at the now famous barber's shop, and he brought chickens and other food as a gesture of respect and friendship at each visit.

It took some time for Mr S to recover from the experience, although he was pleased with the outcome. Perhaps there was some good in this gangster after all! Perhaps he did feel his father's leather belt as a child! Perhaps it was the lack of jobs, the inability to earn money, the lack of food and the lack of self esteem that all contributed towards his decline into a life of crime! Who knows? Mr S didn't.

World War Two was a difficult time for Mrs S, as she struggled to keep her young family of two boys and a girl together. Food was scarce, and what there was, she could hardly afford. Bread was 4d for a large 4lb-loaf, but at 6d a pound, butter was hardly ever on the table. She wasn't keen on the plastic tasting margarine, but at half the price she really had no choice.

> **Did You Know that during World War Two and beyond, food was rationed from 1940 to 1954, bread was rationed from 1946 to 1948, and clothes were rationed from 1941 to 1949?**

Her husband was fighting on the front, and, like hundreds of others in the city, Mrs S had to cope without him. These hard times had, however, brought everyone together and there was usually someone to turn to in times of difficulty.

The blitz had been a terrible time, but Mrs S and her neighbours had been lucky and were able to help in the rest centres set up for those whose homes had been bombed. She recalled with sadness the state of many of the poor people who came though the doors of Firvale House after the bombing. Shocked, confused and bewildered, many had been unable to talk and just sat there staring about. Most had to sleep on the floor at nights, wrapped in a blanket when one was available, but at least they were safe.

In the days that followed, hundreds of volunteers like Mrs S made bread in the kitchens, brought food and clothes to the home, and helped to care for those in need. Scouts gave concerts to cheer people up, and the young girl guides ran errands and looked after the babies and children, as well as anything else that was needed.

The worst, however, was now over, but the sirens still sounded without notice and the evening black-out still had to be observed.

"Mummy, I don't know why we keep on hiding under this table with a big blanket over it every time that awful noise comes on," her daughter said on one such occasion. "Mind you, I do like it because it's like being in a tent."

Mrs S didn't always rush off to the air-raid shelters every time the warning broke the evening silence. It happened too regularly now, and with three children it was quite a job dragging them all down the street. The big old dining room table wouldn't really have been much help if the house had been hit, but at least she felt a bit more secure.

It was with enormous relief that the war had come to an end in 1945, and life could be almost normal again. The children could play in the streets and feel safe, and they were always able to entertain themselves without much problem. Hopscotch and skipping were favourites with the girls, whilst Mrs S's two boys played for hours with a whip and top and an old wooden Yo-yo.

Even shopping was a pleasure for the children, particularly at the Co-op on Middlewood Road.

> **Did You Know that shops bought foodstuffs in bulk rather than in bags in 1940s? Huge slabs of butter or cheese were a common sight on the "Co-op" counter, and were cut to size while the shopper waited! Sugar was dealt with the same way, being poured into little blue bags on the weigh-scale before being handed over.**

They loved to watch in amazement as the shop assistant pulled a fine steel wire through the huge round cheese, which always seemed to be sitting on the counter. It took several such cuts to obtain a piece of two ounces, which was all that their mother could afford. It was the same with butter which was "an enormous great lump", and they loved the way the assistant sliced a bit off and "slapped" it into a piece of grease-proof paper.

The best part of the visit, however, was paying for the goods and waiting for the change. The bill and the money were always put in little brown torpedo-shaped carriers which whizzed around on overhead wires when the assistant pulled a lever. The man or woman in the office at the end of the shop always put in the correct change before he too sent the "torpedo" racing back to the counter to the delight of the waiting children. It was often a "race" to see which customer got theirs back first, and a cheer from the kids often welcomed back the winner.

Luckily for Mrs S, the children were all of school age, which gave her some time on her own, which she richly deserved. However, Jimmy, her youngest, was quite a handful and things didn't always go well at school. The other day, for example, he'd been flicking folded-up paper across the classroom with a large elastic band, much to the consternation of Mr Withers, his rather stern teacher.

"Come out here young James," he had demanded, "and hold out your hand."

The swishing noise that the long yellow cane made as it cut through the air on its downward stroke of punishment had always made Jimmy wince, but the pain was something different. The first stroke was bad enough, but the fourth, fifth and sixth were sheer agony, and it was always several weeks before he felt the urge to misbehave again.

"That's nothing to the punishment that Mum puts us through everyday, though, is it?" said Jimmy's sister unsympathetically when he showed her his sore hand. "She makes us have school dinners, and they're yuk!"

Now she did have a point. The large cylindrical containers which were delivered to the school each day contained all the hot meals, and some even tasted quite good. But the tough, gristly stew, the hard stringy turnips and the revolting looking sago were just too much to bear. Even smothering them with thick brown sauce, smuggled into the dining room in one of Mrs S's empty Aspirin bottles, didn't help a great deal, and the teacher in charge always made the children eat everything up!

But, of course, those were the joys of childhood, and Jimmy was growing up, with plenty of adventures of life to look forward to!

*   *   *   *   *   *   *   *   *   *

It had been overcast all morning, and flakes of snow had begun to settle again on the already icy roads by lunchtime. Mrs S had just heard the Home Service weather forecast on the wireless which had issued warnings of further heavy snow all over the country.

"I hope you're not thinking of going on that trip to Grindleford tonight, Jimmy my lad," she said to her son. "Your dad says its thick out in Derbyshire already and the buses are struggling to get through."

Jimmy had his head buried in the sports section of Monday's early edition of *The Star*, and wondered why it was that a bit of snow and ice could affect such important things as football matches.

"It's 1947, after all," he muttered to himself, "and we did win the war. You'd have thought in this day and age that a bit of snow in February wouldn't bring the country to a standstill, especially football!"

"Did you hear what I was saying, Jimmy?" persisted his mother as she looked out of the window at the snow, which now seemed to be falling a bit faster.

"Mother, I wish you and Dad wouldn't fuss so much when I go out. I checked with the Transport Department and the buses are still running, so it must be alright. Anyway," he added mischievously, "Dad can come and dig me out if I get stuck. After all, he is in charge of snow clearing at the Town Hall, isn't he?"

Mrs S knew there was no point in pursuing the matter any more. Jimmy was as stubborn as his father, and if he'd made his mind up to do something, then he would do it.

It was early evening when Jimmy boarded the bus to Grindleford and paid his 8d (3p) fare to Arthur Hobson, the conductor. He and the driver, Henry Thorpe, were a bit concerned about the weather, which was getting worse, but at least they'd got one person brave enough to make the journey with them.

Jimmy felt rather strange being the only passenger on board the single deck Corporation bus as it battled its way along Hathersage Road. Strong winds were now whipping the snow into a frenzy and causing it to drift. The last place anybody wanted to be on a night such as this was on a lonely bus travelling over the tops of the open moors; but of course, Jimmy knew best!

The downhill journey past the Fox House Inn from Stony Ridge was a bit of a relief, although the driver could hardly see where he was going as he negotiated the sharp bend on the last lap down to Padley and Grindleford. A small car had appeared in the bus headlights, and was cautiously crawling its way forward when suddenly, it happened. The car skidded to one side, hit a snowdrift, and the road was blocked. no one could move.

Jimmy's walk back to the Fox House Inn with the driving snow stinging his raw cheeks was a sobering reminder of his mother's warning to stay in that evening. The raging blizzard was now at its peak, and the little group of travellers know that they would be in for a long stay if the appalling weather continued.

"I told him not to go out tonight," sobbed Mrs S as her husband tried to comfort her later that night. "He's just like you. He won't listen to anything I say."

"Don't worry love, he'll be alright. I'll get the bulldozers out tomorrow morning and we'll soon have him home."

The landlord of the Fox House Inn had, by now, telephoned the Corporation to tell them that they were completely cut off, but that the bus driver, conductor and passenger were safe and well with him. Mr S was, of course, aware of this, but knew that getting out there would be no easy task.

That day, Monday, 3 February and the Tuesday morning following, saw the worst blizzards in Sheffield for more than 40 years. Towns and villages were cut off and yet the snow persisted. Food and milk stocks everywhere were becoming scarce, and the Fox House Inn was no exception. Bread and mild had more or less run out by the Wednesday evening, and by Thursday, things were getting desperate.

Persistent white flakes were still mischievously swirling about on that dull Thursday morning as Jimmy stood at the Inn doorway, staring in desperation at the mountains of snow in front of him. The 15ft drifts looked as though they would be there for ever, and the gleeful winds laughed triumphantly at the huge white barriers they had created. Mother nature had done her best to punish Jimmy, and now he was afraid.

It was a faint, but definite roaring sound that interrupted his depressed thoughts. A tingling sensation ran through his body as he hardly dared to think what it might be. Another huge roar, more determined than the first, now sounded nearer, and it was more recognisable. The wind howled back in protest as two forces battled for supremacy, and for a minute or two, both sides echoed their defiance around the white wilderness of this lonely spot.

Suddenly, without warning, tons of snow parted like a wall of soft flour as the huge, gleaming blade of Mr S's most powerful bulldozer thrust its way into view. Clouds of thick, black exhaust fumes shot triumphantly skywards from its hot exhaust port on top of the engine, and everyone was cheering.

Jimmy was trying hard to choke back tears of pride as his father gave him a wave, and he was safe at last.

Everyone was shaking hands with each other with huge grins of relief on their faces. Rescue had arrived just in time and nature had lost its battle on this occasion. Mr S explained to the grateful men who stood round him that Sheffield was

Handshakes all round as Sheffield Corporation break through huge snowdrifts to reach the Fox House pub during the terrible winter of 1947.

in the grip of a milk famine, and there were virtually no potatoes in town. Five foot drifts had blocked residents back or front doors, and getting about anywhere was very difficult. The City Engineer, Jim Collie, had even suggested that the trams might have to stop running; things had to be bad for that to happen.

Sheffield Councillors join the party as Mr S congratulates his bulldozer driver in the background.

But life is strange isn't it? The landlord himself was low on provisions and Mr S wanted a cup of tea for his tired, cold men who had fought for hours to reach their goal. Gratitude on this occasion was, unfortunately, short lived, and the men never did get their well-deserved cuppa!

* * * * * * * * *

It was now the mid 1950s and Mr & Mrs S's son Jim, as he preferred to be called now that he was quite an "old teenager", had decided to go and work at the Town Hall. His father had moved on to different pastures, and to some degree Jim was relieved. Working for the same organisation as your dad

would be fraught with difficulties, he'd decided, as you can't really be yourself!

"Have you seen what he's wearing today Mother?" Mr S blasted as Jim sauntered into the room a few days before his interview at the Town Hall. "He's got one of them "Teddy Bear" outfits on and he looks a right tea-cake if you ask me!"

Mr S always called his wife "Mother" when he was upset, and he never could remember that the trendy young teenager of today was a Teddy "Boy", not a "Bear".

"Now just calm down love," Mrs S responded quietly. You might not like the way he looks, but at least he's clean and smart."

"CLEAN AND SMART!" retorted Mr S, trying hard not to burst a blood vessel. "He's got half a jar of Brylcream on that mop of hair of his, AND its twisted into all sorts of weird shapes."

"Look Dad," said Jim, in an attempt to calm things down. "There's nothing wrong with my hair. I've simply got a "Tony Curtis" at the front and a "D.A." at the back. It's all in now you know."

Did You Know that it was common in the 1940s and '50s for young ladies who were not very well off to paint "seams" down the backs of their legs with black "eye-liner" as they couldn't afford to buy the stockings? It was also quite common to use boot polish on eyebrows as even the eyebrow pencil was expensive.

Mr S was speechless as he looked at the way Jim's hair was shaped to resemble the rear end of a duck at the back. His gaze drifted slowly to the long blue jacket which finished just above knee level, below which skin-tight black trousers resembled two drainpipes searching for a grate. In between the felt lapels of the jacket, Jim's pink shirt sported a tie shaped as boot laces, and still Mr S was speechless.

"Forgive me for asking," he croaked eventually, "but haven't you grown about two inches in this last half hour?"

"No, no. It's my crepe soled "brothel creepers" Dad," Jim replied calmly. They're supposed to be this thick."

After a brief, stunned silence, Jim made a move to the door.

"I'll have to go now, anyway," he said, giving his black greasy quiff one last touch with his comb. "Me and my mates are popping down to the Locarno now. There's a Rock and Roll dance on and they're playing Bill Haley and Little Richard records tonight. See ya' later, alligator!"

Mrs S looked at her bewildered husband and sympathised with his feelings to some degree. Accepting change is never easy, but for the generation who fought with strict discipline in the war, it was particularly difficult.

"He'll get over it, don't you worry," she comforted. "He's starting work at the Town Hall next week remember; that will sort him out."

It was, of course, a different Jim who started work a week later. The hair hadn't changed much, but the smart, pale grey suit and black shiny leather shoes were certainly "different" to his previous attire. His tie rather resembled a cod skin as it glistened silvery grey against the "whiter than white" shirt, but all in all Jim looked quite like a "Town Hall worker".

If Jim thought that everything would be beyond reproach at this famous seat of learning and administration, then he was to be very surprised. There was plenty of work to be done, and by-and-large the staff with whom he worked were highly professional and very dedicated. It was a friendly place, although respect for the hierarchy was insisted upon.

He'd started in the general office when he arrived, in order to gain some broad experience. It was on the second day that the phone started to ring in a continuous tone. Jim was most surprised, particularly when two or three members of staff almost fell over themselves to pick it up.

The Town Hall, showing the statue of the Roman god Vulcan who, according to mythology, was the god of metalworkers.

"Jones speaking Sir. Yes Sir. Of course Sir. Immediately Sir."

That was the day Jim learnt about "The Chief", as the City Engineer was referred to in those days. He always had to be referred to as "Sir", and his personal, continuous ring had to be answered immediately. The step from "Bill Haley" to "The Chief" was quite a large one for Jim to make but, as his job depended on it, make it he did.

But, as in any very large organisation, the Corporation had its characters at the other end of the scale to "The Chief". Take Charlie, for example. He was a surveyor, but he was also a genius at mechanics. This was soon made apparent to Jim on his second week in the office when an old motor bike engine appeared on the wide shelf at the back of the office one morning. Not wishing to sound naïve, the young newcomer asked no questions, but could hardly contain himself in amazement at its appearance.

"I saw you looking at my engine lad," Charlie suddenly said halfway through the morning. "If you're interested, I'll show you how to strip it down at lunchtime."

True to his word, lunchtime found Charlie spreading a large sheet of paper over his desk and lifting the engine on to it. Jim's head was spinning as he watched each oily piece in turn being taken off and cleaned, the whole process lasting several weeks as most lunch breaks were only half an hour or so. In between time, of course, Charlie was one of the best surveyors in the office, but Jim couldn't quite get over his unusual lunchtime hobby.

Then there was Ted. He was excellent at his job as a draughtsman, but Tuesdays and Fridays were hair washing mornings in the "gents" at the end of the corridor.

"Do you want to borrow the shampoo lad?" offered Ted as Jim walked into the "gents" that first "wash morning".

"No, its all right thank you," came Jim's rather feeble reply as he watched Ted froth up his mop of black hair over the end wash basin. "I washed it last night."

The weekly issue of the "town hall towel" finished off the job to perfection for Ted who, with a damp but freshly cleaned head, buckled down with extra vigour to his duties on returning to the office.

Martin was another twice a week visitor to the same little room at the end of the corridor. This time, his visits were more legitimate than those of Ted. Unfortunately, they lasted at least 30 minutes each and Jim was warned not to venture anywhere near the place for at least an hour afterwards!

Despite these surprising encounters, Jim managed to learn a lot over the next few years. One job he was given was the Tram Track Abandonment Scheme. This involved the surveying and costing of resurfacing works on many miles of tram track in a large area of the city, in preparation for the removal of the trams from the streets towards the end of 1960.

"You know Dad," said Jim one evening as they all sat round for family tea, "it's strange doing something that you don't quite agree with."

"Well son, it happens to us all from time to time," his father explained. "The politicians make the final decisions after considering the views and recommendations of their officers.

Once they've decided, you've just got to get on with it as best you can."

He was right of course, but Jim remembered with some fondness the hundreds of tram journeys he had made from Meadowhead to Sheffield Lane Top year after year, to and from school. He could never remember a day when the tram never made it.

It was 8 October 1960 when the last tram ran in Sheffield. Jim had taken the afternoon off to witness the event and it was pouring with rain. The last service tram was number 222, and as it made its way into the Tinsley Depot, he noticed that its final destination poignantly read "Cemetery Gates".

The final procession consisted of 15 trams, and left the Tenter Street Depot about six-o'clock. Despite the torrential rain, people were out in their thousands, with many putting coins on the track in order that they could save the bent metal as a souvenir of their favourite method of transport.

All 15 trams travelled out as far as Beauchief before reversing on their last final drive to the Town Hall. The atmosphere was electric as they approached. Flood lighting reflected in the wet street, and the bouncing rain appeared like tiny stars which shimmered and sparkled to the resounding sound of the Transport Band.

Number 510 brought up the rear amidst tears, cheers and a magnificent rendition of *Auld Lang Syne*. This was the end

of over 60 years of magic and history, and Jim felt rather sad.

During the next 30 years or so, Jim made good progress with his work, and experienced many changes at the Town Hall. It was, however, the city itself which changed most dramatically, as new roads were built, traffic increased, and pedestrianisation took place on the Moor and Fargate. Huge buildings arose, both good and bad, and subways were built and then filled in. The huge shopping complex of Meadowhall was built on the site of Hadfield's demolished steelworks, and massive sports facilities sprang up nearby.

A plane droned overhead, and Supertram glided silently down Commercial Street on to the large, steel bridge over Park Square. Jim stood there and watched it disappear into the distance on its way out to Crystal Peaks.

It was the middle of the afternoon, but Jim wasn't at work. He was now in his fifties and had left the Town Hall a few years previously. Freelance photography was now his pleasure in life, and he'd just taken a good shot of the tram as it passed between the huge bowed girders of the bridge.

"I must let Dad have a copy of that," he muttered to himself.

Jim's dad, Mr S was old now and couldn't get out much. He loved it when his son popped over to see him with photographs showing how the city had changed. He would often reminisce as he studied the brightly coloured images.

Jim smiled to himself as he recalled the first time he'd shown his dad a photograph of the tram.

"Well, I'll go to'foot of our stairs!" he'd exclaimed. "It's nowt like I expected. Now when your mum's sister Elsie was a 'clippie' on the trams, they made 'em proper; you know, big and strong. This 'un looks more like a slug than a tram!"

Jim moved further down the street and took another shot, this time of the rows of growling cars which waited impatiently for the glaring red lights to change on the huge roundabout.

"It gets more like the Grand Prix every day down here," he thought to himself as the lights changed to green and shouted Go! Go! Go! and the race for lane position began. "I bet Damon Hill would have been pleased with that start!"

This was really Jim's day off, but he was thinking of producing a calendar for the millennium, and he thought that a few photographs of the changes which had taken place in this area might come in useful.

"If only those early settlers of a thousand years or so ago could see the area now," he muttered. "They'd think it was another world."

It was time to go back to his car which he'd left in Cole's car park, and he decided to take a few more shots on the way. The "Hole in the Road", where the Shambles market once stood, had itself been filled in, and Jim thought that a photograph of this spot wouldn't go amiss.

He continued up High Street to the Cathedral, where hundreds of years ago the Normans had set fire to the first little church built there. A brightly coloured fair was now attracting children on to the forecourt, and they were having fun. He turned into Fargate, with its wide paved area crowded with shoppers. This was where water once rushed down from Barker's Pool, washing away rubbish and filth that had collected in its open gutter hundreds of years ago.

> **Did You Know** that the 89 computer controlled jets of the new Goodwin Fountain and Holberry Cascades in the Sheffield Peace Gardens, create 70 tons of airborne water every second of the day for the enjoyment of the viewing public?

By this time Jim had reached the Town Hall, and he paused for a moment. As he gazed at the huge columns of water which gushed out from the new fountain in the re-modelled Peace Gardens, he tried to imagine the magnificent Church of St Paul which once stood there.

He arrived at the car park at last and climbed the small winding staircase up to his car. Gone was the laughter of years gone by, when crowds of excited theatre goers had climbed a much grander set of steps on this spot, at the entrance to the old Albert Hall.

Old Mr S was delighted with the photographs that Jim took him a few days later. He could hardly believe the changes that had taken place but, as a Sheffielder born and bred, he was proud of what he saw.

" I tell you what son," he said. "There's one thing that they'll never change."

"What's that Dad?" asked Jim.

"It's the people, son. There's nowt like us Yorkshire folk, and there never will be. They'll always be the same!"

The Cathedral bells were chiming in the New Year. The new millennium was almost upon them, and a hush fell over the huge street party in the centre of town. Jim wished his dad could be there to see it, but knew that time goes on, and he was now Mr S.

"I wonder what Sheffield will be like in another thousand years?" he said quietly as he gazed up into the clear black sky. "And who will be here to tell the story?"

APPENDIX 1

Some Interesting Name Changes

Pudding Lane became King Street

Truelove's Gutter became Castle Green Head then Castle Street

Castle Folds became Exchange Street

Under-the-water became Bridge Street

Pinson Lane became Pinstone Street

Well Gate became Townhead Street

Workhouse Lane became Paradise Street

Pepper Alley became Norfolk Row

Pond Well became Pond Hill

The Shambles became Castle Square

Change Alley became Arundel Gate

Beast Market became Bull Stake then Haymarket

High Street became Prior Gate then High Street again

Virgin's Row became St James Row

Coal Pit Lane became Cambridge Street

Blind Lane became Holly Street

Sembly Green became the Wicker

Paradise Square was known as Pot Square

Goose Green became London Road (at Highfield)

Black Lamb Lane became Broomhall Street

Lamb Pool Lane became Jansen Street (Attercliffe)

Walkley Road became Infirmary Road

South Street became The Moor

APPENDIX 2

Sheffield's Population Changes

Year	Township Population	Outer Districts Population		Combined Borough/City Population
1000	About 200	100		
1100	400	200	1851	135,300
1200	700	350	1860	184,779
1300	900	450	1871	240,000
1400	800	400	1891	324,000
1500	1200	600	1900	409,070
1600	2000	1000	1911	460,000
1615	2207	1100	1921	518,300
1736	9695	4400	1951	514,700
1778	20,000	10,000	1967	534,000
1800	30,000	15,000	1991	526,000
1851	83,400	52,900	2000	Approx 526,00

APPENDIX 3

Town Halls

There have been at least Four Town Halls in Sheffield:

1. 'Sheffield Towne Halle' (Referred to in "Survey of the Manor of Sheffield", 1637).

   This building was large enough to have eleven shops underneath it. Tenants included William Skargell (possibly a carpenter), 'Widdow Eyre' and 'Widdow Elmore'. It is not known where the building was located. However, in "Reminiscences of Old Sheffield" published in 1876, local historian R.E. Leader stated that No. 10 Pinfold Street was thought to be the first Town Hall. It apparently had chains attached to the walls which were used to detain prisoners.

2. Town Hall Two. 1700-1808

   Built in 1700, this small brick building was erected at the south-east corner of the churchyard. It faced down High Street and had steps leading to the door from which parliamentary candidates made speeches during elections.

   Underneath the hall were three dark and dirty prison cells. There were also shops facing what is now Church Street and a Belfry in which hung the Town Bell. The hall was used for much of the century as court-house, but was also used for dances, plays and meetings.

   The building was demolished in 1808, and had come to be regarded as a disgrace.

3. Town Hall Three. 1808

   The replacement to the demolished Town Hall was built on a grander scale. The architect was Charles Watson and the foundation stone was laid on 23 June 1808. The building was enlarged in 1833 and 1867 and was used as a prison, prison offices for Petty and Quarter Sessions and for town meetings.

Originally owned by the Town Trustees, the lease was taken over by the City Council in1866. In 1867, the hall was enlarged and internally re-modelled. A clock tower was constructed from earlier portions of the building which had been demolished and a drinking fountain, the first of its kind in Sheffield, was inserted into the wall facing Castle Street in 1859. An underground passage was also built which connected the Town Hall with the newly constructed police offices in Castle Green.

4. Town Hall 4. (Present Town Hall) 1897.
   A number of premises had to be cleared to allow for the new municipal buildings as the area between Surrey Street, Norfolk Row and Pinstone Street was filled with housing, shops and businesses. It was designed so it could be easily extended. A new portion of the building was opened on 29th May 1923 which was designed by F.E.P. Edwards, using exactly the same materials as those used on the 1897 building.

5. "New Town Hall". 1977
   Plans for further extensions were shelved until the 1970's when the "egg box" was built on the east side of Norfolk Street. The shape was chosen "so that it would not dominate its surroundings, but blend harmoniously with the existing… Victorian buildings."
   The new extension cost £9 million.

APPENDIX 4

English Kings & Queens

Saxons
Egbert	827-839
Aethelwulf	839-858
Aethelbald	858-860
Aethelbert	860-865
Aethelred I	865-871
Alfred the Great	871-899
Edward the Elder	899-924
Aethelstan	924-939
Edmund	939-946
Edred	946-955
Edwy	955-959
Edgar	959-975
Edward the Martyr	979-978
Aethelred II the Unready	978-1016
Edmund Ironside	1016

Danes
Cnut	1016-1035
Harold I Harefoot	1035-1040
Harthacnut	1040-1042

Saxons
Edward the Confessor	1042-1066
Harold II	1066

House of Normandy
William the Conqueror	1066-1087
William II	1087-1100
Henry I	1100-1135
Stephen	1135-1154

House of Plantaganet
Henry II	1154-1189
Richard	1189-1199
John	1199-1216
Henry III	1216-1272
Edward I	1272-1307
Edward II	1307-1327
Edward III	1327-1377
Richard II	1377-1399

House of Lancaster
Henry IV	1399-1413
Henry V	1413-1422
Henry VI	1422-1461

House of York
Edward IV	1461-1483
Edward V	1483
Richard III	1483-1485

House of Tudor
Henry VII	1485-1509
Henry VIII	1509-1547
Edward VI	1547-1553
Mary I	1553-1558
Elizabeth I	1558-1603

House of Stuart
James I	1603-1625
Charles I	1625-1649
Commonwealth	1649-1660

House of Stuart (restored)
Charles II	1660-1685
James II	1685-1688
William II jointly	1689-1702
Mary II	1689-1694
Anne	1702-1714

House of Hanover
George I	1714-1727
George II	1727-1760
George III	1760-1820
George IV	1820-1830
William IV	1830-1837
Victoria	1837-1901

House of Saxe-Coburg
Edward VII	1901-1910

House of Windsor
George V	1910-1936
Edward VIII	1936
George VI	1936-1952
Elizabeth II	1952-

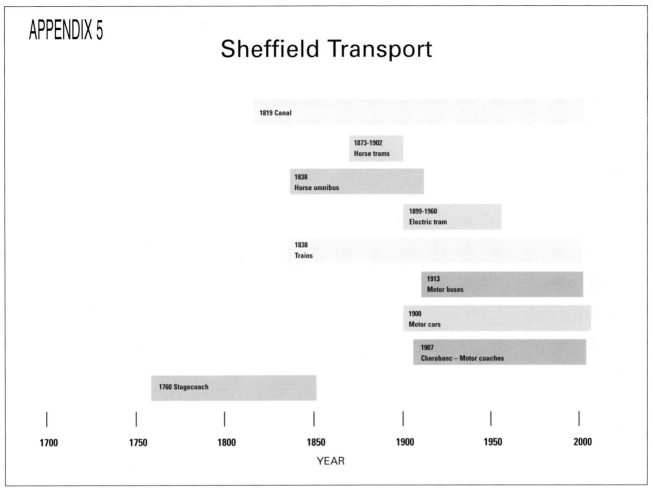

APPENDIX 5

Sheffield Transport

1819 Canal

1873-1902
Horse trams

1838
Horse omnibus

1899-1960
Electric tram

1838
Trains

1913
Motor buses

1900
Motor cars

1907
Charabanc – Motor coaches

1760 Stagecoach

| 1700 | 1750 | 1800 | 1850 | 1900 | 1950 | 2000 |

YEAR

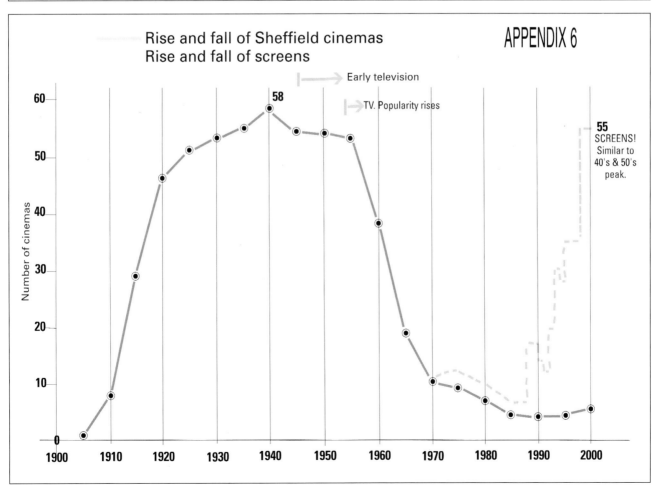

APPENDIX 6

Rise and fall of Sheffield cinemas
Rise and fall of screens

Early television

TV. Popularity rises

58

55
SCREENS!
Similar to
40's & 50's
peak.

Number of cinemas

60 —
50 —
40 —
30 —
20 —
10 —
0 —

1900 1910 1920 1930 1940 1950 1960 1970 1980 1990 2000

Subscribers

1 Michelle Jackson
2 David Edmundson
3 Gary Grimes
4 Peter Charlton
5 Richard Sharpe
6 Tracy Dockray
7 Mark Rodgers
8 Christine Ball
9 Angela Burgess
10 Lisa Higham
11 Mark Maloney
12 Frank Lincoln
13 Micheal John Bolsover
14 Rod Marshall
15 Jennifer Mary McDermott
16 Kevin Wells
17 John Francis Thompson
18 Dorothy Holland
19 George Ernest Lilley
20 Rebecca Sue Reid
21 Ronald E Goodyear
22 Tony & Barbara Whitaker
23 Ronald Aspland
24 Richard Hobson
25 William Barrie Garton
26 George William Revill
27 Eric Shipley
28 Ronald Pearce
29 Micheal Young
30 Barbara Anne Hossell
31 John Kenneth Tomlinson
32 David Holberry
33 Keith Thompson
34 Peter Bryan Conway
35 Albert Leek
36 Robert Michael Prestwood
37 Graham Ernest Simpson
38 John Broughton
39 Frank Carrington
40 David James Gains
41 Sheila Franks
42 Charles Ronald Rawlings
43 Herbert Shawcross
44 Glynn Fox
45 Norma Crossland
46 Janet Ann Martin
47 Roy F Bott
48 Andrew John Deane
49 Lesley Waller
50 Paul Watson
51 James Lingard
52 Anthony James Cawthorne
53 James Larkin
54 John Barrett
55 Tony Tew

56 Paul Butcher
57 John Mason
58 Kevin Steers
59 Lilian Steers
60 Verronica Waller
61 Anita Cole
62 George Deakin
63 Albert Slack
64 Peter Haythorne
65 Harry Shillito
66 Mr K Larkins
67 Neil Andrew Stringer
68 Esther Crawshaw
69 Anne Nuttall
70 Elsie Arabian
71 Joseph Knapp
72 Harry Walker
73 Grace Isabella Beeley
74 Duncan Beeley
75 David Alan Simmons
76 Keith Beckton
77 John William Booth
78 David Mark Wickett
79 Mary Costello
80 Louise Docherty
81 Craig Bowring
82 John Richard Smith
83 Gordon K C Powell
84 Alan G Leafe
85 Richard Brenchley
86 Matthew Houghton
87 Janet Toulson
88 Madge Armitage
89 Michael Andrew Rhodes
90 John Brian Sutcliffe
91 Raymond Keith Longden
92 Sandra Gillott
93 James Wainwright
94 Graham Peter Burdett
95 William Henry Frudd
96 George Edward Hanson
97 Michael Stanley Maher
98 Stephen John Allen
99 Charles Henry Palmer
100 Hilda Evans
101 Ernest Atherton
102 David Buxton
103 Joan & Les Giles
104 Evelyn Pearson
105 Stephen Lawrence Pickering
106 Ethel Rezler
107 George Samuel Millhouse
108 Gordon Frederick Wakefield
109 Debbie Adams
110 Mr & Mrs E R Morton

111 Terry Jackson
112 Jack Bingham
113 Irene Barlow
114 Eric Taylor
115 Richard W Taylor
116 Kevin Vine
117 John Wrighton Shepherd
118 Graham Lomas
119 Thomas William Pownall
120 Patricia Jukes
121 John Greaves
122 Alan Barraclough
123 Roy White
124 Patricia Cundy
125 David Richardson
126 Pam Swinard
127 Paul Milner
128 Margaret Lee
129 David Alan Burkinshaw
130 Irene Peech Atkin
131 Laura Leadbeater
132 Ray Fisher
133 Ruth Broadhurst
134 Rosa James
135 Peter Jenkinson
136 Edith Godbehere
137 Maureen Mace
138 Thelma Ballard
139 Olga Slocombe
140 Douglas Barker
141 Irene Eastwood
142 David Pitts
143 Malcolm Winter
144 Arthur Job
145 Nellie Hall
146 Roger Wall
147 James Frederick Flewitt
148 Frank Shaw
149 Gertrude Hukin
150 Dorothy Sampson
151 Robert A Wright
152 Albert Bagshaw
153 Willie Hartley
154 Kevin A Briggs
155 Terence Hearnshaw
156 Trevor Louis Harvey
157 Dennis Gray
158 Philip Wigfield
159 Claire Elizabeth Wigfield
160 John Keith Dodd
161 Mary Marshall
162 Stuart Cooke
163 Rita Estelle Carr
164 Janet Farkas
165 Craig McGuiness

166 John William Hurd
167 Brenda Tarrant
168 Mary Parsisson
169 Chloe Leigh Jones
170 Elizabeth Ann Stringer
171 Laura Nicole Baines
172 Alex Graham Baines
173 Annette Gillott
174 Morcia Kay Platt
175 Ron Dawtry
176 David Thomas
177 Malcolm Hodgson
178 John Brown
179 James C Cutts
180 Ralph Miles
181 Christine & James Pickering
182 Nancy Grayso
183 David Keir
184 Valerie Stenton
185 James Shepherd
186 Dorothy & Joseph Muscroft
187 Joanne Taylor
188 Peter Simpson
189 Geoff Wales
190 Robert Mullins
191 Keith Jepson
192 Kenneth M Savage
193 John S Carnelley
194 Nancy Jepson
195 Kathleen Sharman
196 Barry Stephen Todd
197 Ernest Sidney Brunt
198 Helena P Wilson
199 Christine Lovett
200 Kevin
201 John Barrie Hobson
202 Mary Roper
203 Edgar Eastwood
204 Winifred Mottram
205 Trevor Albert Evans
206 Leonard Evans
207 Mark David Dooley
208 Patricia Mary Hall
209 Irene Townsend
210 Dorothy Bullock
211 Victor Roy Hellewell
212 Barbara Ravenhall
213 Barry Wilson
214 Mary Blanche Hudson
215 Dallice Merrick
216 Ronald Fryer
217 Wendy Gilson
218 Freda & Tony Moore
219 John Renshaw
220 Irene Castleton

221 Dorothy Wright
222 Gordon Gregory
223 William Arnold Rayne
224 Janet Twigg
225 Annie Maria Weston
226 Brian Molloy
227 Valerie & Dennis Bock
228 Jane Chrissikou
229 Jakki Freeman
230 Mr & Mrs F Stansfield
231 Mr & Mrs A Shaw
232 Robert Whitham
233 James S Eccles
234 Ernest Casson
235 Mrs P A Leadbeater
236 Alan Taylor
237 Claire Elaine Rennie
238 Joan Newland
239 John Jordan
240 Kenneth Thurston
241 Matthew Cullen
242 Andrew Clarkson
243 Mary Haigh Glover
244 Pauline Gant
245 David M Hill
246 Leslie Damms
247 Edana Oakley
248 Henrietta Ruth Hanby
249 Gerald, Stanley, J Standage
250 Brian Whitham
251 Maureen Owen
252 Brian Travis
253 Kathleen Lillian Smith
254 Robert Arthur Thornton
255 David Bartles
256 Violet Renshaw
257 Margaret Hadwin
258 Julie Diane Spencer
259 Lorraine Hardy
260 Edna May Woodhead
261 Maude Helen Townsley
262 Margaret Gregory
263 Maureen Carnall
264 Alan Bingham
265 David Varley
266 Margaret Wedgewood
267 Reginald Drabble
268 Pat & John Gillingham
269 Christina Oxley
270 Neil Robinson
271 Norma Gambles
272 Grace Marion Bateman
273 Martyn Stanley Schole
274 William Henry Hudson
275 Mrs Christine Mary Lee
276 Joseph W Stockdale
277 Anthony Robert Bradbury
278 Howard Mealing
279 Arthur Whitehead
280 Johnathan Janiszewski

281 Desmond Pass
282 Brian Woodward
283 Eric Sims
284 Mavis Lem
285 Wilfred Wren
286 Peggy Scott
287 Steven W Murdoch
288 Michael J Crossland
289 Donald Turner
290 J Barry Swift
291 Betty Armitage
292 Gill Radley
293 Laurence Heath
294 Cyril Mather
295 Derick Wilks
296 Arnold B Milner
297 Florence Swallow
298 Mr & Mrs K Turner
299 B Gibbs
300 Morgan Drew Meredith Davis
301 Hilda (Tilly) Priestley
302 Hilda Bentley
303 Beryl A Johnson
304 Joseph William Goddard
305 Susan Williams
306 Irene Graham
307 Anthony Roger Turner
308 Simon James Watkinson
309 Stephen Woolley
310 Susan Eastwood
311 David Fletcher
312 Gavin D Miller
313 David V Miller
314 John B Mosley
315 Sara Louise Watkinson
316 Mrs Joan Naylor
317 Jayne Griffin
318 David Squire Abbott
319 Sidney Vallance
320 Margaret Carr
321 George Barker
322 Paul Ratcliffe
323 John Bernard King
324 Mrs A E Wade
325 Peter C R Downing
326 Alison Jane Crookes
327 Margaret Grant
328 Leonard Forrester
329 Derek Lovett
330 Doreen H Speight
331 Christopher Andrew Peet
332 Betty Vizor
333 William Kidgell
334 Catherine Gibson
335 Maureen Martin
336 Harry Wright
337 Trevor Wilson
338 Keith Tompkins
339 Jessica Broadhead
340 Stella Preece

341 N Thorpe
342 M J Thorpe
343 Brian Chisell
344 John William Earnshaw
345 Mrs Constance Lillian Hague
346 John David Aldam
347 Walter Edward Spooner
348 Ian Lilleyman
349 Mary Thompson
350 Madge Barber
351 Fred Thursby
352 Niel Hopewell
353 Bob Palmer
354 Elka Will
355 Frank Macedo
356 Harry & Lily Flinders
357 Kathryn Dumelow
358 Clifford Boot
359 K Bennett
360 Cyril Ewart King
361 Roger Stevenson
362 Stella Loomes
363 Margaret Maxfield
364 Wendy Bell
365 Vivian Tompkins
366 Eileen M O'Shaughnessy
367 William Charles Cawthorne
368 Linda Griffiths
369 Patricia Ann Chapman
370 C M Baxendale
371 Mr Daniel Daley
372 Raymond White
373 Patricia Platts
374 Alan Marshall
375 Alan Beatson
376 Gilbert Perkins
377 Gladys Allen
378 Anthony W Rider
379 Keith Robinson
380 Graham & Carolyn Spurr
381 Dennis Anthony Cerrone
382 Christine Hamilton
383 Malcolm Robert Beeden
384 Geoffrey Edward Warren
385 George Whitehead
386 Linda Mary Degenhart
387 Alice May Gardner
388 Brian Thompson
389 John Micheal Hobson
390 Alice T Jefferson
391 Terence Dalton
392 Mark David Gregory
393 Hilda Barks
394 Gordon Waist Nidge
395 Robert William Spencer
396 Lilian Spencer
397 Patrick Widdowson
398 James Berrell
399 Carol Birkett
400 Freda Hodgkinson

401 Mary Evans
402 Jack Sowerby
403 Alfred Wilkin
404 Muriel Parker
405 Frank Chadwick
406 Joyce L Jenkinson
407 Ron Platts
408 Peter Edward Smith
409 Frank Trevor Stubbins
410 Peter Ernest Bradshaw
411 Olga Dora Fitzroy Hall
412 Alan E Barber
413 Dennis Wood
414 Eric Thornton
415 Derek Furniss
416 Hazel Goodison
417 Les Morris
418 Gordon Hodgkinson
419 Marjorie Round
420 Denis Fox
421 Mr & Mrs G Cottam
422 Alan Ernest Roddis
423 Linda Jean Britt
424 Maureen Woolcott
425 Philip R Perry
426 Fay Catherine Ramzan
427 Brenda Storr
428 Graham Slater
429 Mary Haslam
430 Dorothy Robinson
431 Trevor Gall
432 Annie Jeffries
433 Barbara Anne Senior
434 Brian Pashley
435 Robert L Pashley
436 William Smith
437 Philip Levick
438 Margaret McCay
439 Moira & Terry Woolley
440 Harry Middleton
441 Ernest Woodhead
442 Steven P Goulding
443 David John Blagburn
444 Stuart L Travis
445 Frank Renshaw
446 Charles Digby
447 Graham Barker
448 Derek Collier
449 Lynda Clarke
450 Margaret Dukes
451 Frank Carl
452 Walter Beighton
453 Alan Thornton
454 Frank Brian Taylor
455 Ann Womersley
456 Peter Fearnehough
457 T Green
458 Mr E & Mrs C M Pownall
459 Patricia A Bowles
460 John Birchell Hughes

461 Ian Douglas Tevendale
462 Stephen Alexander Caunt
463 Jack Birch
464 M A Stringer
465 Susan Roberts
466 Philip T Collier
467 Sheila Pasley
468 Paul Johnson
469 Norman J Johnson
470 Geoffrey Ward
471 Mrs Jessie Watson
472 Stuart M Watson
473 Susan & John Turner
474 Mary B Tong
475 Edna Young
476 Melvyn Roberts
477 George Smith
478 David Norman Storey
479 Gary Robert Barrass
480 Thomas Surr
481 Hannah Ludlam
482 William Sanderson
483 Susan Patricia Myers
484 Geoffrey Asquith
485 May Gibson
486 Peggy & Harry Cocker
487 Albert Carnall
488 Stuart Andrew Brooks
489 John Hague
490 Ronald Rodgers
491 David Goulding
492 Raymond Homar
493 Connie Sweet
494 Arthur Outram
495 Nellie Brooke
496 Geoffrey Piers Ward
497 Thomas Beardshaw
498 Eric Barnsley
499 Raymond Allwood
500 Derek Tingle
501 John Anthony Watson
502 Ernest Callinswood
503 Grace Mary Bailey
504 John E Towler
505 Elizabeth M Didlock
506 Don Owen
507 Margaret Owen
508 Bertha Cann
509 Terence Reaney
510 Joyce Malkin
511 Brian Gregory
512 Mavis Gosney
513 Jennifer Marie Henderson
514 Michael Peter Brookes
515 Mark Ernest Moore
516 Michael G Thickett
517 Dennis & Margaret Otter
518 Keith M Cotterill
519 Terry George Yeardley
520 Dr Ivy Oates

521 Thelma Brown
522 Daphne Marshall
523 Graham Cadel
524 William Hodkinson
525 Ray Monica Bond
526 Arthur Young
527 Ronald Sturgess
528 Tony Kenny
529 Paul D Cadel BSc Hons
530 Eleanor Marsh SEN
531 Allan G Podoski
532 Trevor Drabble
533 Doug Moorhouse
534 Bella Malcolmson
535 James Patrick Cooper
536 Royce Hoskings
537 Russell Bown
538 Jane Nashvili
539 Jack Barnett
540 Peter Hopper
541 Irene Mary Priestley
542 Dorothy Audrey Riley
543 David & Patrick Naylor
544 Shirley Janet Bilton
545 Lynne Cooper
546 John Roddis
547 Jonathan Roddis
548 Clifford Wright
549 Ronald Ellis
550 Margaret A Joel
551 Mr & Mrs B Marples
552 Ashleigh Victoria Marples
553 Audrey E Bark
554 Walter Gill
555 Ian Francis Daley
556 Bill E Crowder
557 Lee Anthony Unwin
558 Jean Malcolmson
559 Thomas Antony Broomhead
560 Samuel Lath
561 Edith Hearnshaw
562 Marjorie Lesley Dixon
563 Roger Ward
564 Julie Hinchcliffe
565 Ken Senior
566 Brian Harry Smith
567 Paul Casbolt
568 Thomas Eric Mills
569 Ronald Gilberthorpe
570 Ronald Gilberthorpe
571 Vincent Thompson
572 Cyril Spooner
573 Margaret Bannister
574 Ann Roche
575 Brett Griffin
576 Lorna E Marsh-Thomas
577 Kenn Swallow
578 John Blincow
579 J David Simpson
580 Ecclesall Local History Society

581 Kathryn Mary Atkin (née Mckenna)
582 Brenda Jean Rose
583 Ethel Marion Parker
584 Norma Bush
585 Alan Reynolds
586 Derek Tingle
587 John Hugh Stanley
588 Kathleen Satterthwaite
589 Edna Bramall
590 Donald Golby
591 Joseph Lewis Ward
592 Melvin D Eyre
593 John Birch
594 Dennis Rooke
595 Alison Jane Carr
596 Jessie Grayson
597 Mrs Constance Fisher
598 Malcolm & Hilary Reynolds
599 Florence Mary Hannah
600 John Michael Ashley
601 Edna Mary Ashley
602 Leslie Smith
603 Robert Byron Broad
604 Lee John Lindley
605 Ronald Abbott
606 Mabel Haines
607 Wayne Bridgeman
608 S & P Habeshaw
609 Sandra C Murgatroyd
610 W E Watterson
611 Mr & Mrs W G Shaw
612 Mrs Mary Collins
613 Colin Richards
614 Ian D Brooks
615 Christopher Steven Dickinson
616 Mr E J Edwards
617 Leonrad Brooks
618 Brian Wood
619 John Leybourne
620 Keith Beeden
621 Anne Ballamy
622 Bernard Cooper
623 Tom Bromley
624 David Ward
625 Scott Andrew Seaton
626 John Barry Staniland
627 Marion Sales
628 Bill Hubard
629 Margaret Barnes
630 Betty May Playforth
631 Kate & David Hardy
632 Thomas Edward Hinchliffe
633 Brian Haglington
634 Alan John Hardy
635 Roy Powell
636 Robert Barnes
637 John & Sheila Baker
638 Ken Button
639 Mavis Hitchcock

640 Harry W Leaper
641 Peter J Shepherd
642 David L Heighington
643 Marjory Irene Richardson
644 Constance Campbell
645 Robert Thomson
646 Cyril Sedgwick
647 Stuart Grafton
648 Daisy Avena Toothill
649 Mr Keith Machin
650 Ann Heath
651 Mary Brown
652 Susan Deehan
653 Doreen & Bernard Allen
654 Anne Jessop
655 Graham Marshall
656 Olive Liversidge
657 Barry Malpass
658 John Charles Whiting
659 Clara Ludbrook
660 Clive C Sheldon
661 Matthewman
662 Bruce Bridgeman
663 Hilda Billam
664 Eva & Reg MArsh
665 Eddie Wardill
666 Roy Hatfield
667 Robert Young
668 Arthur Edwards
669 Derrick Arthur Edwards
670 Susan Carol Edwards
671 Janet Ethel Edwards
672 Maureen Alice Edwards
673 Stephen Robert Edwards
674 Colin Truelove
675 Terence Ward
676 Gordon W Bell
677 J Walker
678 D & G Johnson
679 Gregory William Barry Chapman
680 Mrs Carole Elaine Haynes
681 Ann Crookes
682 Mavis M Bradbury
683 Brian Shepherd
684 Keith M Liddelow
685 David Briggs
686 John Briggs
687 Walter Briggs
688 Christine H Holland
689 Serena Natalie Lomas
690 Andra Dionne Birch
691 Neil Ashley John Lomas
692 Darryl Graham Lomas
693 C J Pheasey
694 George Cooke
695 Michael Warren
696 Kenneth Bower
697 Brian Darwent